The

NO-SALT

Cookbook

Reduce or eliminate salt without sacrificing flavor

David C. Anderson
and Thomas D. Anderson

ADAMS MEDIA CORPORATION
Avon, Massachusetts

Published by
Adams Media, an F+W Publications Company
57 Littlefield Street, Avon, MA 02322
www.adamsmedia.com
ISBN 13: 978-1-58062-525-8
ISBN 10: 1-58062-525-8

Printed in Canada.

J I H G

Library of Congress Cataloging-in-Publication Data
Anderson, Thomas D.
No salt cookbook : reduce or eliminate salt without sacrificing flavor /
David C. Anderson and Thomas D. Anderson.
p.   cm.
Includes index.
ISBN 1-58062-525-8
1. Salt-free diet--Recipes. I. Anderson, David C., 1942– II. Title.
RM 237.8 .A534   2001
641.5'632--dc21   2001033538

This publication is designed to provide accurate and authoritative information with regard to the subject matter covered. It is sold with the
understanding that the publisher is not engaged in rendering legal,
accounting, or other professional advice. If legal advice or other expert
assistance is required, the services of a competent professional person
should be sought.
— From a *Declaration of Principles* jointly adopted by a
Committee of the American Bar Association and
a Committee of Publishers and Associations

This book is available at quantity discounts for bulk purchases.
For information, call 1-800-289-0963.

CONTENTS

I. INTRODUCTION

We Still Eat Well. So Can You.

This book is a report from the front lines. The advice and recipes that follow are based on a quest for ways to make food taste good without salt that spans nearly two decades, along with a four-year effort to organize and expand upon it for publication, first on the Internet, now as a book.

The authors, the father a journalist, the son a self-taught chef—approach this task unapologetically as amateurs. Accepting that the physicians and nutritionists are right when they order a reduction in sodium intake for the management of a medical problem, how is the patient who loves food supposed to cope?

Other diet orders, if troublesome, are less challenging. Reducing cholesterol or fat, for example, means substitutions of ingredients or shifts in menus. Replace the butter with margarine; forget the cheeseburgers and ice cream; go for chicken, fish, fruits, and vegetables. You may have to give up on foods that have comforted you since childhood, but you can still go out to a restaurant with friends, still frequent familiar aisles of the supermarket. Most important, you can still make the food you are allowed to eat taste good to you in the conventional ways.

It's not the same when a doctor orders you to cut out salt. A quick investigation lays the basis for panic. Reduce sodium intake to 1,500 milligrams per day: Okay, take a calculator shopping and start checking the nutritional analyses printed on labels. Bread: 135 milligrams of sodium per slice. Butter: 85 milligrams per tablespoon. Bacon: 290 milligrams in two strips. Cheerios: 280 milligrams per cup. Cheddar cheese: 180 milligrams per ounce. Tuna fish: 750 milligrams in a six-ounce can. Mustard: 50 milligrams per teaspoon. Mayonnaise: 80 milligrams per tablespoon. Canned green beans, pasta sauce, and chicken noodle soup: 390 milligrams, 610 milligrams, and 980 milligrams in half a cup of each.

At this rate, you'll hit the 1,500 milligram ceiling halfway through lunch. The reality sinks in: Whole sections of the supermarket—virtually all the processed foods—are now off limits. And 1,500 milligrams a day isn't all that strict. Some doctors want you below 750 or 500.

Restaurants are equally discouraging. McDonald's and Burger King now post nutritional analyses of their fare, and the sodium amounts are forbidding: 1,380 milligrams in Burger King's Whopper with cheese, 1,070 in McDonald's Big Mac. Fish and chicken sandwiches exceed 1,000 milligrams at each place.

To handle the low-sodium diet, you'll have to forget the fast food and think more than twice about the ethnic places you've learned to love over the years, especially the Asian restaurants that depend so much on soy sauce (1,319 milligrams per tablespoon). Higher-end continental and American cuisine offer some hope, but you have to be aggressive about ordering dishes prepared without salt, pinning down the waiter and the chef.

Home cooking offers the best hope for continued enjoyment of food, but here, too, the challenge is serious. A single teaspoon of table salt (sodium chloride) contains 2,132 milligrams of sodium, more than even a liberal daily limit, and you also need to count the sodium that occurs naturally in the food you prepare. These amounts are significant: 150 milligrams of sodium in 8 ounces of boneless broiled chicken, 180 milligrams in 8 ounces of broiled sirloin steak.

The arithmetic leads to an uncompromising bottom line: Cooking for yourself, you can get decent nourishment within the confines of a low-sodium diet, but given the naturally occurring sodium in food, you will have to do so without adding any salt whatsoever, either when you prepare the food or when you sit down to eat it. For all too many people, that's a devastating idea.

Do the doctors who order a low-sodium diet understand what it can mean? We wonder.

A young woman we know recently moved in with her aging parents, no longer able to live by themselves because of multiple medical problems. Attempting to prepare tasty meals, the daughter found herself stumped by the 750-milligram-per-day sodium limit her father's doctor had imposed. "They gave us no guidance," she says of her efforts to cope. "I was just stumbling around, reading labels." She wound up preparing flavorless and totally monotonous combinations of rice and steamed vegetables day after day.

An older friend speaks despairingly of the low-sodium diet that reduced her cuisine to unadorned rice and chicken breasts. The restriction dealt a serious blow to her quality of life: Retired from a successful career as an educator, she now lives alone; sharing good food with friends had been a basic source of enjoyment.

Shortly after we began uploading salt-free recipes on our Web site a man wrote to us with startling gratitude. "You have literally saved my wife's life," he declared. "Since we found out she couldn't eat anything with salt in it she had almost stopped eating. The doctor warned her about weight loss, but it didn't help."

These are frustrating stories, because monotony, despair, and near starvation are wholly unnecessary for the sake of a salt-free diet.

Our own interest in a low-sodium cuisine began more than 20 years ago when David Anderson was diagnosed with high blood pressure and ordered off salt by his doctor. He began experimenting in the kitchen and embarked on the often frustrating hunt for salt-free products off the shelf. Several years later, his son Tom began to pursue a passion for cooking and brought his imagination and a fascination with gourmet cuisine to his father's continuing quest for flavor.

While life without salt has meant the sacrifice of some foods we used to love—pastrami, hot dogs with sauerkraut, bacon for breakfast, the Easter ham—it has also meant the discovery of new dishes that are just as satisfying, if not more so, through a process that is always creative and often fun. We feel that we eat very well, whether at home with our families or entertaining our friends. So can you.

The Salt-Free Palate

Salt is cheap and plentiful; it all too easily becomes a habit, if not an addiction. As you use it, your numbing palate demands more and more. This makes it easy to build up a big daily salt intake without much effort, but the good news is that the process may be reversed. Breaking the habit is entirely possible, and success entitles you to a sense of liberation.

Palates adjust. After you eliminate salt from your diet, food will taste bland for a week or so; then you'll begin to notice a lot of interesting flavor you may never have tasted before in mundane items: a good variety of rice, fresh potatoes, certain green vegetables, a ripe tomato. Meanwhile, canned soups and snacks like pretzels and chips will taste so salty as to be inedible.

You could stop there, simply following recipes in the standard cookbooks minus the salt. But the problem intrigued us: The new flavors revealed by the absence of salt invited enhancement and experimentation with herbs and spices, vinegar, lemon juice, and wine. The recipes and advice that follow are the result.

Like any recipes, they must speak for themselves; the proof of their value is in the tasting. We believe, however, that our experience of giving up salt and finding our own way to cooking without it may yield a cuisine more valid and useful than those commissioned as "special-diet" projects from chefs trained to believe salt is an essential ingredient and who like the taste of it. As with appreciation of art, there is a big subjective element to appreciation of food. Salt-free cooking based on a salt-free palate and unencumbered by culinary traditions produces a cuisine we are proud to serve to family and guests alike.

A cautionary note: The recipes and advice that follow are intended only to help people reduce salt intake—a concern of millions who have no need for further dietary restrictions. They are not designed with the idea of reducing cholesterol, fat, carbohydrates, sugar, or other elements of diet that physicians might restrict along with sodium in order to treat some medical conditions. People seeking to manage additional restrictions may well be able to adapt these recipes—for example, by substituting salt-free margarine for butter. The principles of preserving and deepening flavor without salt that one can learn from this book should remain valid for a dieter facing other limitations as well. If in doubt, show the recipes in this book to a medical professional and follow his or her advice about how to use them.

Counting Milligrams

How much sodium do you ingest each day from salt and from the sodium that occurs naturally in foods? That's the first question that comes up when a doctor imposes a limit, and sometimes it's a hard one to answer with precision. Processed food packages list sodium contents, permitting calculations based on how much of them you eat. It's important to shop carefully. Terms on labels follow rules established by the Food and Drug Administration. Only products containing fewer than 5 milligrams of sodium per serving may be labeled "sodium free." Those labeled "very low sodium" may contain no more than 35 milligrams per serving, while a "low sodium" product may contain up to 140 milligrams per serving or per 50 grams of the food.

A "low sodium" serving may therefore contribute a sizable piece of one's 1,500-milligram-per-day limit. It's also important to check the serving sizes as well as the sodium counts. Campbell's "Healthy Request" vegetable soup, for example, contains 480 milligrams of sodium in a ½ cup serving of the condensed soup. The ½ cup "serving" makes one cup of soup when diluted with an equal amount of water, but one cup doesn't look like much in a soup bowl; a lot of people will want more, especially if that is their main dish for lunch or supper.

For foods you prepare at home, you'll want to learn the sodium values for common ingredients (see our chart on page 316). In general, you'll find natural sodium concentrated in meats, poultry, and fish; a large egg contains about 60 milligrams, a cup of whole milk has 122.

Most vegetables are very low in sodium, with some notable exceptions: celery (151 milligrams per cup, chopped), spinach (90 milligrams per cooked cup), beets (81 milligrams per cup), and Swiss chard (125 milligrams per cooked cup). A cup of grated carrot contains 52 milligrams, while a cup of mashed boiled turnips contains 78. While these amounts are significant, they are not, in our opinion, worth worrying about if the vegetable in question is part of a larger dish. Adding celery or spinach to a soup or stew, for example, won't add enough to the sodium content of a serving to make a big difference. On the other hand, the sodium values of such vegetables are worth remembering when planning meals. If the meat dish is high in sodium (250 milligrams per serving, say) serve it with broccoli (16 milligrams per cup, cooked) rather than spinach or beets.

If you are computer literate and you want more detailed nutritional information, you can consult the huge national database maintained by the United States Department of Agriculture which gives complete nutritional analyses for thousands of foods. You can find it on the Internet at *www.nal.usda.gov/fnic/foodcomp*. It's an excellent resource, if a bit cumbersome to use. Enter the name of a food product in the search engine, and the database will deliver two pages of nutritional information for you to read and print out. You have to search through all the ingredients to find the sodium count in milligrams, then do a bit of arithmetic to translate the quantities for the food you want to prepare.

To save time, you can purchase software to run on your computer that analyzes individual food products and recipes. To calculate sodium contents of recipes in this book and on our Web site, we've been using Food Analyst Plus, produced by Hopkins Technology of Hopkins, Minnesota (612-931-9376 or *www.hoptechno.com/faplus.htm*). You enter the food product and quantity (for a recipe, you also break it down by serving size). The software then consults databases loaded onto its CD-ROM and calculates nutrient contents, including sodium in milligrams.

If you don't have a computer, you can purchase a basic reference book like Bowes and Church's *Food Values of Portions Commonly Used,* a 481-page tome (Lippincott, located in Philadelphia and New York). In truth, however, you may soon decide that the chart we've provided in this book, based mostly on the USDA database, is all you need. You're likely to settle into a routine based on salt-free ingredients and recipes you like, and after looking up the sodium contents of your favorite foods a few times, you'll know them by heart.

The Salt-Free Shopper

Forbidding as they remain today, supermarkets were much more frustrating for the salt-free dieter two decades ago. In those days, the only place worth frequenting was the short section of shelves designated "special diet." Here you might find overpriced and not very tasty versions of a few familiar condiments and other processed foods bearing labels such as Weight Watchers or Pritikin that emphasized their contents' relevance to medical advice rather than good eating.

Today, it's worth spending more time in the main aisles of the big stores. Food producers, aware of growing demand, are offering more and more salt-free versions of common products like peanut butter, chicken broth, catsup, and mustard and putting them on the shelves alongside the mainstream products rather than confining them to the special-diet section.

Even so, you're likely to find more useful purchases in a health-food or natural-food store. We've been gratified to watch the health-food retail business shift from boutiques and mom-and-pop storefronts to big warehouses, at least in urban centers. The mood is much more encouraging than in the supermarkets; everyone should eat this way, the store suggests, not just people under doctor's orders. And many of the salt-free products are more satisfying than the supermarket brands. The catsup or can of beans originally conceived as organic, simple, and salt-free look better and taste better than low-sodium variants of older products that grew to commercial maturity under the influence of chemical additives and consumer testing.

Shopping is more problematic if you don't have access to a health-food store. Again, a computer may be helpful, as more and more producers of low-sodium products are advertising them on Web sites, and are sometimes selling them on the Internet. You can also develop your personal file of connections by calling the producers directly. Most food labels list the producer's name and headquarters city; some list toll-free numbers as well. Ask for the customer service or sales departments. They should be able to give you a list of retailers near you who sell the product as well as mail order distributors. Some producers are willing to fill mail orders themselves.

A mail order house that distributes one salt-free product, of course, is likely to distribute many others as well. Get its catalog and see what else it has to offer. Start a master list of products you'll want on a continuing basis and ways to get them through the mail, by phone, or online. All the calling around takes time and runs up telephone charges, but the return—a customized salt-free shopping network—makes it a sound investment.

Bread Without Salt

Brother Peter Reinhart, author of *Brother Juniper's Bread Book*, declares flatly that "Bread needs salt," reflecting a view common to many bakers. "If we forget to put salt in the dough, it takes off faster than usual and the crust does not brown evenly. The bread tastes dull and flat. . . . Saltless bread is barely bread. . . . If you have a salt problem or are on a restricted diet, try to eliminate it from other elements of your diet."

Such is the conventional wisdom, yet we've been baking bread without salt for years and never had a problem with unevenly browned crust or controlling its rise. And we've discovered that there are many ways to bake tasty bread without salt.

We're not alone. In Northern Italy, Tuscan bakers have baked salt-free bread since the sixteenth century, when they decided they didn't like paying the tax imposed on salt. Travel there today, and you'll find a warm loaf of saltless bread at the center of the buffets the hotels set out each morning for breakfast.

It's possible to buy fairly good commercially produced salt-free bread, usually in health-food stores. The best are whole-wheat or whole-grain breads; satisfying as they are, they leave a lot of cravings unfulfilled. What to do if you hanker for a good sour rye or, perhaps, the soft, full-flavored white bread that makes great breakfast toast or a classic tomato sandwich?

The answer is to bake your own—this book contains our recipes for rye, white, and many other breads. While some bread bakers, like winemakers, try to invest the craft with intimidating mumbo jumbo, in truth, baking your own bread is not hard to do. And it grants a satisfying measure of control over your cuisine.

You can learn enough to bake good bread at home by reading a good basic bread cookbook (see page 9). Or you may have access to a cooking school that offers a short course (two or three sessions) in bread baking. When we enrolled in such a class recently, we explained that we wanted to make our bread without salt. As it happened, we lucked out: Instead of recoiling in horror, the instructor welcomed the challenge and made it part of the group's learning experience. Asked about the advice of bakers like Brother Peter, he agreed that it's nonsense. People who like the way salt tastes in bread, he suggested, think up a lot of elegant reasons for why it's essential. The challenge is to find ways to make bread flavorful—simply omitting salt from many traditional recipes produces a loaf even people with well developed salt-free palates may find bland.

Here are a few general rules gleaned from classes and our own experience:

Substitute sweet for salt. A quarter cup of full-flavored honey or molasses greatly enhances the flavor of wheat and distracts the palate from its memory of salt in bread. Some salt-free bakers also add a touch of sweetness by cooking a half cup of bulgur wheat or cracked wheat in a cup of fruit juice (apple works best), allowing it to cool, and adding it to the liquid ingredients before stirring in the flour.

Use unbleached, stone ground, organically grown flours. These develop more flavor than the processed flours sold under major brand names in supermarkets; the difference is especially noticeable with both white all-purpose flours and the "bread" flours that contain more gluten. It's worth a trip to the health-food store to find unbleached organic flour; if yours doesn't have a good flour section (many don't) you can always purchase excellent flours by mail or phone order from King Arthur Flour of Norwich, Vermont (1-800-827-6836).

Learn to start breads with sponges and sourdough starters. Dissolving yeast, adding a small amount of flour, and allowing it to rise and then fall in a warm place creates a "sponge" to which the rest of the ingredients are added to make the dough. Fermentation gives the sponge an assertive sweet-sour flavor that remains an important feature of the finished loaf. A new sponge is prepared for each new batch of dough. Sourdough starters are sponges that begin with smaller amounts of yeast, often only the wild yeast present in the atmosphere, and are allowed to ferment over a period of days. Typically, the baker uses only a portion of the starter for each new dough, then replenishes it with fresh flour so that it continues to ferment and will be ready for the next baking day.

We encourage you to try our bread recipes (which incorporate all these principles) as a way to teach yourself the basics. You can also find good discussions of sourdough baking and recipes for starters, as well as a lot of other bread baking lore, in *The Village Baker* by Joe Ortiz (Ten Speed Press, Berkeley, California); *Bread Alone* by Daniel Leader and Judith Blahnik (William Morrow and Company, New York); and *Bernard Clayton's New Complete Book of Breads* by Bernard Clayton, Jr. (Simon & Schuster, New York).

If you don't have time to learn a new craft—and you don't mind adding another small appliance to your kitchen counter—you can get a bread machine. While the more complicated bread recipes are better carried out by hand, you may be satisfied with the simpler ones, and a machine may be the best way for you to make good salt-free bread. Here's one recipe that works; when we tried it with a machine, the bread it produced had a light crust, good texture, and plenty of flavor—a fine option for breakfast toast and sandwiches.

BREAD MACHINE BREAD

6 oz. water (¾ c.)
2 tbsp. milk
2¾ c. bread flour
2 tbsp. sugar
2 tbsp. unsalted butter
2¼ tsp. active dry yeast
   (1 package)

Put the liquid in the canister of the machine, then add the flour and sugar. Cut up the butter and place it at the corners of the canister. Make a well in the mixture, add the yeast, and turn on the machine. (Follow the instructions that came with your machine; some may call for adding dry and liquid ingredients in a different sequence.)

YIELD: 1 loaf of bread
SODIUM CONTENT: 3 mg. of sodium per ½ inch slice

Cheese Options

Traditional cheese makers, like bread bakers, consider salt an essential ingredient and don't have much patience with people who want cheese without it. This is a problem. Exploring all the wonderful varieties of cheese is fun, if fattening; this is an area where adherence to a low-sodium diet requires some sacrifice.

You'll have to give up the generous dustings of Parmesan on pasta, the invitingly ripe Camembert with wine or fruit, the sturdy wedge of New York or Vermont Cheddar with your slice of apple pie. These may contain 200 to 500 milligrams of sodium per ounce.

There are, however some good substitutes:

Low-Sodium Gouda. This is by far the most useful of the salt-free cheeses. Its full, slightly sharp flavor and smooth texture make it perfectly presentable to serve before dinner with low-sodium crackers, in a grilled cheese sandwich, or with fruit or desserts. And it contains only 10 milligrams of sodium per ounce. We also grate it up to sprinkle on top of pastas or other dishes calling for doses of sharp grated cheese. In two decades, we've never tired of its flavor.

The problem is finding it. Low-sodium Gouda, imported from Holland, appears sporadically, cut into wedges, in the cheese or deli cases of supermarkets. If you live near a cheese shop or specialty food store, ask for it; if they don't have it in stock, they may be able to order it. If you do request a special order, the retailer may ask that you purchase an entire wheel. Consider it. The cheese keeps well, and you'll be surprised how quickly it disappears, given its great versatility.

Swiss Lorraine. This lacy, delicately flavored cheese seems to be available more and more often in delicatessens and at supermarket deli counters. Get it sliced paper thin for use in sandwiches; it also tastes great on pizza, and it contains only 35 milligrams of sodium per ounce.

Fresh Mozzarella. Speaking of pizza, if you want to make your own (see pages 275–281), you'll want a good source of unsalted mozzarella cheese, which has only 40 milligrams of sodium per ounce compared with 150 or so for salted versions. The best salt-free mozzarella is made fresh daily; you'll find it in Italian delicatessens and specialty shops. We've learned to love the light, milky flavor of this cheese all by itself; in August and September, when the tomatoes are ripe, we make the most of them by cutting big slices, topping each one with a slab of unsalted mozzarella and a single basil leaf, then sprinkling them with olive oil, balsamic vinegar, and black pepper.

Salt-Free Swiss. This may be the most widely available of all the salt-free cheeses, but it also has the least satisfying flavor. You're likely to find it in supermarkets in the dairy case, cut into long rectangular chunks, alongside other mainstream packaged cheeses. Typically, it bears a bright little sticker identifying it as salt free, and it contributes a modest 10 milligrams of sodium per ounce. It's basically just traditional Swiss cheese without the salt, and we're the first to agree that it's an acquired taste. We also have to say that we've acquired it over the years; even if the flavor is a bit watery, the nutty quality of Swiss survives. Use this cheese sliced thin for a sandwich on whole-wheat bread with one of the salt-free mustards (see page 315) and a handful of unsalted potato chips, put it out for your guests before dinner with low-sodium crackers, or grate it up and sprinkle it on pasta. The flavor is best if you allow it to warm to room temperature before serving.

Quark. No, we don't mean the subatomic particle; we mean yogurt cheese, the thick, tasty stuff you get when you drain much of the liquid out of fresh yogurt. It makes a fine substitute for cream cheese with little fat (depending on the yogurt used to make it) and no salt. Hawthorne Valley Farm of Ghent, New York, makes a commercial version, available in health-food stores, with only 10 milligrams of sodium per two-tablespoon serving; a similar amount of traditional cream cheese contains anywhere from 75 to 150 milligrams.

If you can't find commercially produced quark, you can always make your own. Start with good yogurt that contains no gelatin or other texture enhancing additives. Line a large strainer with cheesecloth or a coffee filter and suspend it over a bowl. Dump the yogurt into the strainer, put it in the refrigerator, and allow it to stand for several hours. (We like to set it up before going to bed, then enjoy quark with toast for breakfast.) Liquid will drain out of the yogurt, leaving a nice batch of quark. The sodium and fat contents of homemade quark depend on the amounts of sodium and fat in the yogurt you use to make it.

The Best Breakfasts

For the most part, the famous cereals we were sold on as kids are all loaded with sodium: 300 milligrams in a cup of Kellogg's Corn Flakes, 350 milligrams in a half cup of Post Grape-Nuts, and 280 milligrams in a cup of General Mills' Cheerios. But there's a fortunate exception: shredded wheat.

This product, biscuits made of wheat kernels that have been run through a mechanical shredder, layered, and baked, contains no salt; in fact it contains nothing at all but wheat and therefore no sodium. It has plenty of all-American flavor on its own. A bowl of it complemented by milk, banana slices, and a bit of brown sugar makes a great way to start the day on a regular basis. (Be aware, however, that a half cup of milk adds about 65 milligrams of sodium to the dish.)

Some people object to the shape and texture of traditional shredded wheat, unkindly comparing this useful food to a scouring pad. But a decade or so ago, manufacturers of the product addressed that problem by offering bite-sized or "mini-wheat" versions that reduced the basic biscuit to the more manageable size of a postage stamp.

Shredded wheat was invented more than a hundred years ago by Henry Drushel Perky, who set up a manufacturing operation for it in Niagara Falls, New York. Nabisco, which produced shredded wheat for many years with a picture of the falls on the box, sold its cereal to Post, which is now owned by Kraft Foods. You'll find other brands in health-food stores, but we see no reason to substitute them for the supermarket product, which has the richest wheat flavor of those we've tried.

If you tire of shredded wheat, you can shift to granola, which is often made without salt. Some of the best granolas are available in health-food stores and sold in bulk rather than packaged under

a brand name. But make sure they are salt free! (Since you'll prob-
ably want to eat granola with that half cup of milk, it's important to
get a zero-sodium variety.) Find a store manager and be sure he or
she really knows the ingredients. Otherwise, you can find packaged granola-like concoctions in both health-food stores and
supermarkets. Again, check the labels, since many commercially
prepared granolas contain salt. Products bearing the same brand
name may contain salt or not depending on the particular combination of grains, sweeteners, nuts, and dried fruits.

The Condiment Crisis

Good condiments—mustard, catsup, mayonnaise, etc.—make so
much everyday food worth eating, yet the common commercial
recipes for them are loaded with salt, enough to knock them off
your shopping list forever. And for many folks, that may be the
most devastating part of a low-sodium diet. Burgers without catsup? A roast beef sandwich without mustard? Tuna fish without
mayonnaise? How can life be lived?

If this looks like a crisis, however, panic isn't warranted. A number of salt-free catsups and mustards are available in health-food
stores and often in supermarkets. As for mayonnaise, for years
we've been using a viable substitute—Hain eggless mayonnaise
dressing—but without a lot of satisfaction. It's sodium free, and the
taste, based on soy oil, vinegar, lemon juice, and honey, approxi-
mates familiar mayo well enough in a tuna or chicken sandwich.
But the consistency is denser and oilier than an egg-based mayonnaise, and a classic element of flavor seems conspicuously missing.

The obvious answer is to make an egg-based mayonnaise at
home, and once upon a time that would have been easy to recommend. Now there's a problem: Mayonnaise recipes call for
raw eggs, and eggs on the market today aren't guaranteed to be
free of salmonella; eating raw eggs is considered high-risk behav-
ior. Most people who want to make their own mayonnaise, therefore, turn to the pasteurized raw eggs or egg products commonly

found in supermarket dairy cases. But many of the pasteurized egg products contain salt.

You can get around this problem if your supermarket carries pasteurized egg whites. This product is designed for the low-cholesterol dieter, and the versions we've seen, unlike those based on pasteurized whole eggs, are salt free. Because eggs contain a certain amount of natural sodium, the unsalted pasteurized egg whites are not sodium free, either. A quarter cup portion contains 70 milligrams of sodium. Even so, when diluted with oil, vinegar, and other mayonnaise ingredients, the salt-free egg whites make a mayonnaise that contains only 8 milligrams of sodium per tablespoon. It's also a great mayonnaise, with a nice light texture and an authentic egg flavor. Here's our recipe:

EGG WHITE MAYONNAISE

¼ c. pasteurized
   unsalted egg whites
2 tsp. white wine
   vinegar
1 tsp. lemon juice
2 tsp. unsalted Dijon
   mustard
freshly ground black
   pepper to taste
¾ c. mild-flavored
   vegetable oil

Add the egg whites, vinegar, lemon juice, mustard, and pepper to a blender and pulse a few times to combine. Then turn the blender to high speed and add the oil in a thin stream through the hole in the top of the cover. Close the cover completely and allow the blender to continue running until the mayonnaise firms up, about 2 minutes. You may want to stop the blending after a minute or so and use a rubber scraper to push mayonnaise down from the sides of the canister.

Feel free to elaborate on this mayonnaise. You'll find our recipes for basil, garlic, sun-dried tomato, and raspberry mayonnaises on pages 95–98.

YIELD: 16 tablespoons
SODIUM CONTENT: 8 mg. of sodium per tablespoon

Horseradish at Home

The root of *Armoracia rusticana,* also known as horseradish, produces a versatile condiment when finely grated and mixed with cider vinegar and black pepper. While many commercial producers also add salt, it's hardly necessary, given the root's fine, bold flavor. Your supermarket may carry a few commercially prepared products that are either salt free or extremely low in sodium, with only 5 milligrams or so per teaspoon.

For the best salt-free horseradish—deepest flavor, strongest bite—we strongly recommend making your own. To do that, you need some raw horseradish root. The best pieces are long and slim, from younger plants. You may be able to find them at farmers' markets or high-end groceries. Or you can grow them yourself (see page 17). Here's our recipe:

HORSERADISH

2 c. horseradish root, scrubbed clean, peeled, and cut into 1-inch pieces
1 tbsp. vegetable oil
1 tbsp. cider vinegar
freshly ground black pepper to taste

Put the horseradish root in a blender or food processor and blend until finely grated. Then add the oil and vinegar and continue to blend to the consistency of a coarse sauce. If you prefer a more liquid horseradish, add small amounts of vinegar. Stir in a generous grinding of pepper and remove to a jar for storage until ready to use.

YIELD: 2 cups
SODIUM CONTENT: 2 mg. of sodium per 2-tablespoon serving

If you have access to a garden plot, you can guarantee yourself a steady supply of fresh horseradish root. Horseradish is easy to grow—too easy, some would say, since the plants are aggressive, crowding whatever else is growing nearby. *Armoracia rusticana* is a member of the cabbage and mustard family. The dark green leaves grow big and coarse; some recommend picking the younger ones for use in salads, though we've never tried it.

To start your own stand of horseradish, get a few roots from a garden supply store or a produce market. The pieces of root for planting should be about ½ inch in diameter and 3 to 4 inches long. Choose a site with deep, moist soil and full sun or partial shade. Bury the roots vertically, covered with soil, about a foot apart. The plants will grow to a height of 2 feet, with a horizontal spread up to 18 inches. If you plant in the spring, you should have good roots to harvest by fall.

Garden books warn that the horseradish is invasive and will choke out other plants if not removed completely every fall. In our experience, that's easier said than done. The roots do grow wildly, and we've never been able to dig them all out. As a result, the pieces of root left in the ground generate new, bigger plants each year. While this can create problems of garden management—you might consider planting your first roots along the edge of the garden plot or in a corner—it also guarantees a steady supply of fresh horseradish through the spring, summer, and fall.

Hot and Helpful

We use a lot of salt-free chili powder, and not just because we like our recipes for vegetarian chili or chili con carne. Some time ago, we discovered that the addition of a half teaspoon of salt-free chili powder followed by a teaspoon of lemon juice brings up the flavor in a whole range of soups, stews, and vegetable dishes that otherwise seemed bland, without lending a noticeable chili taste. And if the chili powder adds a little bite, that's all to the good, we think. Hot spice adds a bit of distraction for palates that might still be missing salt.

Some popular brands of chili powder contain salt, and while the amounts cited on labels seem small (10 milligrams per quarter teaspoon), they add up to a lot if you are dumping a couple of teaspoons (for a large soup or stew) or two or three tablespoons (for chili) into the pot. Besides, there's no reason chili powder should contain salt. It's a gratuitous addition, given the good ground hot pepper, oregano, garlic, and other spices that go into the chili powder mix. You may be able to find a salt-free version in a supermarket—the last time we checked, Durkee offered one. Otherwise, try a health-food store.

We think of curry powder in the same way we think of chili powder, and we like to have a lot of it around. It's essential, of course, for meat and vegetable curries, and the great pork vindaloo (an Indian curry dish) we created in response to a cooking school teacher who insisted on loading his version of the dish with salt (see recipe on page 189). But the flavors of curry also invite experimentation. We routinely sprinkle it on the low-sodium tuna fish increasingly available in supermarkets, along with black pepper and a little lemon juice. We also add a bit to salad dressing and the flour or salt-free bread crumbs we use to coat chicken before broiling or frying. Commercial salt-free curry powders are somewhat easier to find than salt-free chili powders, but once we learned how to make our own curry powder by grinding up common spices, we no longer bothered to put a commercial version on the shopping list. Curry powder is easy to prepare, and a whiff of the results should persuade you that fresh grinding is worth the trouble.

For this and other do-it-yourself spice blends, it's best to work with an electric spice grinder—a mini electric blender that holds about a half a cup of dry ingredients. Such grinders are commonly available at housewares stores and are not expensive; people use them for grinding a pot's worth of coffee beans just before brewing. (If you get one for spices, however, don't use it for coffee; otherwise, coffee will taste like spices, and spices will taste like coffee.) If you don't like the idea of another electric appliance in the kitchen, you can invest in a mortar and pestle—effective so long as you are willing to expend the elbow grease. You can even improvise a mortar and pestle with a heavy bowl or coffee mug and the thick handle of an implement like an ice cream scoop.

CURRY POWDER

2 tsp. whole coriander
  seed
1 tsp. whole
  cumin seed
1 tsp. mustard
  seed
1 tsp. black peppercorns
1 stick of cinnamon,
  about 1 inch long
1 tsp. crushed
  hot pepper flakes
1 large bay leaf,
  crumbled

Put all the ingredients in a small bowl and stir to combine. Put the mixture in a hot skillet and roast over low to medium heat for two minutes, shaking the skillet so the spices don't burn. Transfer the mixture to a spice grinder and grind to a uniformly blended powder, or use a mortar and pestle to achieve the same result.

YIELD: 2 tablespoons
SODIUM CONTENT: 0 mg. of sodium per teaspoon

Pure Peanut Butter

Millions of Americans develop a taste for peanut butter in child-hood and carry their love for the standard sandwich—Peter Pan or Skippy with grape jelly—into adulthood. Unfortunately, most producers of peanut butter don't seem to recognize the prod-uct's greatest virtue, the flavor of peanuts, and insist on adding a lot of sugar and salt. Two tablespoons of Skippy, for example, contain 150 milligrams of sodium; Peter Pan contains a similar amount; for Jif the figure is a whopping 250 milligrams. Jif does produce a low-sodium, low-sugar version, but it still contains 65 milligrams of sodium in a two-tablespoon serving, and it tastes pretty salty to us.

We are constantly on the lookout for pure peanut butters, the kind that depend entirely on peanuts for flavor, and in recent years, they have become more available. California-based Hunt-Wesson, which produces Peter Pan peanut butters, offers a "very low sodium" version containing only peanuts and the hydrogenated vegetable oils that prevent separation of nut-meats and their oil while the jar is standing on the shelf. Smucker's, another ubiquitous supermarket brand, also offers no-salt-added peanut butters, with deeper and nuttier flavor than Peter Pan's.

Baking Essential

Beyond salt, a low-sodium diet means avoiding the sodium in baking powder and baking soda, common leavening agents for cakes, cookies, pancakes, waffles, muffins, and other sweet breads. It's easy enough to leave the small amounts of salt out of such dishes, but in most cases there is no natural substitute for the chemical leavener.

There is a good chemical substitute, however: Featherweight baking powder, distributed by the Hain Food Group of Uniondale, New York, and often available at health-food stores.

Featherweight is made of monocalcium phosphate, potato starch, and potassium bicarbonate. It contains no sodium, compared with 110 milligrams per quarter teaspoon in a conventional baking powder. The label recommends substituting equal amounts of Featherweight for conventional baking powder in recipes, though we habitually use a bit more.

The Salt-Free Pie

Fruit and berry pies make great desserts and a great way to celebrate the progress of summer and fall harvests. Pumpkin and pecan pies are holiday traditions. For the most part, you can prepare low-sodium fillings for all such pies simply by eliminating salt from your favorite recipes. As for crusts, we've come to rely on three.

The first is just a traditional crust without salt and with a touch of sugar. Here's the recipe, which makes enough for a top and bottom crust on a 9-inch pie. Reduce the quantities accordingly for a pie with only a bottom crust or with a lattice crust on top. Assuming you cut the pie into six pieces, this crust adds 5 milligrams of sodium per piece.

TRADITIONAL PIE CRUST

1 c. (2 sticks) cold
   unsalted butter or
   margarine
2½ c. all-purpose flour
2 tsp. white sugar
3 tbsp. ice water

Slice the butter into small pieces and put in a food processor fitted with a metal blade. Stir together the flour and sugar and put them in with the butter. Process until the butter and flour begin to mix, then dribble in the ice water while the processor continues to run. When the dough comes together into a large ball, remove to a bowl and refrigerate. (To make the dough by hand, mix the flour and sugar and cut them into the butter with a pastry blender, two knives, or your fingertips. Add the water and continue to mix until the dough clings together.)

To make a really flaky crust, it's important not to handle the dough too much when rolling it out, and to chill the crust again before adding the filling and putting it in the oven. The idea is to make the crust as cold as possible so that it gets a big shock from the heat of the oven. We like to put the bottom crust in the freezer for 10 or 15 minutes after we've rolled it out and put it in the pie tin. You can't do that with the top crust, of course, since it has to go on the pie after you've put in the filling. You might want to cut out circles of crust, put them on a piece of waxed paper, and put them in the freezer with the bottom crust, then float them on top of the filling before putting the pie in the oven.

YIELD: Crust for 9-inch pie (top and bottom)
SODIUM CONTENT: 5 mg. of sodium per ⅙ of crust

The second crust is based on crumbs of low-sodium melba toast, a product you can look for in supermarkets, cheese stores, and specialty food shops. Melba toast is a yeast-raised bread that has been baked, sliced, and baked some more so that it becomes dry and crisp. For a pie crust, you pulverize it, then mix it with sugar, a touch of nutmeg, and melted butter or margarine, then press it into a pie tin and bake until it solidifies before adding the filling. If you find a melba toast with 5 milligrams of sodium in two slices, this crust will add only 9 milligrams of sodium to one-sixth of a 9-inch pie.

MELBA TOAST CRUST

1½ c. of crumbs made from low-sodium melba toast (5 mg. in 2 slices)
¼ c. white sugar
1 tsp. nutmeg
6 tbsp. unsalted butter or margarine, melted

Preheat the oven to 350 degrees. To make the crumbs, place slices of the toast in a food processor fitted with the metal blade and pulse several times. If you don't have a food processor, you can put the toast slices between sheets of waxed paper and crush them with a rolling pin. Put the crumbs in a bowl, add the sugar and nutmeg, and stir to blend. Then stir in the melted butter or margarine until all the crumbs are moistened. Transfer the crumbs to a 9-inch pie plate and spread them around with your fingertips so that they cover the bottom and sides of the plate in an even layer. Bake on the middle rack of the oven for 10 minutes, until the crust begins to brown and hold together. Remove from the oven and allow to cool before adding the filling.

YIELD: Crust for 9-inch pie
SODIUM CONTENT: 9 mg. of sodium per ⅙ of crust

The third crust is even simpler to make and adds great elegance to a berry or cream pie. It's based on the amaretto cookies imported from Italy and available, often in large metal tins, in Italian delicatessens or specialty food shops. Because the cookies are quite sweet you will want to brush off any large grains of sugar adhering to them (many come sprinkled with it), and you should consider reducing the sugar content of the filling. This crust contributes 9 milligrams of sodium to one sixth of a 9-inch pie.

AMARETTO CRUMB CRUST

1½ c. amaretto cookie crumbs
6 tbsp. unsalted butter or margarine, melted

Preheat the oven to 350 degrees. Pulverize the cookies by putting them in a food processor fitted with the metal blade and pulsing several times or placing them between sheets of waxed paper and

crushing them with a rolling pin. Put the crumbs in a bowl, add the melted butter or margarine, and stir so that all the crumbs are moistened. Transfer the crumbs to a 9-inch pie plate and spread them around with your fingertips so that they cover the bottom and sides of the plate in an even layer. Bake on the middle rack of the oven for 10 minutes, until the crust begins to brown and hold together. Remove from the oven and allow to cool before adding the filling.

YIELD: Crust for 9-inch pie
SODIUM CONTENT: 9 mg. of sodium per ⅙ of crust

A Restaurant Story

One day someone smart may decide to open a chain of no-salt eateries; until then, dining out remains problematic for the salt-free dieter.

In general, we've found it's best to go to higher-end restaurants (assuming you can afford it), where chefs prepare most of the dishes from scratch. But a big element of chance remains. Some laudable chefs take the customer's request as a creative challenge and are glad to do more than simply omitting the sauce (and most of the interest) from the broiled fish or chicken. These, in our experience, tend to be the exception, however. Far more common are the waiters and chefs who glibly agree to prepare your dish with no added salt, neglecting to tell you that the piece of meat in question has been soaking for hours in soy sauce or some other heavily salted marinade.

We are pleased to report, however, on one happy experience that suggests a possible strategy: patronize a restaurant you like well enough so that you get to know the waiters; tip them well, chat them up, and eventually ask if they can get the kitchen to give you something that's not on the menu, made to order without salt.

We were able to do this in, of all places, a Chinese restaurant down the block, known as Charlie Mom. Over the years, we've given them a lot of business, ordering takeout for gatherings at the house and meeting there for dinner with other families, while doing our best to dodge the sodium in dishes we ordered for ourselves. With a lot of the waiters, our order came down to a standard exchange. We'd like the chicken with broccoli, we say, "No soy sauce, no salt, no MSG."

"No soy sauce? No salt? No MSG?" the waiter responds with dismay. "No taste!" We assure him that that's fine. We will eat a dish with no taste. And that is what usually follows.

One night, however, a particular waiter showed more interest. Why did we always order this way, he wanted to know. We explained our need to avoid sodium. He frowned and stared at the menu, then pointed to a dish called Shrimp and Scallops Royal. This was described as shrimp and scallops in a white sauce with pineapple and green onion. "How about this?" he said. "No soy sauce, no salt, no MSG, but we will add garlic, ginger, and dried red peppers." We readily agreed; it certainly sounded better than anything else on the menu we could possibly eat. And when the dish arrived, it was delicious—we had reclaimed our ability to eat Chinese food without compromise.

We asked the waiter to write down the order, which he did in Chinese characters. We kept the precious slip of paper and presented it a few weeks later at the takeout counter. This did not faze the woman who waited on us. She simply copied down the characters and shipped them into the kitchen, where the cooks easily duplicated the dish we had had before.

So on our next trip to Charlie Mom, we hope to find the same waiter and talk him into crafting another super low-sodium dish just for us. The possibilities, after all, are infinite.

II. BREAKFAST

BASIC PANCAKES

You can't go wrong with this recipe so long as you don't mix the batter too much and you turn the pancakes as soon as the batter begins to bubble. In addition to basic pancakes, you can use this batter for blueberry, raspberry, or banana pancakes.

2 c. flour
4 tsp. low-sodium baking powder
2 tsp. cinnamon
2 eggs
2 c. milk
¼ c. vegetable oil
1 tsp. vanilla

Sift the flour together with the baking powder and cinnamon, and set aside. Break the eggs into a bowl and beat lightly. Add the milk, oil, and vanilla, and stir to blend. Add the flour mixture and stir only until it is completely moistened. Do not overmix.

Heat an oiled griddle or frying pan until a drop of water thrown onto it quickly boils away. To make pancakes, drop generous tablespoons full of batter on the griddle. If you are making blueberry, raspberry, or banana pancakes, add the fruit on top of the batter just after you drop it on the griddle. When bubbles form on the surface of the batter, turn the pancakes quickly and cook a minute or so longer until cooked through. Serve immediately.

YIELD: 12 medium pancakes
SODIUM CONTENT: 32 mg. of sodium per pancake

BASIC MUFFINS

1½ c. whole-wheat flour
2 tsp. low-sodium
  baking powder
½ tsp. cinnamon
3 tbsp. unsalted butter
  or margarine
3 tbsp. honey or light
  molasses
1 egg
¾ c. milk

Preheat oven to 375 degrees. Sift the dry ingredients together and set aside. Cream the butter and honey or molasses in a bowl. Beat in the egg. Add the milk and stir to blend. Add the dry ingredients and stir only until they are moistened. Do not overmix. Fill cups of a greased muffin tin three-quarters full and bake for 10 to 15 minutes until the tops have browned and a toothpick inserted into the center of a muffin comes out clean.

Variations: For fruit-flavored muffins, substitute fruit juice for milk. Or you can stick with the original recipe and add fresh fruit, stirring it into the wet ingredients before you add the dry (see the following recipes for apple cinnamon and orange-cranberry muffins). If you use blueberries or raspberries, omit the cinnamon. If you use peaches (peeled and diced), substitute nutmeg for the cinnamon; if you use pears (peeled and diced) substitute ground ginger.

YIELD: 12 muffins
SODIUM CONTENT: 14 mg. of sodium per muffin

APPLE CINNAMON MUFFINS

2 c. flour
2 tsp. low-sodium
  baking powder
¼ c. sugar
1 tbsp. cinnamon
¾ c. milk
2 medium apples,
  peeled, cored,
  and diced
3 tbsp. unsalted butter,
  melted
2 eggs

Stir the dry ingredients together in a large bowl. Add the milk and stir until all the dry ingredients are moist. Do not overmix. Add the apples, butter, and the eggs, and stir to incorporate. Let the batter rest while you heat the oven to 400 degrees. When the oven is hot, drop the batter into cups of a greased muffin tin, filling to just below the top of each cup. Bake for 10 to 15 minutes or until the tops have browned and a toothpick inserted into the center of a muffin comes out clean.

YIELD: 12 muffins
SODIUM CONTENT: 20 mg. of sodium per muffin

ORANGE CRANBERRY MUFFINS

To make these muffins you need to find sweetened dried cranberries, not the fresh ones sold for cranberry sauce. This makes a festive muffin for breakfast; if you have the right muffin tin, you can also make little 2-inch muffins to serve with dinner.

¾ c. dried cranberries
1¼ c. all-purpose flour
¾ c. whole-wheat flour
2 tsp. low-sodium
    baking powder
1 tsp. cinnamon
3 tbsp. vegetable oil
¼ c. honey
2 eggs
¾ c. orange juice

Put the cranberries in a small bowl, cover them with water, and allow them to soak until softened (at least an hour; more if possible).

Preheat the oven to 350 degrees. Sift together the flours, baking powder, and cinnamon in a large bowl. Combine the oil, honey, eggs, and orange juice, and stir to blend. Add the cranberries and a small amount (no more than ¼ cup) of the water in which they have soaked; stir. Pour this mixture over the flour mixture and stir gently, only until all the dry ingredients are moistened. Spoon the mixture into cups of a lightly greased muffin tin; the cups should be nearly full. Bake on the middle rack of the oven for about 15 minutes until the tops begin to brown and a toothpick inserted into the center of a muffin comes out clean. Turn the muffins out onto a rack to cool a bit before serving.

YIELD: 12 muffins
SODIUM CONTENT: 13 mg. of sodium per muffin

MAPLE PECAN MUFFINS

1½ c. roughly chopped
pecans
¼ c. wheat bran
1 c. whole-wheat flour
1¼ c. all-purpose flour
1 tbsp. low-sodium
baking powder
⅓ c. plain yogurt
⅔ c. milk
2 tbsp. unsalted butter,
melted
1 egg, lightly beaten
1 c. maple syrup

Preheat the oven to 350 degrees. Spread the chopped nuts and bran on a baking sheet and toast them briefly in the oven until the bran begins to turn brown, then remove. Sift together the flours and baking powder; add the toasted bran and pecans and stir to blend. In a separate bowl, combine the yogurt, milk, and melted butter, then add the egg and maple syrup and stir to blend. Pour the liquid ingredients over the dry and stir until the dry ingredients are moistened. Fill the cups of a lightly greased muffin tin to just below the rim with the batter and bake on the middle rack of the oven for about 15 minutes, until the tops begin to brown and a toothpick inserted into the center of a muffin comes out clean.

YIELD: 12 muffins
SODIUM CONTENT: 18 mg. of sodium per muffin

PINEAPPLE COCONUT MUFFINS

Be sure to use raw grated coconut unadulterated with anything else; look for it in a health-food store if your supermarket doesn't carry it. Avoid the packaged coconut commonly sold with baking supplies; it's likely to be loaded with sugar, salt, and other sodium compounds.

1 c. raw grated coconut
½ c. whole-wheat flour
1½ c. all-purpose flour
2 tsp. low-sodium
   baking powder
1½ tsp. cinnamon
1 c. canned crushed
   pineapple, plus juice,
   or chopped fresh
   pineapple
5 tbsp. brown sugar
4 tbsp. unsalted butter,
   melted
1 egg
½ c. plain yogurt
¼ c. milk

Preheat the oven to 350 degrees. Spread the coconut on a baking sheet and bake for a few minutes until it begins to turn golden brown. Sift together the flours, baking powder, and cinnamon; add the toasted coconut and stir to combine. In a separate bowl, combine the pineapple, brown sugar, and melted butter and stir to blend; then stir in the egg, yogurt, and milk. Pour this mixture over the dry ingredients and stir only until the dry ingredients are well moistened. Fill the cups of a lightly greased muffin tin with the batter to just below the rim and bake on the middle rack of the oven for about 15 minutes until the tops begin to brown and a toothpick inserted into the middle of a muffin comes out clean.

YIELD: 12 muffins
SODIUM CONTENT: 20 mg. of sodium per muffin

PUMPKIN MUFFINS

For fresh pumpkin purée, seed the pumpkin, cut the shell into chunks, and peel off the outer skin. Steam the chunks until tender in a large pot, then purée them in a blender or food processor.

4 tbsp. unsalted butter, softened
⅓ c. molasses
1 egg
¾ c. puréed pumpkin, fresh or canned
½ c. golden raisins
1 tsp. cinnamon
½ tsp. ground ginger
½ tsp. allspice
½ tsp. ground cloves
1 tbsp. salt-free baking powder
1½ c. all-purpose flour

Preheat the oven to 350 degrees. Cream the butter and molasses together until well blended. Stir in the egg. Add the pumpkin and stir to blend, then stir in the raisins. Sift together the spices, baking powder, and flour. Mix the dry ingredients with the pumpkin mixture and stir only until the dry ingredients are moistened. Do not overmix. Spoon the mixture into a lightly greased muffin tin, filling each cup to just below the rim. Place the tin in the oven and bake for about 15 minutes, until the tops of the muffins begin to brown and a toothpick inserted into the center of a muffin comes out clean. Turn the muffins out onto a rack to cool a bit before serving.

YIELD: 12 muffins
SODIUM CONTENT: 12 mg. of sodium per muffin

BASIL MUFFINS

We like these savory muffins best in miniature— get a muffin tin with 2-inch (rather than the standard 3-inch) cups and fill it twice. Made that way, the muffins take less time to cook, so watch them carefully.

½ **c. coarsely chopped fresh basil leaves**
1 **heaping tbsp. pine nuts or chopped walnuts**
1 **clove garlic**
¼ **c. plus 2 tbsp. olive oil**
1 **c. low-sodium chicken broth, vegetable broth, or water**
1 **c. milk**
1 **egg**
2 **tsp. honey**
3 **c. all-purpose flour**
1 **tbsp. low-sodium baking powder**

Preheat the oven to 350 degrees. Put the basil leaves, nuts, garlic, and 2 tablespoons of oil in a blender or food processor and process to form a smooth paste. Combine the broth or water, milk, egg, honey, basil mixture, and the rest of the oil in a bowl and stir until well blended. Sift together the flour and baking powder in a separate bowl. Pour the wet ingredients over the dry and stir with a spoon just until the dry ingredients are thoroughly moistened.

Lightly grease a muffin tin. Fill the cups with equal amounts of the batter. Cook on the middle rack of the oven for about 15 to 20 minutes for 3-inch muffins, 10 to 15 minutes for 2-inch muffins, or until the tops are lightly browned and a toothpick inserted into the center of a muffin comes out clean.

YIELD: 12 (3-inch) or 24 (2-inch) muffins
SODIUM CONTENT: about 29 mg. of sodium per 3-inch muffin, 15 mg. per 2-inch muffin. Sodium amounts are for muffins made with chicken broth; if made with vegetable broth (see page 103), count 19 mg. per 3-inch muffin, 10 mg. per 2-inch muffin; if made with water, count 17 mg. per 3-inch muffin, 9 mg. per 2-inch muffin.

TOMATO MUFFINS
WITH ROSEMARY

2 c. salt-free tomato
sauce, tomato purée,
or canned tomatoes
with liquid
1 c. cornmeal
1 tbsp. plus 1 tsp.
unsalted chili powder
⅓ c. finely chopped
onion
2 tbsp. dried rosemary
leaves
2 eggs
2 tbsp. molasses
¼ c. plus 2 tbsp. olive
oil
1½ c. all-purpose flour
4 tsp. low-sodium
baking powder

Preheat the oven to 350 degrees.
Combine the tomato sauce or
tomatoes and cornmeal in a large
bowl; stir in the chili powder, onion,
and rosemary. Allow to stand for a
few minutes. In a separate bowl
combine the eggs, molasses, and olive
oil, then add them to the tomato
mixture and stir to blend. Sift together
the flour and baking powder and add
them to the tomato mixture. Stir
gently to combine, only until all the
dry ingredients are moistened.

Lightly grease a muffin tin and fill
the cups just to the rim with the
batter. Bake on the middle rack of the
oven for 15 to 20 minutes or until the
tops of the muffins begin to brown
and a toothpick inserted into the
middle of a muffin comes out clean.

YIELD: 12 large muffins
SODIUM CONTENT: about 22 mg. of sodium per muffin

HASH BROWN POTATOES

**2 lbs. (6 medium)
potatoes, peeled
2 tbsp. olive oil
½ c. finely chopped
onion
2 cloves garlic, minced
2 tsp. lemon juice
1 tsp. unsalted chili
powder**

Boil the potatoes whole until just tender partway through. Cut them into 1-inch cubes. Heat 2 tablespoons of oil in a large skillet or sauté pan, add the onion, and cook over medium heat until it wilts and turns golden brown. Add the cubed potato and toss with the onions to combine. Sprinkle with the minced garlic, lemon juice, and chili powder, and stir so that all the ingredients are evenly distributed. As the potato begins to stick to the pan, scrape bits of it off with a wooden spoon and stir it into the larger mixture. After 5 minutes of cooking this way, turn the heat to low, cover the pan, and allow the potatoes to continue cooking until completely tender.

YIELD: Serves 6
SODIUM CONTENT: 10 mg. of sodium per serving

BREAKFAST SAUSAGE

1 lb. ground beef or pork freshly ground black pepper to taste
½ tsp. dried sage
½ tsp. onion powder
½ tsp. garlic powder

Sprinkle the spices over the meat and mix them in by kneading the meat by hand for 5 minutes. Be sure the spices are evenly distributed. Shape the meat into round patties about 2 inches in diameter and ¾-inch thick. Put them on a plate, cover with foil or plastic wrap, and refrigerate for at least a half hour or overnight. This allows the spice flavors to permeate the meat.

Fry the patties in a nonstick pan over medium heat until they are nicely browned on the outside and thoroughly cooked on the inside. Place on a dish lined with paper towel to drain for a few minutes before serving.

YIELD: Serves 4
SODIUM CONTENT: 63 mg. of sodium per serving

BAKING POWDER BISCUITS

2 c. all-purpose flour
1 tbsp. low-sodium
  baking powder
6 tbsp. unsalted butter
1 c. milk

Sift together the flour and baking powder. Cut the butter into small pieces and add it to the flour mixture. Use two knives, a pastry blender, your fingertips, or a food processor to mix the flour and butter to the consistency of cornmeal. Add the milk and stir to blend. Turn the dough onto a lightly floured board and knead for a minute or so; the dough should be evenly soft, the same consistency throughout. Dust your hands with flour. Cut pieces of dough 2 to 3 inches square and roll them into balls between your palms. Place them on a greased, floured baking sheet and press them gently to flatten them slightly. Chill in the refrigerator for at least a half hour before baking.

While the biscuits are chilling, preheat the oven to 450 degrees. Bake the biscuits on the top rack of the oven until they begin to brown, about 15 minutes.

YIELD: 12 biscuits
SODIUM CONTENT: 11 mg. of sodium per biscuit

SCONES WITH BRAN AND APRICOTS

1½ c. white flour
½ c. bran
1 tbsp. low-sodium baking powder
3 tbsp. sugar
3 tbsp. unsalted butter, softened
½ c. finely diced dried apricots or raisins
1 egg
¼ c. milk
¼ c. plain yogurt

Preheat the oven to 425 degrees. Stir together the flour, bran, baking powder, and sugar. Cut in the butter using a pastry blender or your fingers until it is totally absorbed into the dry ingredients. Add the apricots and stir to distribute them evenly. Combine the egg, milk, and yogurt in a bowl, then add to the flour mixture and stir only enough to moisten all of it. Turn the dough onto a floured surface, knead several times, and pat it down until it is about an inch thick. Flour the rim of a 2- to 3-inch diameter glass and use it to cut scones out of the dough, gathering the scraps and patting them flat until you have used all the dough. Put the scones on a baking sheet and bake for about 15 minutes or until golden brown.

If you wish, you can glaze the scones: Beat 2 tablespoons water into 1¼ cups confectioners' sugar to form a thick glaze. Add a little more water if you prefer a thinner glaze. Stir in ½ teaspoon vanilla or 1 teaspoon lemon juice, whichever you prefer. Drizzle the glaze over the scones while they are warm from the oven.

YIELD: 8 scones
SODIUM CONTENT: 19 mg. of sodium per scone

MAPLE-PECAN STICKY BUNS

Unless you like to get up really early in the morning, you should begin these yeast-raised buns the night before you want to serve them for breakfast and allow them to do their second rising slowly in the refrigerator overnight.

FOR THE DOUGH:

4½ tsp. (2 packages)
   dry yeast
1 c. lukewarm water
½ c. milk
2 eggs
4 tbsp. unsalted butter,
   softened
4 c. all-purpose flour
1 tbsp. plus 1 tsp.
   cinnamon
1 c. raisins

FOR THE GLAZE:

½ c. tightly packed
   brown sugar
½ c. maple syrup
4 tbsp. unsalted butter
1½ c. pecan halves

Dissolve the yeast in ½ cup of lukewarm water and allow to stand a few minutes, until it begins to foam. Add the rest of the water, milk, eggs, and 2 tablespoons of butter, and stir until well blended. Then stir in the flour, half a cup at a time, until the mixture becomes too stiff to handle in the bowl. Turn it out onto a floured board and knead by hand, adding flour as needed, for 8 to 10 minutes, until the dough becomes soft and elastic. Put the dough in a lightly oiled straight-sided bowl, cover loosely with plastic wrap, and put in a warm place to rise until double in bulk, about 1 hour.

While the dough is rising, grease a 9-inch by 13-inch baking pan lightly with vegetable shortening. Combine the brown sugar, maple syrup, and 4 tablespoons butter in a small saucepan and heat gently on top of the stove until the sugar melts and the mixture is smooth. Spread the topping mixture evenly in the greased pan. Then add the pecan halves, curved side down, so that they are evenly distributed.

When the dough has risen, punch it down, turn it out on a floured board, and knead it a few times. Then flatten it out, using a well-floured rolling pin if necessary, to form a large rectangle. Melt the

(Continued)

remaining 2 tablespoons of butter and brush it evenly over the surface of the dough; then sprinkle with the cinnamon and spread the raisins across it. Starting on a long side of the rectangle, roll up the dough to form a cylinder, pinching the seam tightly together along the bottom. Starting at one end of the cylinder, use a sharp knife to cut off 16 equal rounds. Place them horizontally on the topping in the baking pan so that they are evenly spaced. Cover the pan loosely with plastic wrap and set the buns aside to rise for about half an hour, while you preheat the oven to 375 degrees. When the buns have risen for the second time, bake them on the middle rack of the oven for about 25 minutes, until nicely browned.

(If you wish, you can put the buns in the refrigerator to rise for the second time overnight. If you do this, allow them to warm up at room temperature for 20 minutes before baking at 375 for 30 to 35 minutes.)

When the buns are baked, allow them to cool for about 10 minutes. Then invert the baking pan over a large serving dish or tray and tap the bottom so that the buns fall out together; scrape out and add back any topping that remains in the pan.

YIELD: 16 buns
SODIUM CONTENT: 23 mg. of sodium per bun

POPOVERS

A warm popover fresh from the oven should be crisp, and to our taste even a little chewy, on the outside, smooth on the inside. The cooking can be a bit tricky, since these are muffins that rise only because of the steam generated during baking; there's no yeast or baking powder. We did best when we started the popovers out at 450 degrees, then reduced the temperature to 350 after 10 minutes. It's important not to peek at them as they cook (unless your oven door has a window), since a puff of cool air could cause them to collapse. And we used bread flour rather than all purpose; the added gluten produced a sturdier popover filled with the big cavities that invite butter and jam.

1½ c. bread flour
1 tbsp. plus 2 tsp. sugar
1½ c. milk
3 eggs
1½ tbsp. unsalted butter, melted
2 tbsp. grated low-sodium Gouda cheese (optional)

Preheat the oven to 450 degrees. Sift together the flour and sugar and put them in a mixing bowl. Combine the milk and eggs in another bowl and beat lightly; slowly pour in the melted butter, stirring to prevent it from cooking the eggs. Add the liquid ingredients to the dry, using an electric mixer to combine them until they are thoroughly blended and smooth. (Or you can put the ingredients in a blender or food processor fitted with the steel blade and blend or process briefly to create the smooth batter.)

Lightly grease the cups of a muffin tin and fill them with the batter to just below the rim. Put the tin on the middle rack of the oven and bake at 450 degrees for 10 minutes, then turn the heat down to 350 degrees and cook for another 20 minutes. The popovers are ready when the tops are nicely browned. Sprinkle with Gouda cheese, if desired. Serve warm with butter and jam.

YIELD: 12 popovers
SODIUM CONTENT: 35 mg. of sodium per popover

YEAST-RAISED BUCKWHEAT PANCAKES

This recipe and the one that follows are adapted from ones in Marion Cunningham's 1987 The Breakfast Book; *the pancakes also resemble ones in* English Bread and Yeast Cookery *by the great English food writer Elizabeth David. Yeast gives pancakes and waffles a special salt-free tang and wonderfully light texture. Buckwheat gives the pancakes terrific flavor. Both are especially good when served with maple syrup or with yogurt and fruit. They are easily cooked for breakfast if you do part of the preparation the night before and allow the batter to rise overnight.*

1 package (2¼ tsp.) dry yeast
½ c. lukewarm water
½ tsp. sugar
1 c. milk
¾ c. buckwheat flour
¾ c. white flour
2 eggs
2 tbsp. melted butter
¼ c. plain yogurt
juice of ½ lemon

Dissolve the yeast in the lukewarm water. Add the sugar and let stand a few minutes until it begins to foam. Heat the milk to lukewarm (no hotter) and add it to the yeast mixture. Stir in ¼ cup buckwheat flour and ¼ cup white flour. When thoroughly blended, cover loosely with plastic wrap and allow to rise in a warm place for 1 to 2 hours, until doubled in size.

Then stir in the rest of the flour and the eggs, butter, and yogurt. Let the batter rise for at least another hour, or in the refrigerator overnight.

After it has risen again, stir in the lemon juice. Heat and lightly oil a skillet or griddle, then cook the pancakes by dropping generous tablespoons of batter onto the hot surface, waiting for bubbles to form, and turning. The pancakes should be golden brown.

YIELD: 12 medium pancakes
SODIUM CONTENT: 25 mg. of sodium per pancake

YEAST-RAISED WAFFLES

½ c. lukewarm water
1 package (2¼ teaspoons)
  dry yeast
2 c. milk
⅓ c. plain yogurt
2 tbsp. melted butter
1 tsp. sugar
½ c. whole-wheat flour
1½ c. white flour
2 eggs
½ tsp. low-sodium
  baking powder

Dissolve the yeast in the lukewarm water and let stand a few minutes until it begins to foam. Add the milk, yogurt, butter, sugar, whole-wheat flour, and white flour to the yeast mixture and stir until blended. Cover and let stand overnight at room temperature.

Heat up the waffle iron. Just before you cook the waffles, stir in the eggs and baking powder. To cook a waffle, drop ¼ cup of batter in the center of the heated waffle iron. Close the top and wait until the light goes off, then goes on again (or follow whatever other device the iron offers for indicating when the waffle is cooked through). You may want to leave the waffles on a bit longer for a crisper texture. Serve immediately with maple syrup, yogurt and fruit, or fresh lemon juice and powdered sugar.

YIELD: 12 medium waffles
SODIUM CONTENT: 35 mg. of sodium per waffle

III. BREAD

HONEY WHEAT BREAD

This is a good basic bread to bake on a regular basis. The addition of vital wheat gluten, available in health-food stores, specialty food stores, and some supermarkets, adds a bit of lift to the loaf and gives it a chewier quality. If you can't find it, however, just leave it out.

2 packages (4½ tsp.) dry yeast
2 c. lukewarm water
¼ c. vegetable oil
¼ c. honey
1 c. whole-wheat flour
½ c. cornmeal
2 tsp. vital wheat gluten (optional)
2½ to 3 c. white bread flour

Dissolve the yeast in ½ cup of lukewarm water. When it begins to foam, add the rest of the water, oil, and honey, and stir to blend. In a separate bowl, combine the whole-wheat flour, cornmeal, and vital wheat gluten. Add them to the liquid mixture, stirring to combine. Then begin adding the white bread flour, ½ cup at a time, to create a stiff dough. When it becomes too hard to handle in the bowl, turn it out onto a floured surface and knead for 10 minutes or more, adding small amounts of white bread flour to prevent sticking, to create a smooth, elastic dough. (Or you can use an electric mixer with a dough hook. Pour in the liquid ingredients; add the whole-wheat flour, cornmeal, and vital wheat gluten and mix for a minute. Then add the white bread flour, ½ cup at a time, until the dough clings together and cleans the side of the bowl. Remove from the mixer bowl and knead a few times by hand to give the dough a uniform texture.) Lightly oil a straight-sided bowl, put the dough in it, cover it with plastic wrap, and put it in a warm place to rise until double in bulk. This should take about 1 hour.

When the dough has risen, punch it down, remove it from the bowl,

(Continued)

knead it a few times, and return it to the bowl to rise for a second time, about 45 minutes.

When the dough has finished rising for the second time, turn it out of the bowl onto a floured surface. Divide it into two equal portions. Using your fingertips or the heel of your palm, flatten one piece of the dough into a large circle. Starting at the top of the circle, fold it toward you by quarters, pressing together the seam of each fold, to create a cylinder. Then fold the ends of the cylinder to the center, pressing together the seams, to create a loaf. Press the loaf into a lightly greased 4½" × 9" loaf pan, seams side down. Repeat with the second piece of dough. Cover the loaf pans loosely with plastic wrap (sprinkle a little flour on top of each loaf to prevent the plastic wrap from sticking) and set them aside in a warm place to rise for the third time.

Preheat the oven to 450 degrees. When the loaves have doubled in bulk (about ½ hour), use a sharp knife to make three diagonal slashes across the top of each one. Then put them on the bottom rack of the oven. Bake for 10 minutes at 450 degrees, then reduce the heat to 350 degrees and continue baking for another 25 to 30 minutes until the tops are well browned and the loaves sound hollow when thumped on the bottom, or a long toothpick or bamboo skewer inserted into the middle of a loaf comes out clean.

YIELD: 2 loaves
SODIUM CONTENT: less than 1 mg. of sodium per ½-inch slice

GOOD WHITE BREAD

Cooking semolina flour in milk to create a wheat-meal mush for incorporation into the dough enhances both flavor and texture. Thick slices of this bread make a great salt-free substitute for a hamburger roll.

1½ c. milk
½ c. semolina flour
2 packages (4½ tsp.) dry yeast
1½ c. water
2 tbsp. honey
2 tsp. vital wheat gluten (optional)
2 tbsp. unsalted butter, melted
4 c. white bread flour

Heat the milk in a small saucepan until almost boiling, then add the semolina flour and stir until the mixture thickens into a mush. Continue to stir so that there are no lumps, then set the pan aside to cool. Make sure it has cooled completely before adding to the dough.

Dissolve the yeast in ½ cup of lukewarm water and allow it to stand until foamy. Stir in the honey, add the rest of the water and the vital wheat gluten (if you are using it), then add the semolina mush, followed by the melted butter; stir to combine. Use a wooden spoon to stir in 2 to 3 cups of the flour. When the mixture gets too stiff to handle in the bowl, turn it out on a floured board and knead for several minutes, continuing to add small amounts of flour, until the dough becomes smooth and pliable. (Or use an electric mixer fitted with a dough hook to knead the dough. After the dough becomes too stiff to handle with a wooden spoon, transfer it to the mixer bowl, turn the mixer on to slow speed and add small amounts of additional flour until the ball of dough cleans the side of the bowl.) Transfer the dough to a lightly oiled straight-sided bowl, cover loosely with plastic wrap, and set aside to rise until more than double in bulk; this should take about an hour.

(Continued)

When the dough has risen, punch it down, remove it from the bowl, knead it a few times, and return it to the bowl to rise for a second time, about 45 minutes.

When the dough has finished rising for the second time, turn it out of the bowl onto a floured surface. Divide it into two equal portions. Using your fingertips or the heel of your palm, flatten one piece of the dough into a large circle. Starting at the top of the circle, fold it toward you by quarters, pressing together the seam of each fold, to create a cylinder. Then fold the ends of the cylinder to the center, pressing together the seams, to create a loaf. Press the loaf into a lightly greased 4½" × 9" loaf pan, seams side down. Repeat with the second piece of dough. Cover the loaf pans loosely with plastic wrap (sprinkle a little flour on top of each loaf to prevent the plastic wrap from sticking) and set them aside in a warm place to rise for the third time.

While they are rising, preheat the oven to 375 degrees. When the loaves have doubled in bulk (about ½ hour), use a sharp knife to cut three diagonal slashes in the top of each one, then put them on the bottom rack of the oven and bake until the tops are well browned—35 to 40 minutes. The bread is done when it sounds hollow if thumped on the bottom or a long toothpick or bamboo skewer inserted into the center of a loaf comes out clean.

YIELD: 2 loaves
SODIUM CONTENT: 7 mg. of sodium per ½-inch slice

SHREDDED WHEAT BREAD

Shredded wheat, one of a few mainstream breakfast cereals that contains no salt or sodium, makes a wonderfully tasty loaf of bread. This family recipe comes from the file of our late mother-in-law, Margaret Burke.

3 biscuits shredded wheat or 3 to 4 oz. bite-sized pieces
2 c. boiling water
2 tsp. vegetable oil
¼ c. honey or molasses
2 packages (2 tbsp.) dry yeast
½ c. lukewarm water
5 to 6 c. all-purpose flour

Crumble up the shredded wheat in a large bowl, pour the boiling water over it, and stir to soften the fibers. Stir in the oil and the honey or molasses and set aside to cool. In a small bowl, dissolve the yeast in the lukewarm water. When the shredded wheat mixture has cooled completely, pour in the yeast mixture and stir to blend. Stir in the flour, ½ cup at a time, until the dough becomes too stiff to handle in the bowl. Turn it out on a floured board and knead for several minutes, continuing to add small amounts of flour, until the dough becomes smooth and pliable. (Or use an electric mixer fitted with a dough hook to knead the dough. After the dough becomes too stiff to handle with a wooden spoon, transfer it to the mixer bowl, turn the mixer on to slow speed and add small amounts of additional flour until the ball of dough cleans the side of the bowl.) Transfer the dough to a lightly oiled straight-sided bowl, cover loosely with plastic wrap, and set aside to rise until more than double in bulk; this should take about an hour.

When the dough has risen, punch it down, remove it from the bowl, knead it a few times, and return it to the bowl to rise for a second time, about 45 minutes.

(Continued)

When the dough has finished rising for the second time, turn it out of the bowl onto a floured surface. Divide it into two equal portions. Using your fingertips or the heel of your palm, flatten one piece of the dough into a large circle. Starting at the top of the circle, fold it towards you by quarters, pressing together the seam of each fold, to create a cylinder. Then fold the ends of the cylinder to the center, pressing together the seams, to create a loaf. Press the loaf into a lightly greased 4½" × 9" loaf pan, seams side down. Repeat with the second piece of dough. Cover the loaf pans loosely with plastic wrap (sprinkle a little flour on top of each loaf to prevent the plastic wrap from sticking), and set them aside in a warm place to rise for the third time.

While they are rising, preheat the oven to 375 degrees. When the loaves have doubled in bulk (about ½ hour), use a sharp knife to cut three diagonal slashes in the top of each one, then put them on the bottom rack of the oven and bake until the tops are well browned—35 to 40 minutes. The bread is done when it sounds hollow if thumped on the bottom or a long toothpick or bamboo skewer inserted into the center of a loaf comes out clean.

YIELD: 2 loaves
SODIUM CONTENT: 1 mg. of sodium per ½-inch slice

TUSCAN BREAD

The world's salt-free dieters owe a great debt to the bakers of Tuscany, who have been producing wonderful bread without salt for centuries. This recipe makes a single loaf large enough to impress a dinner party. If you are baking for family use, you might want to separate the dough to bake in two loaves and put one in the freezer.

2 packages (4½ tsp.) dry yeast
2 c. warm water
4 to 5 c. all-purpose flour
1 c. whole-wheat flour

Put the yeast and ½ cup of the warm water in a bowl and allow to stand for a few minutes, until the yeast dissolves. Then add the rest of the water and 1 cup of the white flour. Stir and allow to stand until foamy. Then add the whole-wheat flour and more white flour, handful by handful, until the mixture becomes too stiff to stir with a spoon.

Remove from the bowl and knead by hand, adding the rest of the flour in small amounts. This should take several minutes. Or put the dough in the bowl of an electric mixer and knead with a dough hook, adding small amounts of flour until the dough cleans the side of the bowl.

Lightly oil the sides of a clean bowl, put the kneaded dough in it, and cover it with plastic wrap. Put the dough in a warm place to rise. When it has doubled in bulk, remove from the bowl and knead for a few minutes. Then flatten it out on a floured surface so that it forms a large circle. Starting at the top of the circle, roll the dough toward you, using your hands to shape it into an oblong loaf. Press together the seams created by the folds of dough.

(Continued)

Spread flour on a dish towel and wrap it loosely around the loaf while it rises for the second time, until about doubled in size.

Place a baking tile on the bottom rack of the oven and preheat the oven to 400 degrees. When the dough has risen for the second time, open the oven door and quickly roll the dough out of the towel and onto the baking tile. (If you don't have a baking tile, you can bake the bread on a baking sheet lined with baker's parchment or sprinkled with a mixture of flour and cornmeal. Preheat the oven, roll the loaf out of the towel and onto the baking sheet on your kitchen counter, then put the baking sheet on the bottom rack of the oven.) When the loaf is in the oven, toss three or four ice cubes onto the oven floor and close the door. Don't open the door to peek at the bread for at least 20 minutes. Bake the bread for about 45 minutes or until it sounds hollow if thumped on the bottom or a long toothpick or bamboo skewer inserted into the center of a loaf comes out clean.

Allow the loaf to cool completely before cutting. The crust may soften as the bread cools. If you want a crisper crust, return the bread to the oven for a few minutes.

YIELD: 1 large loaf
SODIUM CONTENT: 2 mg. of sodium per ½-inch slice

RYE BREAD WITH ONION AND CARAWAY SEEDS

The great ryes produced in places like Eastern Europe and Brooklyn may depend on mysterious "sours" maintained with religious devotion for decades or even centuries, but you don't have to get into all that to bake a good loaf of rye at home. All we ask is that you think about it the day before you bake so that your "sponge" can rise and fall, developing its tangy flavor, for several hours or overnight.

FOR THE SPONGE:

2 packages (4½ tsp.) dry yeast
1½ c. lukewarm water
1 c. rye flour
1 c. bread flour
1 tbsp. caraway seeds
½ c. chopped onion

FOR THE DOUGH:

all of the sponge
1½ c. lukewarm water
2 tbsp. vegetable oil
2 tbsp. molasses
1 tbsp. caraway seeds
1 c. rye flour
4 to 5 c. bread flour

To prepare the sponge, dissolve the yeast in ½ cup of the lukewarm water in a large bowl; allow to sit for a few minutes until it begins to foam. Mix together the rye flour, bread flour, and caraway seeds in a separate bowl. Add the rest of the water to the yeast mixture and stir to combine. Then add the flour mixture, ½ cup at a time, stirring until thoroughly blended. Bundle the onion in a piece of cheesecloth and tie at the top so that the onion pieces can't escape into the sponge. Push the bundle of onion into the middle of the sponge so that it is completely immersed.

Cover the bowl loosely with plastic wrap and set aside at room temperature so that the sponge can develop flavor as it rises and falls. It may be used after 6 hours but will be fine if left overnight.

To make the dough, remove the onion bundle, scrape off any of the sponge that clings to it, and discard the bundle. Add 1½ cups of water to the sponge and stir to combine. Then stir in the vegetable oil, molasses, and caraway seeds. Mix the rye and bread flours together in a separate bowl, then add them to the sponge mixture, ½ cup at a time, until the dough becomes too stiff to handle in the

(Continued)

bowl. Remove and knead by hand (or in the bowl of an electric mixer fitted with a dough hook), adding more flour as necessary until the ingredients are well mixed and form a pliable dough. This should take about 10 minutes if kneading by hand; about 5 minutes, or until the dough cleans the sides of the bowl, with the electric mixer. Lightly oil the mixing bowl and return the dough to it. Cover loosely with plastic wrap and put it in a warm place to rise until doubled in bulk. This should take about 1½ hours.

Punch down the risen dough in the bowl and turn it out onto a floured board. Knead it a few times and divide it into two equal portions. Using your fingertips or the heel of your palm, flatten one piece of the dough into a large circle. Starting at the top of the circle, fold it toward you by quarters, pressing together the seam of each fold, to create an oblong loaf. Push the ends in and seal the edges. Repeat with the second piece of dough. Line a heavy baking sheet with baker's parchment or sprinkle it with a mixture of flour and cornmeal, place the loaves on it, seams side down, and cover loosely with plastic wrap (sprinkle a little flour on top of each loaf to prevent the plastic wrap from sticking). Allow to rise until the loaves have nearly doubled in bulk, about ½ hour.

While the loaves are rising, place a baking tile (if you have one) on the bottom rack of the oven and preheat the oven to 425 degrees. When the loaves have risen, use a sharp knife or razor blade to cut three slashes about ½ inch deep diagonally across the top of each loaf. Put the baking sheet in the oven on the tile (or on the bottom rack if you aren't using a tile), toss two ice cubes on the floor of the oven, close the door, and do not open it to peek at the bread for at least 20 minutes. Allow the bread to bake for 35 to 40 minutes; it is done when it sounds hollow if thumped on the bottom or a long toothpick or bamboo skewer inserted into the center of a loaf comes out clean.

Allow the loaves to cool completely before cutting. The crust may soften as the bread cools. If you want a crisper crust, return the bread to the oven for a few minutes.

YIELD: 2 loaves
SODIUM CONTENT: 2 mg. of sodium per ½-inch slice

POTATO BREAD WITH ROSEMARY

1½ lbs. Yukon Gold or
other full-flavored
potatoes
2 packages (4½ tsp.)
dry yeast
¼ c. warm water
3 to 4 c. all-purpose
flour
2 tbsp. olive oil
1 heaping tbsp.
chopped fresh
rosemary leaves

Boil the potatoes in their skins until fork-tender. Then peel and mash or put through a ricer. Set aside to cool.

Prepare a sponge by dissolving the yeast in the warm water and adding 1 cup of the flour. (Add a tablespoon or two of water if the mixture seems too stiff.) Stir, cover with plastic wrap, and set aside in a warm place to rise until double in bulk (1 to 2 hours).

Stir down the sponge and transfer it to a large mixing bowl or the bowl of an electric mixer. Add the olive oil, potatoes, and rosemary, and stir to blend. Stir in the rest of the flour, a handful at a time, until the dough becomes too stiff to handle. Then transfer to a floured board and knead by hand, adding the rest of the flour in small amounts. Or knead with the mixer, using a dough hook, adding small amounts of flour until the dough cleans the sides of the bowl.

Lightly oil a clean bowl, put the kneaded dough in it, and cover with plastic wrap. Allow it to rise in a warm place until it has doubled in bulk. This should take about an hour. Punch down the dough, remove it from the bowl, and knead it for a few minutes. Divide into two equal portions. Use your fingertips or the heel of your palm to flatten one piece of dough into a circle. Fold the edges

(Continued)

of the circle under it toward its center, rotating the dough with your hands, to form a high circular loaf. Repeat with the second piece of dough.

Line a heavy baking sheet with baker's parchment or sprinkle it with a mixture of flour and cornmeal, place the loaves on it, seam side down, and cover loosely with plastic wrap. (Sprinkle a little flour on top of the loaf to prevent the plastic wrap from sticking.) Allow to rise until nearly doubled in bulk, about a ½ hour.

While the loaves are rising, place a baking tile (if you have one) on the bottom rack of the oven and preheat the oven to 400 degrees. When the loaves have risen, use a sharp knife or razor blade to cut two slashes about ½ inch deep across the top of each one. Put the baking sheet in the oven on the tile (or on the bottom rack if you aren't using a tile). Bake for 35 to 40 minutes; the bread is done when it sounds hollow if thumped on the bottom or a long toothpick or bamboo skewer inserted into the center of the loaf comes out clean.

Allow the loaves to cool completely before cutting. The crust may soften as the bread cools. If you want a crisper crust, return the bread to the oven for a few minutes.

YIELD: 2 loaves
SODIUM CONTENT: 3 mg. of sodium per ½-inch slice

OLIVE OIL AND BASIL BREAD

We like to bake this bread in five small loaves; if you prefer, you can divide the dough into two or three equal portions rather than five.

2 tbsp. dry yeast
2 c. lukewarm water
½ c. good quality olive oil
¼ c. chopped basil leaves
4 to 5 c. bread flour
1 tbsp. vital wheat gluten (optional)
cornmeal

Dissolve the yeast in ½ cup of the lukewarm water and allow to stand until it begins to foam. Add the oil, basil leaves, and the rest of the water; stir. Add 2 cups of the flour and stir to blend until the mixture becomes too stiff to handle in the bowl. Remove and knead by hand (or in the bowl of an electric mixer fitted with a dough hook), adding more flour as necessary until the ingredients are well mixed and form a pliable dough. This should take about 10 minutes if kneading by hand, or about 5 minutes with the electric mixer, until the dough cleans the sides of the bowl. Lightly oil the mixing bowl and return the dough to it. Cover loosely with plastic wrap and put it in a warm place to rise until doubled in bulk. This should take about an hour.

When the dough has risen, punch it down, remove it from the bowl, and divide it into five equal sections. Using your fingertips, flatten each section into a circle. To form a small round loaf, fold the edges of the circle into the center, pinching the seams together. Then turn the loaf over on the board and rotate it between your palms to make the loaf rounder and higher. Pinch the seams on the bottom together before placing each loaf, seam side down, on a heavy baking sheet dusted with a mixture of

(Continued)

flour and cornmeal. Spread a sheet of plastic wrap loosely over the loaves and let them rise again until double in bulk. (Sprinkle a bit of flour on top of each loaf to prevent the plastic wrap from sticking.) This should take about a ½ hour.

Place a baking tile (if you have one) on the bottom rack of the oven and preheat the oven to 375 degrees. When the loaves have risen, place the baking sheet on the tile (or on the bottom rack) and toss two ice cubes on the floor of the oven before closing the door. Bake for 30 minutes; the bread is done when it sounds hollow if thumped on the bottom or a long toothpick or bamboo skewer inserted into the center of a loaf comes out clean.

Allow the loaves to cool completely before cutting. The crust may soften as the bread cools. If you want a crisper crust, return the bread to the oven for a few minutes.

YIELD: 5 loaves of bread
SODIUM CONTENT: 2 mg. of sodium per slice

FOCACCIA WITH ROSEMARY

Slices of this classic Italian flatbread make a great accompaniment for pasta, chicken, or fish dishes. It's important to use high-quality olive oil with good flavor. This version calls for rosemary, but you can experiment with other fresh spices. We like to serve the bread with a small plate of olive oil for dipping.

3 packages (6¾ tsps.) dry yeast
2 c. lukewarm water
4 c. all-purpose flour
⅓ c. plus 2 tbsp. olive oil
1 tbsp. finely chopped fresh rosemary
1 tbsp. whole rosemary leaves

Dissolve the yeast in 1 cup of the lukewarm water. Add 1 cup of the flour and stir to blend into a paste. Cover this "sponge" and set it aside in a warm area until double in bulk; this should take about an hour.

Put the sponge in a large mixing bowl, add the rest of the water, and stir to blend. Then add ⅓ cup of the oil and the chopped rosemary. Add more of the flour until the dough becomes too stiff to handle in the bowl. Turn it out on a floured board and knead in the rest of the flour. Continue kneading for a few more minutes until the dough achieves a uniform, elastic texture. (Or put the dough in the bowl of an electric mixer fitted with a dough hook and use it to knead in the rest of the flour until the dough cleans the sides of the bowl.) Put the dough in a lightly oiled bowl, cover loosely with plastic wrap, and set aside in a warm place to rise until double in bulk; this should take about 1½ hours.

You can cook all the dough on a rectangular 15" × 11" jellyroll pan or you can divide it into two pieces and cook them in straight-sided 9-inch cake tins that have been brushed lightly with olive oil. Punch down the dough and, if dividing it, form it into two balls of equal size. Use a rolling pin to roll each ball into a circle about

(Continued)

the diameter of the cake tin. Put the dough in the two tins and use your fingertips to spread the dough so that it reaches the sides of the tins. (If using a jellyroll pan, brush it lightly with olive oil, roll the dough into a large rectangle, put it in the pan, and spread it to reach the sides). Cover loosely with plastic wrap and set aside in a warm area to rise again until double in bulk. This should take 30 to 45 minutes.

While the dough is rising, preheat the oven to 350 degrees. When the dough has risen, sprinkle with the remaining 2 tablespoons of olive oil and "dimple" the surface, spreading your fingers and pushing down firmly with them until they touch the bottom of the pan. Repeat to create an even pattern of holes in the dough separated from each other by an inch. Sprinkle with the whole rosemary leaves. Put the focaccia in the oven and bake for about 20 minutes, or until the crust turns golden brown.

YIELD: 10 slices
SODIUM CONTENT: 10 mg. of sodium per slice

CHALLAH BREAD

This sweet, eggy bread makes the best French toast. Traditionally, you shape the loaves by braiding the dough, which is less complicated than it sounds; we have described how to do that here. If you would rather just shape it into rectangular loaves and cook them in loaf pans, that will work, too.

2 packages (4½ tsp.) dry yeast
2 c. lukewarm water
3 eggs
2 tbsp. sugar
2 tbsp. honey
3 tbsp. unsalted butter, melted
5 to 6 c. bread flour
1 tbsp. milk
poppy seeds

Dissolve the yeast in ½ cup of the lukewarm water and allow to stand until it begins to foam. Break two of the eggs into another bowl and beat them lightly. Add the rest of the water, sugar, honey, and melted butter. (Make sure the butter has cooled and add it slowly so that it doesn't cook the eggs.) When the yeast mixture has turned frothy, stir it into the rest of the ingredients. Stir in the flour, ½ cup at a time, until the dough gets too stiff to stir in the bowl.

Turn the dough out on a floured board and knead in the rest of the flour so that the dough becomes smooth and elastic. Continue to knead for another 5 minutes. (Or, if you prefer, stir 2 cups of flour into the wet ingredients, put the mixture into the bowl of an electric mixer fitted with a dough hook, and use it to mix and knead in the rest of the flour, adding ½ cup at a time until the dough cleans the sides of the bowl.) Put the dough into a lightly oiled bowl, cover loosely with plastic wrap, and set aside in a warm place to rise until doubled in bulk. This should take 1 to 1½ hours.

Divide the dough in half, then divide each half into three pieces. Roll each piece of dough into a ball. Take a ball of dough, flatten it on a floured board, and roll it into a

(Continued)

cylinder. Then continue to roll the cylinder, pushing out from the
middle toward the ends, to form a round strip of dough about a foot
long. Repeat with two more balls of dough. When you have three
foot-long strips of dough, line them up side by side and pinch one set
of ends together. Then braid the dough strips together, as if braiding
rope or hair, and pinch the other ends together. Fold the ends under
the braided loaf and place it in a lightly greased loaf pan. Repeat
with the other three balls of dough.

Break the third egg into a bowl, add the milk, and beat to
combine. Use a pastry brush to daub the egg mixture on top of each
loaf. Sprinkle the loaves with poppy seeds, drape a piece of plastic
wrap loosely over them, and set them aside to rise for about ½ hour,
until doubled in bulk.

Preheat the oven to 400 degrees. Put the loaves on the bottom
rack of the oven and bake for 30 to 40 minutes, until the tops have
turned a rich golden brown and a thump on the bottom of a loaf
produces a hollow sound or a long toothpick or bamboo skewer
inserted into the middle of a loaf comes out clean.

YIELD: 2 loaves
SODIUM CONTENT: 10 mg. of sodium per ½-inch slice

COCONUT AND HAZELNUT BREAD

Use only plain, shredded coconut here, not the familiar packaged varieties loaded with sugar, salt, and other sodium compounds. The trip to the upscale grocery or health-food store is well worth it, for this is a genuinely amazing bread—rich and mystically flavorful. Toasting brings out the best in it; serve it with your breakfast eggs, or for a snack or tea with your favorite low-sodium cheese.

¾ c. shredded coconut
2 packages (4½ tsp.) dry yeast
¾ c. lukewarm water
¼ c. honey
2 eggs
4 tbsp. (½ stick) unsalted butter
3 c. bread flour
¾ c. chopped hazelnuts
1 egg white

Preheat the oven to 350 degrees. Spread the coconut in a baking pan and toast in the oven for about 5 minutes or until it begins to turn golden brown, then remove and allow to cool. Dissolve the yeast in ½ cup of the water and allow to stand until it begins to foam. Then add the rest of the water, the honey, the eggs, and the butter; stir until well blended. Add 2 cups of the flour, ½ cup at a time, stirring to blend. Then stir in all but 1 tablespoon of the coconut and all but 1 tablespoon of the chopped hazelnuts.

Add the remaining flour in small amounts until the dough becomes too stiff to handle in the bowl. Then turn it out onto a floured board and knead by hand for several minutes, adding flour, until it holds together and feels elastic. (Or transfer the dough to the bowl of a mixer fitted with a dough hook and knead at slow speed, adding small amounts of flour, until the dough cleans the sides of the bowl.) After it is kneaded, put the dough in a lightly greased, straight-sided bowl, cover loosely with plastic wrap, and set aside to rise until double in bulk, about an hour.

When the dough has risen, punch it down, remove it from the bowl, and use your fingertips and the heel of your palm to flatten it so that it

(Continued)

forms a large oval. Fold it toward you from the top to form a cylinder, pinching together the seam along the bottom. Then turn it seam side up and fold the ends to the center, pinching together the seams again, to form a loaf. Put the loaf seam-side down in an 8" × 4" loaf pan and press down the top of the loaf so that it fills out the pan. Sprinkle flour lightly on top of the loaf, cover loosely with plastic wrap, and set aside to rise for the second time until double in bulk, about ½ an hour.

While the loaf is rising, preheat the oven to 350 degrees. When the loaf has risen, use a sharp knife to cut a single slash about ½ inch deep down the center of it lengthwise. Mix the egg white with a little water and brush the top of the loaf lightly with the mixture. Then sprinkle the top with the reserved coconut and hazelnuts. Bake on the bottom rack of the oven for 30 to 40 minutes, until the top is golden brown and the loaf sounds hollow when thumped on the bottom or a bamboo skewer inserted into the center of the loaf comes out clean.

Allow the loaf to cool completely before cutting. The crust may soften as the bread cools. If you want a crisper crust, return the bread to the oven for a few minutes.

YIELD: 1 large loaf
SODIUM CONTENT: 15 mg. of sodium per ½-inch slice

HONEY AND SESAME BAGELS

Use this recipe to learn the basic process for making bagels. Once you master it, you can experiment with ingredients for other breads or make up your own. We like these cut in half, toasted, lightly buttered, and smeared with yogurt cheese, also known as quark, the salt-free answer to cream cheese (see page 12).

FOR THE SPONGE:

2 packages (4½ tsp.) dry yeast
2 c. lukewarm water
2 c. all-purpose flour

FOR THE BAGELS:

2 tbsp. vegetable oil
2 tbsp. honey
1½ c. water
½ c. semolina flour
3 to 4 c. all-purpose flour
1 gallon water
sesame seeds

Prepare a sponge by dissolving the yeast in ½ cup of the lukewarm water, allowing it to stand for a few minutes until it begins to foam. Then add the remaining 1½ cups of lukewarm water, stir, and add 2 cups of all-purpose flour. Stir for 100 strokes, until well blended. Cover with plastic wrap and set aside in a warm place for about 2 hours. During this time, it should rise and fall and acquire a bubbly texture.

Mix the vegetable oil and honey with 1½ cups of water. When the sponge is ready, add this mixture to it and stir to blend thoroughly. Stir in the semolina flour, then add the all-purpose flour, ½ cup at a time, stirring to blend until the mixture becomes too stiff to handle. Turn it out onto a floured board and knead for several minutes, adding more flour in small amounts until the dough is smooth and elastic. (Or transfer the mixture to the bowl of an electric mixer after adding the semolina, insert the dough hook and use the mixer to knead in the all-purpose flour, adding it by the ½ cup until the ball of dough cleans the sides of the bowl.)

Lightly oil the sides of a straight-sided bowl, put the dough in it, cover loosely with plastic wrap, and put in a warm place to rise until double in bulk. This should take 1½ to 2 hours.

(Continued)

Check the dough to see how fast it is rising, and about 20 minutes before it has completed its rise, put the gallon of water in a large pot over high heat so that it will boil by the time the dough has risen. Lightly grease two baking sheets and preheat the oven to 375 degrees.

When the dough has risen, punch it down, remove it from the bowl, and divide it into two equal parts. Then divide each part into eight equal portions. Roll each small piece of dough between your palms to form a cylinder several inches long, then form it into a circle by pinching the ends together. When you have shaped four bagels in this way, drop them, one by one, into the boiling water. They should sink to the bottom for a few seconds, then rise to the top. Allow them to remain in the simmering water for about a minute before using a slotted spoon or spatula to remove them to one of the baking sheets. Repeat the process for the rest of the dough pieces, four at a time.

Put eight bagels on each baking sheet. Sprinkle them generously with sesame seeds. Put them on the bottom rack of the oven and cook for about 30 minutes, or until they have turned a rich golden brown.

YIELD: 16 bagels
SODIUM CONTENT: 3 mg. of sodium per bagel

SWEET CORN BREAD

1 egg
½ c. plain yogurt
½ c. milk
3 tbsp. melted butter
3 tbsp. honey
1 c. fresh corn (or
  frozen unsalted corn)
1 c. yellow or blue
  cornmeal
1 c. all-purpose flour
4 tsp. low-sodium
  baking powder

Preheat the oven to 350 degrees. Grease an 8-inch square baking pan. Stir together the egg, yogurt, milk, butter, honey, and corn in a large bowl until well blended. Sift together the cornmeal, flour, and baking powder in a separate bowl and add them to the mixture of wet ingredients. Stir only until the dry ingredients are moistened. Pour the batter into the pan and bake for 20 to 25 minutes, until a toothpick inserted into the center of the cornbread comes out clean.

YIELD: 12 pieces
SODIUM CONTENT: 19 mg. of sodium per piece

CINNAMON RAISIN BREAD

**2 packages (4½ tsp.) dry
  yeast
2¼ c. lukewarm water
1 c. raisins
1 c. whole-wheat flour
3 c. white flour
⅓ c. honey
¼ c. vegetable oil
¼ c. cinnamon
¼ c. sugar
2 tbsp. melted butter**

Dissolve the yeast in ½ cup of the lukewarm water and let stand until it begins to foam. Combine the whole-wheat flour with 1 cup of the white flour in a large bowl. Add the raisins and stir to distribute them evenly through the flour. Stir the honey, oil, and the rest of the warm water into the yeast mixture, then pour it over the flour. Stir until blended. Add the rest of the white flour, ½ cup at a time, until the dough gets too stiff to handle in the bowl. Turn the dough out onto a floured board and knead for about 10 minutes, adding small amounts of flour, until it becomes smooth and elastic. (Or put the dough in the bowl of an electric mixer and knead with the dough hook, adding small amounts of flour, until it cleans the sides of the bowl.)

Lightly oil a clean bowl and put the dough in it, cover loosely with plastic wrap, and put it in a warm place to rise until the dough doubles in bulk, about 1 to 1½ hours.

Punch down the dough and divide into two equal pieces. Flatten out the first piece on a floured board to make a large rectangle. Mix together the cinnamon and sugar and reserve 2 tablespoons to sprinkle on the finished loaves. Spread half of the rest generously over the flattened dough. Fold two

(Continued)

ends of the dough over the center, as if folding a sheet of paper. Then roll up one end of the folded dough to make a cylinder. Pinch the ends of the cylinder together to form a loaf and place it, seam side down, in a lightly greased loaf pan. Repeat for the second piece of dough. Cover the loaves loosely with plastic wrap (sprinkle a little flour on top of each one to prevent the plastic wrap from sticking). Put the loaves in a warm place to rise until almost double in size, about a ½ hour.

Preheat the oven to 325 degrees while the bread is rising. When it has risen, gently brush or blow the flour off the top of the loaves and brush them with melted butter. Then sprinkle them with the reserved sugar and cinnamon. Bake for about 30 minutes, or until the loaves sound hollow when tapped on the bottom or a long toothpick or bamboo skewer inserted into the middle of a loaf comes out clean.

YIELD: 2 loaves
SODIUM CONTENT: 2 mg. of sodium per ½-inch slice

CRANBERRY WALNUT BREAD

1 package (2¼ tsp.) dry
yeast
1 c. lukewarm water
¼ c. molasses
2 tbsp. honey
¾ c. coarsely chopped
walnuts
¾ c. halved cranberries
3 tbsp. unsalted butter,
melted
½ c. whole-wheat flour
2 to 3 c. white bread
flour
1 tbsp. vital wheat
gluten (optional)

Dissolve the yeast in ½ cup of the lukewarm water and let stand until it begins to foam. Add the rest of the water, the molasses, honey, walnuts, and cranberries and stir to blend. Stir in the whole-wheat flour and wheat gluten (if you are using it), then slowly add the melted butter, stirring constantly. Stir in the white flour, ½ cup at a time.

When the dough gets too stiff to handle in the bowl, turn it out onto a floured board and knead it by hand for several minutes, adding small amounts of flour, until it is smooth and elastic. (Or transfer the dough to the bowl of an electric mixer fitted with a dough hook and mix, adding small amounts of flour, until the dough cleans the sides of the bowl.) Put the kneaded dough in a lightly oiled straight-sided bowl and put it in a warm place to rise until double in bulk, about 1 to 1½ hours.

Punch down the risen dough, knead it a few times, and divide it into two equal pieces. Using your fingertips or the heel of your palm, flatten a piece of the dough into a large oval. Starting at a narrow end, roll the dough up into a cylinder. Turn it seam side up, pinch the ends tight and fold them into the center to form an oblong loaf. Place the loaf in a lightly greased loaf pan, seam side

(Continued)

down. Dust the top of the loaf with flour, cover loosely with plastic wrap, and set aside to rise until double in bulk, about 20 to 30 minutes.

Preheat the oven to 450 degrees. When the loaf has risen, use a sharp knife to make a cut about ½ inch deep down the length of the top, then put the loaf on the bottom rack of the oven to bake. After 10 minutes, turn the oven temperature down to 350 degrees. Bake for another 30 minutes, until the loaf sounds hollow when thumped on the bottom or a long toothpick or bamboo skewer inserted into the loaf comes out clean.

YIELD: 1 loaf
SODIUM CONTENT: 4 mg. of sodium per ½-inch slice

DATE AND NUT BREAD

*Another family recipe
from the files of our late
mother-in-law, Margaret
Burke. This, too, is good
with yogurt cheese, or
quark (see page 12).*

¾ c. chopped walnuts
1 c. chopped dates
1 tbsp. low-sodium
   baking powder
3 tbsp. vegetable
   shortening
¾ c. boiling water
2 eggs
1 tsp. vanilla
½ c. white sugar
½ c. brown sugar
1½ c. sifted all-purpose
   flour

Combine the walnuts, dates, and baking powder in a mixing bowl. Add the shortening and pour in the boiling water. Stir to distribute, then allow the mixture to stand for 20 minutes.

Preheat the oven to 350 degrees. Break the eggs into a large bowl and beat them briefly with a fork. Stir in the vanilla, sugars, and flour. Add the date-nut mixture, stirring to blend. Be sure the dates and nuts are distributed evenly through the batter. Grease a 9" × 5" loaf pan and pour the mixture into it. Bake for about 1 hour or until a toothpick inserted into the loaf comes out clean.

YIELD: 1 loaf
SODIUM CONTENT: 13 mg. of sodium per ½-inch slice

ZUCCHINI BREAD

We like this sweet bread best just plain, but some prefer to add a cup of raisins or chopped walnuts.

3 eggs
1¼ c. vegetable oil
1½ c. sugar
1 tsp. vanilla
2 c. finely grated raw zucchini
2 c. all-purpose flour
3½ tsp. low-sodium baking powder
1 tsp. ground cloves
1 tsp. ground cinnamon

Preheat the oven to 350 degrees. Combine the eggs, oil, sugar, and vanilla, and beat until well blended. Add zucchini and stir to combine. Sift the flour and baking powder together with the spices and stir into the oil mixture until the dry ingredients are moistened. Do not overmix. Spoon the batter into a lightly greased 9" × 5" loaf pan, taking care not to fill it more than three-quarters full. Put any leftover batter in a small greased baking dish. Cook for an hour or more on the middle rack of the oven until a toothpick dipped into the middle of the loaf comes out clean.

YIELD: 1 loaf
SODIUM CONTENT: 19 mg. of sodium per ½-inch piece

IV. CONDIMENTS

ANDERSONS' FAMOUS BARBECUE SAUCE

The secret of this recipe is long, slow cooking, which produces a rich, creamy texture. If you like the sauce totally smooth, put it in the blender after it cooks to break down any remaining pieces of onion or other ingredients. Salt-free tomato purée or tomato sauce is increasingly available in supermarkets under familiar brand names. If you can't find it, you can approximate it by thinning one of the readily available salt-free tomato pastes with water.

1 large onion, diced
vegetable oil
28-oz. can salt-free tomato purée
2 fresh tomatoes, chopped
2 c. white wine vinegar
½ c. brown sugar
freshly ground black pepper to taste
2 tbsp. paprika
2 tbsp. salt-free chili powder
¼ c. molasses
1 c. pineapple juice
¼ c. plus 2 tbsp. salt-free Dijon mustard
2 tbsp. dark rum
2 cloves garlic, minced

Sauté the onion in a little oil until translucent. Add the rest of the ingredients, stirring to blend well. Bring the mixture to a boil, then reduce the heat and simmer over very low heat for 3 to 4 hours.

Cool the sauce, then transfer it to a glass jar or bowl and refrigerate until ready to use.

YIELD: 8 cups of sauce
SODIUM CONTENT: 8 mg. of sodium per ¼ cup

ANDERSONS' FAMOUS STEAK SAUCE

This sauce is wonderful with chicken as well as steak; it will keep for up to two weeks in the refrigerator if kept in a sealed jar.

8 medium tomatoes, quartered
1 tbsp. olive oil
1 shallot, minced
½ c. white wine vinegar
½ c. packed brown sugar
¼ c. salt-free pickle relish (see page 315)
¼ c. molasses
¼ tsp. garlic powder

Place the quartered tomatoes in a blender and blend until liquefied. For a really smooth sauce, force the tomatoes through a fine strainer. Heat the oil in a pot to medium heat; add the shallot and cook for several minutes until wilted. Add the tomato and all the other ingredients to the pot; reduce to a simmer and cook for 2½ to 3 hours.

Allow the sauce to cool, and refrigerate overnight before using.

YIELD: 6 cups of sauce
SODIUM CONTENT: 6 mg. of sodium per ¼ cup

TEXAS-STYLE BARBECUE SAUCE

This sauce is not as sweet as our Andersons' Famous Barbecue Sauce (see page 81) and it goes well with all meats. The recipe calls for 4 dried red chilies; adjust the amount for the degree of heat you and your guests prefer. For salt-free catsups, see page 315.

2 tbsp. vegetable oil
1 onion, diced
1 c. salt-free catsup
28-oz. can salt-free tomatoes, chopped, or 3 large fresh tomatoes, chopped
1 c. white wine vinegar
¼ c. molasses
1 tbsp. cayenne pepper
4 dried red chili peppers
freshly ground black pepper to taste

Heat the oil in a large saucepan; add the onion and sauté over medium heat for 10 minutes. Then add the rest of the ingredients. Stir to combine. Simmer over low heat for at least an hour.

YIELD: 6 cups of sauce
SODIUM CONTENT: 13 mg. of sodium per ¼ cup

SPICY BARBECUE SAUCE

2 tbsp. oil
1 medium onion,
  chopped
4 jalapeño peppers,
  seeded and diced
1 tbsp. chopped fresh
  ginger
4 medium tomatoes,
  chopped
2 tbsp. honey
2 tbsp. white wine
  vinegar
½ tsp. dried coriander
½ tsp. dried cumin
1 c. fresh cilantro leaves

Heat the oil in a medium saucepan; add the onion, peppers, and ginger. Cook for 10 minutes over medium heat. Then add the rest of the ingredients and stir to combine. Bring the mixture to a simmer and cook for 45 minutes. If the vegetables don't release enough liquid to keep the mixture moist as it cooks, add a little water. Remove from the heat and let cool.

When cool, transfer the mixture to a blender or food processor and blend to a liquid. Brush the sauce onto meat before charcoal grilling or broiling in the oven, then use it to baste the meat as it is almost done. (Note: If you prefer a hotter sauce, add cayenne pepper to taste.)

YIELD: 3 cups of sauce
SODIUM CONTENT: 5 mg. of sodium per ¼ cup

FRESH CORN RELISH

Use this great condiment for hamburgers and grilled or poached chicken and fish.

4 ears fresh sweet corn, husked and silk removed, or 3 c. frozen salt-free corn
1 tbsp. olive oil
3 tbsp. diced red onion
2 tbsp. diced orange sweet pepper
2 tsp. balsamic vinegar
freshly ground black pepper to taste

Strip the kernels from the corncobs by running a knife lengthwise down the ear of corn (or defrost the frozen corn). Heat the oil in a nonstick pan until moderately hot. Add the corn to the pan and cook, stirring frequently, for 2 minutes. Then add the rest of the ingredients and cook 1 minute longer. Remove from the heat and allow to cool before serving.

YIELD: About 1¾ cups
SODIUM CONTENT: 4 mg. of sodium per ¼ cup

FRESH TOMATO SALSA

6 ripe tomatoes
½ c. chopped
  red onion
¼ c. chopped scallions
1 tbsp. finely minced
  garlic
1 tbsp. olive oil
¼ c. chopped cilantro
2 tbsp. lime juice
1 tbsp. lemon juice
2 tbsp. cider vinegar
1 small jalapeño pepper,
  finely minced

Peel the tomatoes by dipping each one in a pot of boiling water for several seconds, then running it under cold water; this should loosen the skin so that it pulls off easily when pierced with a knife. Cut the tomatoes open, remove the seeds, and cut the flesh into pieces. Put the tomato, chopped onion, and chopped scallion in a blender or food processor and blend slowly or pulse to achieve a coarse blend. Pour the mixture into a bowl. Stir in the rest of the ingredients. Serve as an appetizer or snack with unsalted corn chips, or as a sauce for chicken or fish with rice.

YIELD: 4 cups
SODIUM CONTENT: 5 mg. of sodium per ¼ cup

SPICY AVOCADO DIP

3 ripe avocados, peeled
juice of ½ lemon
2 jalapeño peppers,
  seeded and finely
  diced
1 shallot, finely diced

Slice the avocado into a bowl and mash it with a fork to create a lumpy paste. Add the lemon juice, jalapeño, and shallots; mix well to combine, and chill before serving.

YIELD: Serves 6
SODIUM CONTENT: 11 mg. of sodium per serving

HORSERADISH CREAM FOR STEAKS

With a large portion of horseradish, this sauce is not for the fainthearted. Reduce the horseradish as you prefer.

½ c. grated fresh horseradish root
⅓ c. sour cream
freshly ground black pepper to taste
1 tbsp. lemon juice

Mix all the ingredients together and place in a serving dish.

YIELD: 1 cup
SODIUM CONTENT: 6 mg. of sodium per 2-tablespoon serving

ROASTED SHALLOT SALAD

1 dozen shallots, ends removed, papery skin peeled off
2 tbsp. olive oil
freshly ground black pepper to taste
3 tbsp. balsamic vinegar

Preheat the oven to 350 degrees. Put the shallots in an ovenproof baking dish, drizzle with oil, sprinkle with pepper, and bake for 1 hour and 15 minutes. Remove the pan from the oven; add the balsamic vinegar and stir to blend. Remove to a bowl; serve warm with meats.

YIELD: Serves 6
SODIUM CONTENT: 4 mg. of sodium per serving

BASIC PESTO

*A marvelous addition to
pasta salads, tomato sauce,
or as a pasta sauce on its
own, this version of pesto
eliminates the salt-laden
Parmesan cheese. If fresh
basil isn't in season,
substitute parsley, cilantro,
or a mixture of all your
favorite leafy green herbs.*

2 c. chopped fresh basil
½ c. good quality olive oil
¼ c. pine nuts or walnuts
2 cloves garlic

Blend all the ingredients in a food
processor or blender until smooth. For
a creamy texture, add a bit more oil.

YIELD: 2 cups
SODIUM CONTENT: 2 mg. per 2-tablespoon serving

HUMMUS

*This classic Middle Eastern
dip and the baba ganouj
recipe (see page 90) make
a great way to start off an
evening meal built around
grilled shish kebabs. Add
more lemon juice and oil
to achieve the texture you
like, or add scallions, hot
sesame oil, cumin, or
cayenne pepper to vary
the flavor. You can find
sesame tahini in health-
food stores and many
supermarkets.*

2 c. chickpeas, cooked without salt,
    or 2 14-oz. cans unsalted
    chickpeas (see page 315)
2 cloves garlic, sliced
⅔ c. sesame tahini
⅔ c. lemon juice
¼ c. olive oil
2 tbsp. chopped parsley

Blend all the ingredients except
parsley in a blender or food
processor to a smooth purée. Stir in
the parsley or sprinkle it over the top
before serving. Serve with triangles of
toasted salt-free bread or salt-free
pita pockets (see page 315).

YIELD: 3½ cups
SODIUM CONTENT: 9 mg. of sodium per ¼-cup serving

ROASTED GARLIC HUMMUS

2 c. chickpeas cooked
without salt or 2
(14-oz.) cans unsalted
chickpeas (see page
315)
1 whole head of garlic
8 fresh basil leaves,
chopped
freshly ground black
pepper to taste
¼ c. low-sodium chicken
broth
juice of ½ lemon

Preheat the oven to 350 degrees. Put the head of garlic, whole, in a small baking dish and roast it until the cloves are soft; this should take about an hour. Remove the garlic from the oven and slice off the top, then squeeze the head over a small dish to extract the cooked garlic flesh from the papery skin. Combine the drained beans, cooked garlic, and the rest of the ingredients in a food processor and process to a smooth purée. Chill for an hour before serving.

YIELD: Serves 6
SODIUM CONTENT: 19 mg. of sodium per serving

BABA GANOUJ

Devoted followers of this dish (pronounced baba ganoosh) recommend roasting the eggplant over a charcoal grill or open flame for a slightly charred, smoky flavor.

1 medium eggplant
3 cloves garlic, minced
¼ c. sesame tahini
⅓ c. lemon juice
freshly ground black pepper to taste
sprigs of parsley for garnish

Preheat the oven to 350 degrees. Place the eggplant on a lightly greased baking sheet and put it in the oven to roast until the flesh inside it cooks through and it collapses on itself (about 45 minutes, depending on the size of the eggplant). After it has cooled, cut the eggplant open, scoop out the flesh and put it in a food processor or blender. Add the garlic, tahini, and lemon juice, and blend until smooth. Stir in a generous grinding of black pepper. Garnish with parsley. Serve with triangles of salt-free bread or salt-free pita pockets (see page 315).

YIELD: 3 cups
SODIUM CONTENT: 16 mg. of sodium per ½-cup serving

ORANGE GINGER MARINADE FOR CHICKEN

It's hard to go wrong with grilled or broiled chicken soaked in a good orange-based marinade. This one works well with chicken headed for the charcoal grill. Francine Prince, who published a number of wonderful diet cookbooks, suggests adding a tablespoon or so of crushed juniper berries for a touch of earthy mystery.

6-oz. can frozen orange juice concentrate
1/4 c. vegetable oil
2 tbsp. lemon juice
2 tsp. finely minced garlic
1 tsp. ground ginger
1 tbsp. finely chopped parsley
2 tsp. Bell's seasoning (see page 315) or 1/2 tsp. each of rosemary, oregano, sage, marjoram, and thyme

Thaw the orange juice concentrate, then pour it into a large bowl. Add all the other ingredients and stir to combine. To prepare chicken for the grill or broiler, immerse chicken pieces in the marinade and allow to stand for a few hours in the refrigerator, then baste them with the marinade as they cook. To maximize the flavor of the marinade, cut boneless chicken breasts into 1-inch chunks before marinating and cook them on skewers.

YIELD: 1 cup of marinade
SODIUM CONTENT: 3 mg. of sodium per 1/4 cup

BALSAMIC VINEGAR AND MUSTARD MARINADE

An excellent all-around marinade to prepare beef, lamb, or chicken for grilling or broiling.

½ c. **balsamic vinegar**
½ c. **olive oil**
2 tbsp. **salt-free Dijon mustard**
2 cloves **garlic, minced**
freshly ground black pepper to taste

Put the vinegar, oil, and mustard in a bowl and stir with a whisk until the oil and vinegar emulsify and the mustard is evenly distributed. Stir in the minced garlic and pepper.

If you are going to grill a steak, place it in a shallow baking dish and pour the marinade over it. After it has soaked for an hour, turn it over and let it soak for another hour. Use the marinade to baste the steak as it cooks on the grill. To maximize the flavor of the marinade, cut the meat into 1½-inch cubes and grill them on skewers. If you like, you can alternate the pieces of meat with cherry tomatoes, whole mushrooms, and pieces of onion and green pepper.

YIELD: 1 cup of marinade
SODIUM CONTENT: 15 mg. of sodium per ¼-cup serving

PEANUT DIPPING SAUCE

Serve this sauce and the one that follows with chicken tenders (see page 165) or fried chicken wings. They both depend on the addition of coconut milk—look for cans of it in urban supermarkets with Hispanic or Asian clienteles. If you can't find it, you can omit it from the recipes. The flavors of the dips will be that much stronger (minus, alas, the beautiful hint of coconut), and guests will use less. If you are using rice wine vinegar be sure to get a pure, unseasoned version, since others may contain a lot of sodium.

2 tbsp. plus 2 tsp. brown sugar
¼ c. salt-free rice wine vinegar or white wine vinegar
2 tbsp. salt-free peanut butter
2 tbsp. salt-free tomato paste
2 tbsp. water
1 large clove garlic, chopped
¼ c. coconut milk

Put all of the ingredients except the coconut milk in a blender or food processor and blend until smooth and creamy. Transfer to a bowl and stir in the coconut milk. Keep the sauce refrigerated if you are not going to use it right away.

YIELD: 1 cup of sauce
SODIUM CONTENT: 3 mg. of sodium per tablespoon

ORANGE DIPPING SAUCE

3 tbsp. water
3 tbsp. dry vermouth,
  sherry, or white wine
1 shallot, chopped
1 clove garlic, chopped
2 tsp. chopped fresh
  ginger
1 tbsp. frozen orange
  juice concentrate
1 tbsp. salt-free tomato
  paste
3 tbsp. coconut milk

Put all of the ingredients except the coconut milk in a blender or food processor and blend until smooth and creamy. Transfer to a bowl and stir in the coconut milk. Keep the sauce refrigerated if you are not going to use it right away.

YIELD: ¾ cup of sauce
SODIUM CONTENT: 3 mg. of sodium per tablespoon

BASIL MAYONNAISE

For our basic salt-free mayonnaise recipe, based on pasteurized egg whites, see page 15.

¼ c. salt-free
   pasteurized egg
   whites (see page 14)
2 tsp. white wine
   vinegar
1 tsp. lemon juice
1 tsp. salt-free Dijon
   mustard
1 medium clove garlic,
   minced
¼ tsp. sugar
6 fresh basil leaves,
   chopped
¾ c. mild olive oil

Combine the egg whites, vinegar, lemon juice, mustard, garlic, sugar, and basil in a blender. Pulse a few times to combine. Then turn the blender on to high speed and add the oil in a thin stream through the hole in the lid. Close the cover completely and allow the blender to continue running until the mayonnaise firms up, about 2 minutes. You may want to stop the blending after a minute or so and use a rubber scraper to push mayonnaise down from the sides.

YIELD: 1 cup of mayonnaise
SODIUM CONTENT: 8 mg. of sodium per tablespoon

GARLIC MAYONNAISE

1 medium clove garlic, chopped
¼ c. salt-free pasteurized egg whites (see page 14)
1 tsp. white wine vinegar
1 tsp. lemon juice
1 tsp. salt-free Dijon mustard
freshly ground black pepper to taste
¾ c. fresh, high-quality olive oil

Combine the garlic, egg whites, vinegar, lemon juice, mustard, and pepper in a blender. Pulse a few times to combine. Then turn the blender on to high speed and add the oil in a thin stream through the hole in the lid. Close the cover completely and allow the blender to continue running until the mayonnaise firms up, about 2 minutes. You may want to stop the blending after a minute or so and use a rubber scraper to push mayonnaise down from the sides.

YIELD: 1 cup of mayonnaise
SODIUM CONTENT: 8 mg. of sodium per tablespoon

SUN-DRIED TOMATO MAYONNAISE

The intensity of flavor in this mayonnaise depends on the number of tomato halves; we liked the result with four, but you can experiment with more or less to suit your taste.

4 halves of salt-free sun-dried tomatoes (see page 315)
¼ c. salt-free pasteurized egg whites (see page 14)
1 tsp. white wine vinegar
2 tsp. lemon juice
¾ c. mild olive oil

Put the halves of tomato in a small bowl, cover with boiling water, and allow to stand for 20 minutes or until soft. Combine the egg whites, vinegar, and lemon juice in a food processor. Drain the sun-dried tomatoes and use scissors or sharp knife to cut them into small pieces and drop them into the mixture as well, then pulse a few times to combine. Turn the blender on to high speed and add the oil in a thin stream through the hole in the lid. Close the cover completely and allow the blender to continue running until the mayonnaise firms up, about 2 minutes. You may want to stop the blending after a minute or so and use a rubber scraper to push mayonnaise down from the sides. Don't worry if some flecks of sun-dried tomato remain; they look fine and add tiny bursts of flavor.

YIELD: 1 cup of mayonnaise
SODIUM CONTENT: 5 mg. of sodium per tablespoon

RASPBERRY MAYONNAISE

Try a dollop of this mayonnaise on a salad of fresh fruit. We love good raspberries, but you should be able to substitute blueberries, strawberries, or other fruit as you wish.

12 fresh raspberries
¼ c. salt-free pasteurized egg whites (see page 14)
2 tsp. lemon juice
1 tbsp. sugar
1 c. mild olive oil

If the raspberries have a lot of seeds, seed them by pushing them through a strainer, capturing the juice and flesh in a bowl. Combine the egg whites, lemon juice, sugar, and seeded raspberries in a blender, then pulse a few times to combine. Turn the blender on to high speed and add the oil in a thin stream through the hole in the lid. Close the cover completely and allow the blender to continue running until the mayonnaise firms up, about 2 minutes. You may want to stop the blending after a minute or so and use a rubber scraper to push mayonnaise down from the sides.

YIELD: 1¼ cups
SODIUM CONTENT: 4 mg. of sodium per tablespoon

CRANBERRY CONSERVE

12-oz. package fresh cranberries
1 c. water
1 c. sugar
½ c. raisins
¼ c. orange pieces
1 c. shelled walnuts

Put the cranberries and water in a saucepan; bring to a boil and cook until the cranberry skins pop. Add the sugar, raisins, and orange pieces, and boil gently for 15 minutes. Stir in the nuts and allow to cool. Serve at room temperature with chicken or turkey.

YIELD: Serves 6
SODIUM CONTENT: 5 mg. of sodium per serving

HOLIDAY CRANBERRY SAUCE

This sauce has a nice sweet-and-sour quality. Be sure to let the sauce cool completely before serving. We like it tart; if you don't, reduce the vinegar and increase the sugar to taste. As for dried fruit, we omitted prunes from the mixture we bought. If you can't find a mix, use equal amounts of dried apricots and raisins.

12-oz. package fresh
   cranberries
¾ c. water
1¼ c. sugar
¼ c. tarragon vinegar
   (or ¼ c. white wine
   vinegar and 2 tsp. dry
   tarragon)
½ tsp. allspice
1 c. mixed dried fruit
   (apples, apricots,
   peaches, raisins) cut
   into small pieces

Put the cranberries in a saucepan, add the water, bring to a boil and cook until the cranberry skins pop.

Stir in the rest of the ingredients and bring to a boil over moderate heat. Reduce the heat to low and simmer for about 10 minutes, stirring constantly. Allow to cool before serving.

YIELD: Serves 6
SODIUM CONTENT: 5 mg. of sodium per serving

V. SOUP

ALL-PURPOSE VEGETABLE STOCK

Many soups, stews, and other dishes call for chicken stock or broth; that's a problem if you want to create a vegetarian version; water makes a pallid substitute, an important issue in a salt-free recipe where every bit of flavor counts. You can address the problem with this simple, tasty vegetable stock. Be sure to include the thyme, which adds a strong dose of flavor.

olive oil
1 large onion, sliced
4 carrots, peeled and cut into
    1-inch pieces
4 stalks celery, cut into 1-inch pieces
1 bunch fresh thyme or 1 tbsp.
    dried thyme
1 bunch fresh sage or 1 tbsp. dried
    sage
1 bunch parsley
freshly ground pepper to taste
4 quarts water

In a stockpot, heat a little oil to medium heat and add the onion, carrot, and celery. Cook for 10 minutes, stirring occasionally, then add all the other ingredients except the water. Allow to cook for another 5 minutes, then add the water and bring to a boil. Reduce the heat and simmer for 1½ hours. Turn off the heat and allow the stock to cool. Strain before using. To save, pour 1- to 2-cup portions into resealable plastic bags and freeze.

YIELD: About 12 cups
SODIUM CONTENT: 21 mg. of sodium per cup

DOUBLE CHICKEN SOUP

The idea of salt-free chicken soup strikes many as an oxymoron; don't you need at least a little salt to bring out the flavor of the meat? There's another way: Cook the soup twice. This recipe gives the procedure for a basic soup of broth and chicken pieces. If you like rice, noodles, and vegetables, add them to the second simmering after an hour and a half.

3 to 4 lbs. of chicken drumsticks and thighs
16 c. (1 gallon) cold water
6 sprigs fresh thyme
1 bunch fresh parsley, washed
1 tbsp. whole peppercorns
2 bay leaves
1 medium onion, peeled and halved
cheesecloth
3 large carrots, peeled and quartered
2 half chicken breasts, bones in

Wash the chicken drumsticks and thighs and remove the skin and all visible fat. Put the cold water in a stockpot and place on high heat. Add the drumsticks and thighs and the thyme to the cold water and bring to a boil. Let the chicken boil for 1 minute, then reduce the heat so that the bubbles just break the surface of the liquid. Skim the top of the stock to get rid of the fat that accumulates as it boils off the chicken. Wrap the parsley, peppercorns, bay leaves, and onion in the cheesecloth and tie off the top with string. Add the cheesecloth bundle and the carrots to the pot. Allow the stock to simmer, covered, for 3 to 4 hours, periodically skimming the fat off the top as it accumulates.

Let the stock cool and strain it through a colander lined with cheesecloth. Discard the chicken, cheesecloth bundle, and carrots. Now return the stock to its original pot; add the chicken breasts, bring to a boil, reduce the heat, and allow to simmer for 2 hours. After the soup has cooked, remove the breasts. Remove the meat from the bones and return it to the soup.

YIELD: Serves 8
SODIUM CONTENT: 65 mg. of sodium per serving

TOMATO SOUP

To make a meal of this soup, cut small medallions of salt-free bread, toast them, then brush them lightly with olive oil. Place two in the bottom of each bowl and pour the soup over them.

2 tbsp. unsalted butter
1 medium onion, chopped
½ carrot, peeled and
**   roughly chopped**
3 cloves garlic, chopped
4 c. unsalted canned
**   tomatoes with their**
**   juice, or 4 c. chopped**
**   fresh tomatoes**
4 fresh basil leaves,
**   chopped, or 1 tbsp.**
**   dried basil**
1 tsp. sugar
freshly ground black
**   pepper to taste**
1 tsp. salt-free
**   chili powder**
2 tsp. lemon juice
2 c. unsalted chicken
**   stock or broth**
milk or cream to taste
**   (optional)**

In a large saucepan or Dutch oven, melt the butter and cook the onion, carrot, and garlic in it for several minutes, until the onion begins to wilt. Add the tomatoes and their juice, basil, sugar, black pepper, chili powder, and lemon juice. Cook for a few minutes, then add the chicken broth or stock and bring to a boil. Reduce the heat and allow to simmer, partially covered, for about 40 minutes.

When the mixture has cooked, transfer it in small batches to a food processor or blender and process to a smooth liquid. Return the blended soup to the pot. At this point you can reheat and serve it as is or add milk or cream as you like before reheating.

YIELD: Serves 4
SODIUM CONTENT: 49 mg. of sodium per serving

ASPARAGUS SOUP

To make this soup, cook the vegetables separately, then blend them together. On a cool day, serve it warm; on a hot day, serve it chilled.

1 large potato, peeled, quartered, and boiled until cooked through
2 dozen asparagus spears, trimmed and boiled or steamed until tender
2 to 3 c. unsalted chicken broth
freshly ground black pepper to taste

Put the potato, asparagus, 2 cups of chicken broth, and a grinding of fresh pepper in a blender or food processor and blend well. If the soup seems too thick, add more chicken broth. The taste and consistency will differ with the relative sizes of the potato and asparagus stalks. Strain the soup through a mesh strainer if you prefer a smooth appearance. Serve chilled or warm.

YIELD: Serves 4
SODIUM CONTENT: 30 mg. of sodium per serving

RED PEPPER SOUP

4 sweet red peppers
1 tbsp. olive oil
1 clove garlic, chopped
1 medium onion,
chopped
1 medium potato,
peeled and cut into
1-inch pieces
1 c. unsalted chicken
broth
½ c. milk
sour cream or yogurt

Preheat the oven to 350 degrees. Cut the peppers in half and remove the seeds. Place the peppers cut side down on a baking sheet and brush with a little olive oil. Bake for 30 to 40 minutes, or until thoroughly tender.

Meanwhile, heat 1 tablespoon olive oil in a saucepan; add the garlic and onion and cook for a few minutes until the onion begins to soften. Add the potato and chicken broth. Bring to a boil, cover, reduce the heat, and simmer until the potato is tender, about 15 minutes. Add a little water if the mixture seems too dry.

When both the peppers and the potato mixture have cooked, cut the peppers into smaller pieces, put them in a food processor or blender, add the potato mixture, and blend until smooth. Return the mixture to the saucepan, stir in the milk, and warm over low heat to serving temperature. Pour the soup into bowls and garnish each serving with a dollop of sour cream or yogurt.

YIELD: Serves 4
SODIUM CONTENT: 40 mg. of sodium per serving

LEEK AND POTATO SOUP

*For a meatier flavor,
substitute salt-free chicken
broth for the water. Be
sure to clean the leeks
carefully to get rid of grit.*

4 leeks, white part only
2 large potatoes
2 tbsp. unsalted butter
3 c. water or low-
    sodium chicken broth
3 tbsp. chopped parsley
2 to 3 c. whole milk
freshly ground black
    pepper to taste

Clean the leeks thoroughly and chop into thin slices. Peel and dice the potatoes. Melt the butter in a large saucepan; add the leeks and cook for about 10 minutes over moderate heat, stirring to prevent burning. Add 1 cup of the water; cover and cook for a few more minutes. Then add the potatoes, parsley and the rest of the water and cook until the potatoes are tender. Add milk to taste and stir until warmed through. Add freshly ground pepper to taste.

The leeks and potatoes retain much of their own identity in this soup. If you prefer a creamier soup, you can transfer the mixture to a blender or food processor before adding the milk and blend until smooth. Then return to the saucepan, add milk and pepper, and heat until warmed through.

YIELD: Serves 8
SODIUM CONTENT: 73 mg. of sodium per serving with chicken broth; 60 mg. of sodium with water

SWEET CORN CHOWDER

3 tbsp. unsalted butter
1 clove garlic, finely
   minced
1 medium onion,
   chopped
2 c. water or low-
   sodium chicken broth
1½ c. peeled and diced
   potatoes
2 c. corn, raw, salt-free
   frozen, or leftover
   cooked without salt
2 c. milk
freshly ground pepper
   to taste
parsley for garnish

Melt 1 tablespoon butter in a
saucepan. Add the garlic and onion
and cook until the onion is
translucent. Add the water or chicken
broth and the potatoes. Simmer until
the potatoes are cooked, about 45
minutes. Add the corn. If it is raw,
allow it to simmer for a few minutes
until the kernels are tender. Stir in the
milk and pepper and cook on low
heat until the chowder is heated
through. Do not allow it to boil. Ladle
into bowls and dot each bowl with a
small piece of the remaining butter.
Sprinkle with chopped parsley and
serve immediately.

YIELD: Serves 8
SODIUM CONTENT: 20 mg. of sodium per serving with
chicken broth, 9 mg. with water

MUSHROOM SOUP

Here's a basic recipe that makes the most of the rich flavor of good mushrooms. We used a combination of porcinis and creminis; supermarket button mushrooms would also work, but might not be quite as flavorful. Experiment with varieties of mushrooms, herbs, and wines.

2 c. low-sodium chicken
   broth
2 tsp. fresh thyme leaves
   or 1 tsp. dried thyme
1 medium potato, cubed
olive oil and unsalted
   butter as needed
1 c. chopped onion
2 cloves garlic, minced
2 c. sliced mushrooms
1 tbsp. lemon juice
freshly ground black
   pepper to taste
½ c. red or white wine
½ c. milk
sprigs of fresh parsley or
   thyme for garnish

Put the chicken broth, thyme, and potato in a saucepan and simmer until the potato is tender. Transfer to a blender or food processor and blend until smooth, then return to the saucepan. Heat a small amount of olive oil and unsalted butter in a sauté pan over medium heat and add the onion, garlic, and mushrooms. Cook for several minutes, until the onions are translucent and the mushrooms are tender. Sprinkle with the lemon juice and black pepper to taste. Add the mushroom mixture to the potato purée. Pour the wine into the sauté pan and stir with a wooden spoon to deglaze; then add to the mushroom-potato mixture. Warm the soup over low heat as you add the milk to thin it out. Serve in bowls, garnished with sprigs of fresh parsley or thyme.

YIELD: Serves 6
SODIUM CONTENT: 34 mg. of sodium per serving

CREAM OF MUSHROOM SOUP

2 tbsp. unsalted butter
2½ c. cleaned, sliced white button mushrooms
1 small onion, finely chopped
3 tbsp. flour
6 c. low-sodium chicken broth
1 tsp. ground thyme
¾ c. heavy cream

Heat a large pot to medium-high heat and add the butter. When the butter has melted, add the mushrooms and the onion. Allow to cook for 10 minutes or so, stirring occasionally, until the mushrooms start to release their liquid. Add the flour, stir to combine, then add the broth and thyme and stir well. Bring the soup to a boil, then reduce the heat to a simmer. Cook for 20 minutes. Add the cream, bring the soup back to a simmer, then turn off the heat and serve.

YIELD: Serves 6
SODIUM CONTENT: 40 mg. of sodium per serving

SQUASH AND APPLE SOUP

1 butternut squash
   (about 2½ pounds)
2 medium apples
2 tbsp. unsalted butter
½ c. chopped onion
1 clove garlic, minced
4 c. low-sodium chicken
   broth
3 tbsp. calvados
1½ tsp. ground cumin
freshly ground black
   pepper to taste
sour cream or yogurt

Preheat the oven to 375 degrees. Peel and seed the squash and apples and cut them into 1-inch cubes. Place the cubes in a baking pan and roast them in the oven until tender, about ½ an hour.

Melt the butter in a heavy pot; add the onion and garlic and cook until they soften. Stir the squash and apples in with the onion and garlic. Allow the mixture to cook for a few minutes, being careful not to let it burn. Then add the chicken broth, calvados, cumin, and black pepper; stir to blend.

Bring the mixture to a boil, reduce the heat to a simmer and cook for about 20 minutes, stirring occasionally. Remove the mixture to a blender or food processor and reduce it to a smooth purée. Return it to the pot over a low flame and keep it warm until you are ready to serve it. To serve, spoon the soup into bowls and garnish each with a generous dollop of sour cream or yogurt.

YIELD: Serves 6
SODIUM CONTENT: 42 mg. of sodium per serving

LENTIL SOUP

Lentils have a great flavor on their own; cooking them with leftover ham brings out more of it. The traditional smoked, salt-cured ham isn't an option for a salt-free diet, of course, but we find that fresh ham or other leftover pork works very well. If you prefer a vegetarian soup, forget the ham and try substituting a few cups of unsalted vegetable broth (see pages 103 and 315) for some of the water.

2 tbsp. olive oil
3 medium carrots, chopped
3 celery stalks, chopped
2 cloves garlic, crushed
1 medium onion, diced
1 c. chopped leftover fresh ham or pork (optional)
1 tsp. dried thyme or 1 tbsp. fresh thyme leaves
freshly ground black pepper to taste
12 c. water
3 tomatoes, chopped
2 c. lentils, rinsed under cold water

Heat the oil to medium-high in a heavy pot or Dutch oven. Add the carrot, celery, garlic, and onion. Cook for 10 minutes until the vegetables wilt, then add the ham, thyme, and pepper. Cook for another 5 minutes, then add the water, tomato, and lentils. Bring to a boil; reduce the heat and allow the soup to simmer, covered, for 3 to 4 hours.

YIELD: Serves 8
SODIUM CONTENT: 52 mg. of sodium per serving

TUSCAN BEAN SOUP

Traditional versions of this dish call for bits of heavily salted pancetta or sausage; we simply omitted them, added a bit of chili powder and lemon juice, and let the good flavors of beans and tomatoes take it from there. We like the result, especially served in the traditional way, over a slice of salt-free bread toasted and brushed with olive oil, then dropped in the bottom of the bowl.

¼ c. plus 2 tbsp. olive oil
1 medium onion, diced
1½ c. salt-free freshly chopped tomatoes or 1 c. salt-free tomato sauce or purée
24 oz. canned salt-free navy beans or cannellini beans (see page 315), drained (or ¾ lb. dried beans soaked in water overnight)
2 cloves garlic, minced

5 c. low-sodium chicken broth
1 tsp. salt-free chili powder
juice of ½ lemon
2 tbsp. fresh sage or rosemary
6 small slices salt-free white or wheat bread, toasted and brushed with olive oil

Heat 2 tablespoons of oil in a large saucepan or Dutch oven; add the onion and cook until golden brown. Then add the tomatoes, beans, and garlic and stir to combine. Add the chicken broth, chili powder, and lemon juice and stir to blend. Heat to a simmer and cook for about 20 minutes if using canned beans; if using dried beans cook for about 40 minutes, or until the beans are tender.

Blend the soup in a blender or food processor or pass it through a food mill, then return it to the pot. Heat the rest of the olive oil in a skillet, add the sage or rosemary, and sauté for a few minutes. Stir the oil and sautéed herb into the soup mixture; bring it to a simmer once more and cook for another 20 minutes. To serve, place a slice of toasted bread in the bottom of the bowl, then pour the soup over it.

YIELD: Serves 6
SODIUM CONTENT: 35 mg. of sodium per serving

PASTA E FAGIOLI

There may be as many
versions of this Italian
classic as there are Italian
cooks, so why not one
without salt? The basic
flavors are fine, strong and
reassuring on their own.
We take our side in a big
debate: whether to cook
the pasta in with the bean
soup mixture or cook it
separately and pour the
soup over it in a bowl. We
prefer the second way; it
allows you to get the
pasta just right.

2 tbsp. olive oil
1 large onion, chopped
2 cloves garlic, finely chopped
2 large carrots, sliced in ¼-inch
    rounds
1 medium zucchini, cubed
2 tbsp. chopped fresh basil
¼ c. flat parsley leaves, tightly
    packed
1 c. fresh spinach, tightly packed
2½ to 3 c. coarsely chopped fresh or
    salt-free canned tomatoes
15-oz. can salt-free navy beans or
    white kidney beans (see page 315)
1 c. salt-free chicken broth or water
1 tsp. dried oregano
1 tsp. ground cumin
juice of ½ lemon
freshly ground black pepper to taste
1 tbsp. white wine vinegar
8 oz. short pasta (spirals, elbows,
    bow-ties) cooked without salt
grated unsalted Gouda or Swiss
    cheese (optional)

(Continued)

Heat the olive oil in a heavy saucepan or Dutch oven. Add the onion, garlic, and carrots and cook until the onions begin to turn brown and caramelize. Add the zucchini, basil, parsley, and spinach. Cook for a few minutes until the basil and spinach are wilted. Add the tomatoes and beans, including the liquid from the canned beans, and the chicken broth. Add the oregano, cumin, lemon juice, pepper, and vinegar, and stir to combine. Bring the mixture to a boil. Turn down the heat and allow to simmer gently for 20 to 30 minutes, until the carrots are soft and the flavors are combined.

To serve, put a generous serving of pasta in a large soup bowl, ladle the bean mixture over it, and sprinkle with grated cheese.

YIELD: Serves 10
SODIUM CONTENT: 4 mg. of sodium per serving

MINESTRONE

1½ c. whole green
  beans, cleaned and
  cut in half
2 tbsp. olive oil
2 large carrots, chopped
1 zucchini, chopped
3 tomatoes, chopped
10 c. salt-free chicken
  broth or water
2 c. canned salt-free
  kidney beans (see
  page 315) or dried
  kidney beans, cooked
  without salt
1 tbsp. chopped fresh
  basil
freshly ground black
  pepper to taste
⅓ c. small pasta (tubes,
  elbows, or
  corkscrews)

Put the green beans in a small saucepan, cover with water, and bring to a boil. Reduce to medium heat and simmer for 20 minutes while you prepare the other ingredients. Put the oil in a large stockpot, add the vegetables and a little water or broth, cover, and cook for 10 minutes on medium to low heat. Stir occasionally to keep them from burning on the bottom. Add the rest of the water or broth, kidney beans, basil, and pepper. Turn up the heat to bring the soup to a boil, then reduce the heat and simmer for 40 minutes. Add the pasta and cook for another 12 minutes.

YIELD: Serves 8
SODIUM CONTENT: 44 mg. of sodium with chicken broth, 17 mg. with water

COLD CUCUMBER SOUP

1 large cucumber,
    peeled
2 c. plain yogurt
½ c. unsalted tomato
    paste
½ tsp. coriander
1 clove garlic, minced
mint for garnish
freshly ground black
    pepper to taste

Dice the cucumber and put it in a blender or food processor. Add the rest of the ingredients except the mint and blend until smooth. Chill in the refrigerator until ready to serve, garnished with sprigs of fresh mint.

YIELD: Serves 4
SODIUM CONTENT: 76 mg. of sodium per serving

MELON SOUP WITH CALVADOS

2 c. diced honeydew
    melon
2 c. diced watermelon
    with seeds removed
1 c. light cream
2 tbsp. calvados
mint for garnish

Combine all the ingredients except the mint in a blender or food processor and blend until smooth. Chill until ready to serve. Garnish with sprigs of fresh mint.

YIELD: Serves 4
SODIUM CONTENT: 34 mg. of sodium per serving

MELON AND RASPBERRY SOUP

The sweeter the melon, the sweeter this soup will be; serve it garnished with mint before a summer meal, or add a dollop of sherbet and serve it for dessert.

1 ripe cantaloupe
1 c. fresh raspberries plus 4 more raspberries for garnish
½ c. orange juice
juice of ½ lemon
juice of ½ lime
4 large fresh mint leaves

Cut the melon in half, clean out the seeds, peel the halves, and cut the flesh into 1-inch pieces. Put the pieces of melon in a food processor or blender and process to create a smooth purée. Pour the melon purée into a large bowl. Put the raspberries in the food processor or blender and process to create a smooth purée. Pour this purée into a strainer and push the juice and pulp through the strainer to a small bowl in order to remove the raspberry seeds. This process should yield about ½ cup of seedless purée (repeat with more raspberries if it comes up short).

Stir the raspberry purée into the melon purée, then add the orange juice, lemon juice, and lime juice, and stir to blend. To serve, ladle the soup into bowls and garnish each serving with a mint leaf and a whole raspberry.

YIELD: Serves 4
SODIUM CONTENT: 12 mg. of sodium per serving

VI. SALAD

COLE SLAW
WITH FRESH HORSERADISH

½ medium head of
  green cabbage
¼ medium head of red
  cabbage
½ c. finely grated raw
  horseradish
3 tbsp. cider vinegar
1 tsp. sugar
freshly ground black
  pepper to taste

Use a grater or food processor to
reduce the cabbages to a fine grain.
Put them in a bowl and stir so that
the two colors are evenly distributed;
then stir in the grated horseradish.
Add the vinegar and stir to blend,
then add the sugar and a generous
grinding of pepper and stir once
more. Allow to sit for at least 30
minutes before serving.

YIELD: Serves 6
SODIUM CONTENT. 19 mg. of sodium per serving

ASPARAGUS SALAD

1 bunch of fresh asparagus (about a dozen spears)
2 hard-boiled eggs
3 tbsp. lemon juice
½ tsp. salt-free Dijon mustard
freshly ground black pepper to taste
1 tbsp. olive oil

Trim the tough ends off the asparagus spears and boil or steam them over moderate heat until they are just tender. Remove the asparagus to cold water to prevent it cooking further and set aside. Remove the hard-boiled eggs from their shells and separate the yolks from the whites. Use a sharp knife to dice the whites and yolks as finely as possible and set them aside. Put the lemon juice, mustard, pepper, and oil in a bowl, and whisk together for the dressing.

Cut the tops off the asparagus and set aside. Slice the asparagus stalks into strips. Reserve 2 tablespoons of the chopped egg and put the rest in the bowl with the asparagus. Pour the dressing over the asparagus and egg mixture and toss. Garnish individual servings of the salad with asparagus tops and a sprinkling of chopped egg.

YIELD: Serves 4
SODIUM CONTENT: 50 mg. of sodium per serving

TABBOULEH

1 c. bulgur wheat
2 c. boiling water
1½ c. chopped parsley
1 c. chopped mint
1 c. chopped scallions
1½ c. chopped, seeded
tomatoes
2 carrots, steamed and
cut into ¼-inch cubes
freshly ground black
pepper to taste
⅓ c. lemon juice
⅓ c. olive oil
½ tsp. salt-free chili
powder

Put the bulgur wheat in a bowl and pour the boiling water over it. Put a pot lid or plate on top of the bowl and allow to stand until the bulgur wheat has absorbed most of the water and has become tender and fluffy. Transfer the bulgur wheat to a strainer and push down on it with a rubber scraper to squeeze out any excess water.

Return the bulgur wheat to the bowl and add the parsley, mint, scallions, tomatoes, and carrots, stirring to distribute after each addition. Sprinkle with freshly ground pepper and stir to combine. Put the lemon juice, oil, and chili powder in a small bowl and stir to combine. Pour this mixture over the bulgur wheat mixture and toss. Chill before serving.

YIELD: Serves 8
SODIUM CONTENT: 15 mg. of sodium per serving

COUSCOUS SALAD

1½ c. couscous
1¾ c. boiling water
1 cucumber
freshly ground black
    pepper to taste
½ small red onion,
    sliced thin
1 tomato, cut in half and
    sliced thin
2 tbsp. olive oil

Put the uncooked couscous in a bowl and pour the boiling water over it. Cover the bowl and allow to stand until all the water is absorbed, about 5 minutes. Remove the cover and let the couscous cool. Peel the cucumber, cut it in half lengthwise, and remove the seeds with a spoon. Dice the cucumber; place in a large bowl and add the pepper, onion, and tomato. When the couscous has cooled, fluff it with a fork and add it to the vegetables. Stir to mix, and drizzle oil over the top. Serve chilled.

YIELD: Serves 6
SODIUM CONTENT: 5 mg. of sodium per serving

CUCUMBER SALAD
WITH TAHINI DRESSING

Our friend Fran Piven, whose vegetable garden is the envy of several counties in upstate New York, contributed this dish to a recent gathering. She recommends skinny cucumbers with small seeds; the long thin European varieties are especially good this way.

¾ c. tahini
juice of 1½ to 2 lemons
1 large clove garlic,
    finely minced
½ tsp. cumin
½ tsp. coriander
pinch of cayenne pepper
freshly ground black
    pepper to taste
2 cucumbers

Stir the tahini and lemon juice together until well blended. Add the rest of the ingredients except the cucumbers and stir to blend. Allow the mixture to stand at room temperature for about 30 minutes. (If you put it in the refrigerator, it will thicken up.) Peel the cucumbers and slice them into thin rounds. Put them in a large bowl, pour the dressing over them, and toss so that it is well distributed.

YIELD: Serves 4
SODIUM CONTENT: 9 mg. of sodium per serving

PICKLED CUCUMBER SALAD

It's important to use a stainless steel bowl for soaking food in vinegar; it's also a good idea to tie up the peppercorns in cheesecloth so they can be removed easily after pickling.

3 cucumbers
1 small red onion,
   sliced thin
2 tbsp. black
   peppercorns
3 c. white wine vinegar
1 tsp. sage
juice of 1 lemon
1 tbsp. sugar

Peel the cucumbers and cut each in half lengthwise. Then cut across each half to create slices about ½-inch thick. Put all the ingredients except the cucumbers and the onion in a saucepan and bring to a boil on top of the stove. Place the cucumbers and the onion in a stainless steel bowl large enough for all the ingredients. When the vinegar mixture is at a boil, pour it over the cucumbers; cover the bowl tightly with aluminum foil or plastic wrap. When the salad cools down refrigerate it overnight. Before serving, drain off the vinegar mixture and remove the peppercorns.

YIELD: Serves 6
SODIUM CONTENT: 6 mg. of sodium per serving

ORZO AND SHRIMP SALAD

In this tasty concoction, orzo, the delicate rice-shaped pasta, makes the perfect vehicle for fresh shrimp. You can devein and otherwise clean the shrimp before or after cooking them.

1 lb. shrimp, peeled, deveined, and washed; boiled for 5 minutes
½ lb. orzo, cooked without salt in boiling water until tender (about 6 to 8 minutes)
olive oil
2 fresh tomatoes, diced
12 basil leaves, chopped
¼ c. chopped parsley
freshly ground black pepper to taste
juice of 1 lemon

After you have cooked and cleaned the shrimp, put them in a bowl of cold water to cool down. Drizzle the cooked orzo with olive oil, stir, and allow it to cool down as well. When the shrimp are cooled, remove them from the water to paper towels and pat them dry. Then toss all the ingredients in a large bowl until well distributed. Serve chilled.

YIELD: Serves 6
SODIUM CONTENT: 112 mg. of sodium per serving

SALADE NIÇOISE

You don't need anchovies or olives to make this hearty, entree-sized salad work, just good potatoes and fresh green beans. It's a great way to use the salt-free tuna fish now available in many supermarkets and health-food stores.

FOR THE SALAD:

2½ c. cooked green beans
8 new potatoes cooked until fork tender and cut into quarters
8 plum tomatoes, quartered
1 small red onion, sliced thin
4 hard-boiled eggs, sliced
2 (6-oz.) cans tuna packed in water without salt

FOR THE DRESSING:

¼ c. snipped parsley
1 tbsp. salt-free Dijon mustard
1 tsp. sugar
¼ c. red wine vinegar
freshly ground black pepper to taste
½ c. olive oil

Arrange the green beans, potato quarters, and tomatoes on a serving plate along with the slices of onion and hard-boiled egg. Drain the tuna and flake it over the top of the vegetables. Whisk together parsley, mustard, sugar, vinegar, and pepper. Then drizzle in the oil while continuing to whisk until it emulsifies and looks cloudy. Pour the dressing over the salad and serve.

YIELD: Serves 8
SODIUM CONTENT: 79 mg. of sodium per serving

SHRIMP SALAD WITH AVOCADO AND GRAPEFRUIT

1 lb. fresh shrimp
1 grapefruit
1 avocado
1 red pepper, diced
2 tbsp. salt-free
   mayonnaise
   (see pages 15
   and 315)
freshly ground black
   pepper to taste

Drop the shrimp into a pot of boiling water and cook for about 5 minutes. After the shrimp are cooked, peel off the shells and devein them. Set them aside in a bowl of ice. Cut the grapefruit in half. Peel one half, then use a sharp knife to remove sections of the flesh from the pulp; set them aside. Squeeze the other half of the grapefruit to extract the juice; set it aside. Cut the avocado in half, remove the pit, separate the flesh from the peel, and slice the flesh into sections. Pour a little of the grapefruit juice over the avocado to keep it from turning brown.

Combine the rest of the grapefruit juice with the diced red pepper, mayonnaise, and ground pepper in a bowl. Drain the shrimp, add them to the bowl, and stir to combine. Spoon a portion of the shrimp mixture onto each plate and place 2 or 3 avocado slices on top. Garnish the plate with the sections of grapefruit.

YIELD: Serves 6
SODIUM CONTENT: 112 mg. of sodium per serving

HEALTHY TUNA SALAD

FOR THE SALAD:

2 (6-oz.) cans tuna packed
in water without salt
1 large carrot, peeled
and grated
1 large cucumber,
peeled, seeded, and
diced
¼ c. finely chopped red
onion

FOR THE DRESSING:

1 tbsp. salt-free Dijon mustard
¼ c. red wine vinegar
1 tsp. sugar
2 tbsp. finely chopped parsley
freshly ground black pepper to taste
½ c. olive oil

Combine the four salad ingredients in
a large bowl. Combine all of the
dressing ingredients except the oil in
a small bowl, then whisk in the oil.
Combine salad and dressing to taste.

YIELD: Serves 4
SODIUM CONTENT: 71 mg. of sodium per serving

CLASSIC TUNA SALAD

2 (6-oz.) cans tuna packed
in water without salt
½ c. salt-free mayonnaise
(see pages 15 and 315)
½ tsp. salt-free curry
powder (see page 19)
2 tbsp. lemon juice
freshly ground black
pepper to taste

Put the tuna fish in a bowl and use a
fork to mash and crumble it to an
even consistency. Add the mayonnaise
and stir until thoroughly blended.
Then stir in the curry powder, lemon
juice, and pepper. Serve on lettuce as
a salad or as a filling for sandwiches on
salt-free bread.

YIELD: Serves 4
SODIUM CONTENT: 35 mg. of sodium per serving

RED POTATO SALAD WITH SWEET ONIONS

10 small red potatoes
1 tbsp. unsalted butter
1 large onion, sliced
2 tsp. sugar
2 tbsp. chopped parsley
1 tbsp. chopped basil
freshly ground black
   pepper to taste

Cut the potatoes into quarters, put them in a saucepan, cover with cold water, bring to a boil, and cook until tender. (Or steam the potatoes until tender if you prefer.) Remove the potatoes from the heat. Cook the butter and onion in a large pan heated to medium-high heat for 10 minutes. When the onions start to brown, add the sugar and cook for another 5 minutes. Add the potatoes and the herbs to the pan, season with pepper, toss, and serve warm.

YIELD: Serves 6
SODIUM CONTENT: 12 mg. of sodium per serving

WARM NEW POTATO AND SHIITAKE MUSHROOM SALAD

10 new potatoes
2 tbsp. olive oil
8 shiitake mushrooms,
   sliced
juice of ½ lemon
freshly ground black
   pepper to taste
1 shallot, minced
2 cloves garlic, diced
2 tbsp. chopped parsley

Wash (but don't peel) the potatoes, then cut them into quarters. Put them in a pot, cover with cold water, bring to a boil, and cook until tender. Remove the potatoes from the heat and drain. Heat olive oil in a large sauté pan over high heat. Add the mushrooms to the pan and cook for 6 minutes, then sprinkle with the lemon juice and black pepper. Add the shallot and garlic, stir to combine, and cook for another minute. Then add the potatoes and parsley; allow it all to warm through and serve.

YIELD: Serves 4
SODIUM CONTENT: 19 mg. of sodium per serving

GREEN BEAN AND SWEET POTATO SALAD

2 lbs. green beans,
cleaned and cut into
thirds
juice of ½ lemon
1 tbsp. unsalted Dijon
mustard
¼ c. red wine vinegar
1 tsp. sugar
¼ c. chopped parsley
freshly ground black
pepper to taste
½ c. olive oil
1 large sweet potato,
peeled, diced, and
boiled until tender

Steam the green beans until tender, about 6 minutes. Remove from the pan and immerse in a bowl of cold water mixed with the lemon juice. Combine the mustard, vinegar, sugar, parsley, and black pepper in a small mixing bowl. Then drizzle in the olive oil while whisking constantly to create a creamy, blended dressing. Drain the green beans and toss with the cooked sweet potatoes in a large serving bowl. Pour the dressing over the top and stir gently to distribute. Chill the salad for an hour before serving.

YIELD: Serves 6
SODIUM CONTENT: 23 mg. of sodium per serving

POTATO AND EGG SALAD

4 large potatoes, peeled
and boiled
6 hard-boiled eggs
1 medium onion, chopped
3 tbsp. olive oil
2 tbsp. balsamic vinegar
freshly ground pepper
to taste
2 tbsp. chopped parsley

Cut the potatoes and eggs into thin slices and combine in a serving bowl. Add the chopped onion and stir gently to combine. Mix the oil and vinegar together, and stir to blend. Pour this mixture over the potatoes and eggs and stir to distribute it evenly. Add the pepper and stir once more. Sprinkle the parsley over the salad and serve.

YIELD: Serves 8
SODIUM CONTENT: 56 mg. of sodium per serving

HEALTHY POTATO SALAD

8 to 10 new potatoes,
  boiled until tender
juice of ½ lemon
¼ c. olive oil
2 tbsp. finely chopped
  dill
freshly ground black
  pepper to taste

When the potatoes are cooked, put them in a colander, run cold water over them, and drain; set aside to cool completely. Whisk together the lemon juice, oil, and dill. Cut the cooled potatoes into quarters and toss with the dressing. Sprinkle with freshly ground pepper and serve.

YIELD: Serves 4
SODIUM CONTENT: 12 mg. of sodium per serving

CLASSIC EGG SALAD

The touch of curry powder makes all the difference in this basic recipe. Embellish it, if you want, with bits of sweet pepper, salt-free sun-dried tomato, or salt-free dill pickle (see page 315).

6 hard-boiled eggs
⅓ c. salt-free
  mayonnaise
  (see page 15)
½ tsp. salt-free curry
  powder (see page 19)
freshly ground black
  pepper to taste

Peel the eggs, put them in a mixing bowl, and use a fork to mash them up. Add the mayonnaise and stir to blend, followed by the curry powder and black pepper. Serve on lettuce as a salad or as filling for a sandwich on salt-free bread.

YIELD: Serves 4
SODIUM CONTENT: 92 mg. of sodium per serving

CHICKEN SALAD
IN RADICCHIO LEAVES

2 chicken breasts
1 tbsp. olive oil
3 tbsp. salt-free
   mayonnaise
   (see page 15)
1 orange
1 yellow sweet pepper
1 head of radicchio
fresh parsley or cilantro
   for garnish

Brush the chicken breasts with the oil and broil until done. Allow them to cool completely. In a mixing bowl, combine the mayonnaise and the juice of half the orange, mixing well. Then cut up the chicken into bite-sized pieces, dice the pepper, and add them to the bowl. Peel the other half of the orange, and use a sharp knife to remove the flesh from the pulp between sections. Stir the orange into the salad. Arrange curved leaves of the radicchio so that they form a cup on each plate, fill with the salad, and garnish with sprigs of fresh parsley or cilantro.

YIELD: Serves 4
SODIUM CONTENT: 86 mg. of sodium per serving

CHICKEN SALAD
WITH MANGO DRESSING

FOR THE SALAD:

2 boneless chicken breasts
2 mangoes, peeled, flesh
cut off the seed, and
diced
12 honeydew melon balls
12 cantaloupe melon balls
radicchio leaves for
garnish

FOR THE VINAIGRETTE:

1 mango
2 tbsp. white wine
vinegar
1 tsp. sesame oil
1 tsp. olive oil
2 tbsp. white wine

Poach the chicken breasts in water for 20 to 30 minutes, until cooked through. Let cool and cut into bite-sized pieces.

To prepare the vinaigrette, peel the mango and remove the pit, cut into cubes, put in a blender, and blend until smooth. Add the vinegar, oils, and wine, and blend to incorporate. Put in the refrigerator to chill.

Toss together the chicken pieces, diced mango, and melon balls. When the dressing is chilled pour it over the salad and toss. Garnish each serving with a leaf of radicchio.

YIELD: Serves 4
SODIUM CONTENT: 90 mg. of sodium per serving

CLASSIC CHICKEN SALAD

Here's a salt-free version of the sandwich filling or everyday lunch special we all learned to love in the 1950s. The gourmet approach is to roast a whole chicken, then lovingly remove equal portions of light and dark meat to chop up and combine with the rest of the ingredients. That's a wonderful gesture for guests you welcome for lunch, or for a contribution to the church or neighborhood potluck. It works just as well, however, with the leftovers from the chicken parts you broiled for last night's dinner.

2 c. diced chicken; roasted, broiled, or sautéed without salt; skin and bones removed
½ c. salt-free mayonnaise (see page 15)
½ tsp. salt-free chili powder
1 tsp. lemon juice

Put the diced chicken in a bowl; add the rest of the ingredients and stir to combine well. Serve as a filling for sandwiches on salt-free bread, or as a salad by placing a scoop of the chicken mixture on a large leaf of romaine or red leaf lettuce, garnished with a sprig of parsley.

YIELD: Serves 4;
SODIUM CONTENT: 83 mg. of sodium per serving

AVOCADO AND BEAN SALAD

*For canned unsalted beans,
see page 315. If you can't
find them, soak 1 pound of
dried beans overnight, then
boil until tender (about 1
hour) and chill.*

**2 avocados, peeled,
pitted, and diced
15-ounce can unsalted
pinto, black, or
kidney beans**

**8 cherry tomatoes, halved
1 shallot, minced
juice of ½ lemon
freshly ground pepper to taste**

Place the first four ingredients in a
bowl and stir to combine. Sprinkle
with the lemon juice and pepper, and
toss well. Serve chilled.

YIELD: Serves 4
SODIUM CONTENT: 31 mg. of sodium per serving

BLACK BEAN SALAD

FOR THE SALAD:

**2 c. cooked black beans
or 15-ounce can salt-
free canned beans (see
page 315)
1 medium onion, diced
1 sweet red pepper, white
membrane removed,
seeded, and diced
2 c. salt-free frozen or
fresh corn
1 tbsp. chopped fresh
cilantro leaves**

FOR THE DRESSING:

**⅓ c. olive oil
¼ c. balsamic vinegar
1 tbsp. unsalted Dijon mustard
freshly ground black pepper to taste**

If using canned beans, drain off their
liquid. Combine the beans, onion,
pepper, corn, and cilantro in a large
bowl. Mix the dressing ingredients
together in a small bowl and stir with
a whisk until thoroughly blended.
Pour the dressing over the bean
mixture and stir to distribute it evenly.

YIELD: Serves 6
SODIUM CONTENT: 19 mg. of sodium per serving

LENTIL SALAD

1½ c. dried lentils
1 medium tomato,
  chopped
2 tbsp. chopped fresh
  parsley
1 tbsp. chopped fresh
  tarragon
1 tbsp. balsamic vinegar
2 tbsp. olive oil

freshly ground black pepper to taste
1 medium red onion, chopped fine

Boil the lentils in unsalted water for 35 minutes or until tender. When the lentils are cooked through, place them in a large serving bowl. Add the rest of the ingredients and toss to combine. Serve chilled.

YIELD: Serves 6
SODIUM CONTENT: 17 mg. of sodium per serving

TUSCAN BEAN SALAD

2 cans salt-free white
  beans (see page 315)
  or 2 c. dried navy
  beans
3 tbsp. chopped parsley
2 tbsp. chopped basil
1 tbsp. chopped sage
freshly ground black
  pepper to taste
juice of ½ lemon
2 tbsp. olive oil

If you are using dried beans, wash them in cool water and boil for 20 minutes. Then drain and boil again until they are tender; this could take up to 2 hours. While the beans are simmering you can flavor them with black pepper and a lemon wedge, fresh herbs, or a couple of garlic cloves.

Drain the beans (whether canned or home cooked), put them in a large bowl with all the rest of the ingredients, and stir to combine. Let stand for 1 hour before serving.

YIELD: Serves 4
SODIUM CONTENT: 31 mg. of sodium per serving

VII. Fish

BROILED SEA BASS

¼ c. olive oil
juice of ½ lemon
freshly ground black
  pepper to taste
2 tbsp. chopped fresh
  parsley
1 tbsp. chopped fresh
  tarragon
2 cloves garlic, crushed
4 (8-oz.) pieces of sea
  bass cut in thick fillets

Mix together all the ingredients except the fish in a shallow dish. Add the fish and turn to coat with the oil-herb mixture. Allow the fish to marinate for 20 to 30 minutes. In the meantime heat the broiler and make sure the rack in the oven is 8 to 10 inches away from the heat source.

After the fish has marinated, remove it from the oil and place it in an ovenproof baking dish. It's not necessary to drain off all the oil—that's where the flavor is. Put the fish under the broiler for 8 minutes, checking occasionally to make sure it doesn't burn. The fish is ready when cooked through and just beginning to brown on top.

YIELD: Serves 4
SODIUM CONTENT: 157 mg. of sodium per serving

STRIPED BASS
WITH BRAISED TOMATO

**2 (12-oz.) fillets of
  striped sea bass
freshly ground black
  pepper to taste
2 tbsp. olive oil
1 small shallot, chopped
3 cloves garlic, sliced
2 medium tomatoes,
  chopped
2 tbsp. chopped parsley
1 tsp. fresh dill
5 large basil leaves,
  roughly chopped
⅓ c. white wine
juice of ½ lemon**

Rinse the fish fillets in cool water and pat dry. Cut each fillet in half to create two squarish pieces. Season with pepper and set aside. Heat 2 tablespoons olive oil in a sauté pan; add the fish, skin side down. Cook for 4 minutes, shaking the pan to prevent sticking. Remove the fish from the pan. Add the shallot and garlic to the pan, season with pepper, and cook for 6 minutes. Add the tomatoes and all the herbs, stirring, and cook for another 5 minutes. Add the white wine and lemon juice and reseason with black pepper. Reduce heat to a simmer, cover, and allow to cook for 12 to 15 minutes.

Return the fish to the pan, skin side down, cover the pan, and cook for 8 minutes. Put a piece of fish on each plate with a dollop of tomatoes. Use a spoon to drizzle some of the pan juices around the fish.

YIELD: Serves 4
SODIUM CONTENT: 126 mg. of sodium per serving

BAKED WHOLE RED SNAPPER OR SEA BASS

Here's the recipe to use when the fisherperson in your family shows up with a large prize at the end of the day. We like it best with red snapper or sea bass, but it should work with almost any sizeable fish.

1 small onion
1 lemon
1 whole fresh fish,
  scaled and cleaned
freshly ground black
  pepper to taste
10 sprigs of fresh
  parsley
½ c. white wine

Preheat the oven to 400 degrees. Peel the onion and slice it very thin. Slice thin cross sections of the lemon. Cut slices crosswise across the top side of the fish to make serving sized pieces. Place the fish in an ovenproof baking dish and sprinkle with black pepper. Distribute the onion, lemon slices, and parsley over the fish and pour the wine around it. Bake in the oven for 25 minutes or until the fish flakes when poked. When the fish has cooked, the slices should lift off the bone easily. Then remove the bone and cut pieces from the bottom side of the fish. Avoid serving pieces containing small bones near the head and fins.

YIELD: Serves 2 or more
SODIUM CONTENT: 124 mg. of sodium per 6 ounces of fish

CAJUN SWORDFISH STEAKS

½ tsp. dried basil
½ tsp. dried parsley
¼ tsp. dried oregano
1 tbsp. paprika
pinch of cumin
pinch of cayenne
  pepper
freshly ground pepper
  to taste
2 (8-oz.) swordfish steaks
1 tbsp. olive oil

Mix all the spices together in a bowl. Wash and dry the fish. Sprinkle the spice mixture evenly over one side of the fish. Allow to sit for 10 minutes. Heat the oil in a nonstick pan and reduce the heat to medium. Add the fish, seasoned side down, and cook for 5 minutes. Turn the fish over and continue cooking for about 3 more minutes, until it is cooked through.

YIELD: Serves 2
SODIUM CONTENT: 125 mg. of sodium per serving

BAKED FLOUNDER WITH FENNEL SAUCE

2 fennel bulbs, cubed
¼ c. white wine
½ c. sour cream or
  quark (see page 12)
2 tbsp. lemon juice
4 (6-oz.) flounder fillets
1 tbsp. fennel seeds
1 clove garlic, minced

Steam the fennel until tender, then purée in a blender or food processor. Add the wine, sour cream or quark,

and 1 tablespoon lemon juice, and stir to combine. Set the sauce aside.

Preheat the oven to 350 degrees. Rinse the flounder fillets and pat dry. Use an electric spice grinder or a mortar and pestle to pulverize the fennel seeds. Combine the seeds, minced garlic, and 1 tablespoon of lemon juice and rub it gently into the surface of the fish. Put the fish fillets in a lightly buttered ovenproof dish and cover with the fennel sauce. Bake until the fish is cooked through, about ½ hour.

YIELD: Serves 4
SODIUM CONTENT: 178 mg. of sodium per serving

FLOUNDER POACHED
IN TOMATO AND WINE

3 oz. salt-free tomato
  paste
½ c. water
¾ c. white wine
juice of ½ lemon
1 tbsp. dried basil or 2
  tbsp. chopped fresh
  basil leaves
4 (6-oz.) flounder fillets
freshly ground black
  pepper to taste
sprigs of parsley for
  garnish

Stir the tomato paste, water, wine, and lemon juice together in a bowl until well blended, then pour into a skillet large enough to accommodate the fish fillets lying flat. Heat briefly and add the basil. Place the fish fillets in the skillet so that they are partially covered by the liquid; sprinkle evenly with the pepper. When the liquid begins to simmer, turn down the heat, cover, and cook until the fish is cooked through, about 10 minutes. Remove the fish to a warm platter, then turn up the heat and allow the liquid to cook down for a minute or so. Pour enough of the liquid over the fish fillets to cover them, garnish with fresh parsley, and serve immediately. Pour the remainder of the liquid into a bowl and serve as additional sauce for the fish.

YIELD: Serves 4
SODIUM CONTENT: 151 mg. of sodium per serving

FLOUNDER BAKED IN PARCHMENT

Baker's parchment, available in supermarkets (usually next to the foil and waxed paper), provides a wonderful way to prepare fish and vegetables—watch for the puff of aromatic steam when you slit the parchment open after cooking. We loved this recipe with flounder, but you should experiment with whatever looks freshest when you go to the fish market. You may also want to try other vegetables and herbs. Use fairly thin fillets so that the fish and vegetables finish cooking at about the same time. Our recipe is for one serving; multiply the quantities by the number of guests.

6-oz. fresh flounder fillet
½ c. finely diced leeks
1 small shallot, finely diced
1 tbsp. olive oil
½ c. carrots cut into julienne strips

4 string beans cut into thin strips
2 sprigs of fresh thyme
2 tbsp. white wine
freshly ground black pepper to taste

Preheat the oven to 400 degrees. Rinse the fish and pat dry. Combine the diced leeks and shallot in a small bowl. Cut a sheet of parchment paper about 12 inches wide and 15 inches long. Fold in half the long way to make a crease. Using your fingers or a pastry brush, spread the olive oil over half of the paper (on one side of the crease), to within an inch of the outside edges. Be sure to leave the edges dry.

Spread a few pieces of carrot and string beans as well as a third of the leek-shallot mixture on the oiled paper and place the fish fillet on top. Pile the rest of the vegetables on top of the fish and place the thyme across them. Sprinkle with the wine and pepper.

Fold the dry half of the parchment over the fish and vegetables and fold the edges tightly, starting at a corner by the crease, to create a semicircular pouch. Fold the edges over two or three times so that they stay together. Put the pouch on a baking sheet, place it in the oven, and bake for 10 to 12 minutes, until the fish is cooked through.

YIELD: Serves 1
SODIUM CONTENT: 164 mg. of sodium per serving

OVEN-ROASTED SALMON WITH TOMATOES AND ASPARAGUS

2 lemons
4 (6-oz.) salmon steaks
8 asparagus spears,
    trimmed
2 medium tomatoes,
    sliced
4 fresh basil leaves
¼ c. white wine
freshly ground black
    pepper to taste
2 tbsp. chopped parsley

Preheat the oven to 375 degrees. Slice one of the lemons into thin circles and distribute them over the bottom of an ovenproof baking dish or pan large enough to hold all the fish. Add the steaks and arrange the asparagus, tomato slices, and basil leaves around them. Then add the wine and sprinkle everything with the pepper and parsley. Roast in the oven until the fish is cooked through, 12 to 16 minutes, depending on the size of the steaks. Serve with slices of the second lemon.

YIELD: Serves 4
SODIUM CONTENT: 120 mg. of sodium per serving

SALMON IN A BASIL BUTTER SAUCE

4 (6-oz.) salmon fillets
1 c. water
juice of ½ lemon
4 tbsp. unsalted butter
1 shallot, finely diced
1 clove garlic, finely diced
8 fresh basil leaves, roughly chopped
sprigs of basil for garnish

Rinse the fish in cold water and remove any bones. Put the fish in a large sauté pan; add the water and lemon juice, and poach the fish in simmering liquid until it has turned pink all the way through, about 8 to 10 minutes. Meanwhile, in a small saucepan, combine butter, shallot, and garlic, and cook over low heat only until the butter has melted—make sure not to brown the butter. Then stir in the basil.

When the salmon is done, remove each fillet to a plate and spoon the butter sauce over and around it. Garnish each fillet with a sprig of basil leaves. Serve hot.

YIELD: Serves 4
SODIUM CONTENT: 114 mg. of sodium per serving

GRILLED SALMON STEAKS
WITH HERBED BUTTER

**4 tbsp. (½ stick)
unsalted butter,
softened
2 tbsp. finely chopped
parsley
1 tbsp. finely chopped
basil
2 sage leaves, finely
chopped
juice of ½ lemon
freshly ground black
pepper to taste
4 (8- to 10-oz.) salmon
steaks**

Put the butter in a bowl; add the
herbs, lemon juice, and pepper, and
stir to blend. Coat each steak liberally
with the herbed butter. Allow to
marinate while you prepare the
charcoal or gas grill. When the grill
reaches medium-high heat, put the
steaks on it and cook about 4 minutes
on one side; turn once and cook 3
minutes more, then remove.

YIELD: Serves 4
SODIUM CONTENT: 187 mg. of sodium per serving

COLD POACHED SALMON
WITH CUCUMBER DILL SAUCE

FOR THE FISH:

1 large salmon fillet, about 24 oz.
water to cover the bottom of the pan, about 1½ cups
6 peppercorns
1 bay leaf
1 tbsp. lemon juice

FOR THE SAUCE:

1 c. plain yogurt or sour cream
½ c. peeled and diced cucumber
1 tbsp. lemon juice
2 tbsp. finely chopped fresh dill

Check the salmon fillet for bones and remove any you find. Bring the water, peppercorns, bay leaf, and lemon juice to a boil in a skillet large enough to hold the fillet lying flat. The liquid should be about ½-inch deep, enough to partially cover the fish. Place the fish in the liquid. When it returns to a boil, turn down the heat so that it continues to simmer gently. Cover loosely and poach for about 10 minutes, or until the fish is tender and cooked through. Allow to cool, then put in the refrigerator to chill.

To make the sauce, put the yogurt or sour cream and cucumber in a blender or food processor and blend until the cucumber is puréed. Add the lemon juice and dill and pulse several times to mix.

To serve, put the fish on a platter, pour some of the sauce over it, and garnish with a few whole sprigs of dill. Serve the rest of the sauce in a bowl.

YIELD: Serves 4
SODIUM CONTENT: 137 mg. of sodium per serving

SALMON CAKES

Get good fresh salmon; fillets are easier to dice, although you can try it with steaks. Just be sure to avoid all the bones. For salt-free bread crumbs, see page 315; if you can't find them, toast two or three slices of salt-free bread and use a knife or food processor to reduce them to crumbs.

1-lb. salmon fillet, diced very small
1 tsp. chopped fresh dill
1 tbsp. chopped parsley
1 tbsp. salt-free Dijon mustard
2 tbsp. finely diced sweet red pepper
1 c. salt-free bread crumbs
1 tbsp. unsalted butter

Combine all the ingredients except the bread crumbs and butter in a bowl and mix them together with your fingers until well blended. Then begin adding bread crumbs a small amount at a time, continuing to mix them in by hand, until the mixture thickens enough so that you can form it into balls that hold together. Each cake should be the size of a large meatball, slightly flattened. Put the cakes on a plate, cover loosely with plastic wrap and refrigerate for a ½ hour.

Heat the butter in a nonstick skillet to medium heat; add the cakes and cook, turning once, 3 to 4 minutes per side, taking care not to let them burn. The cakes will be fragile; it is all right to let them fall apart a bit as they cook.

YIELD: Serves 6
SODIUM CONTENT: 62 mg. of sodium per serving

SEARED SCALLOPS
WITH SPRING VEGETABLES

1 c. baby carrots, peeled
and washed
1 c. green beans washed
and cut into 2-inch
strips
1 c. fresh baby spinach,
washed
1 red pepper, seeded
and cut into thin strips
vegetable oil
12 large sea scallops,
cleaned and rinsed
juice of 1 lemon

Steam the carrots until just tender; do the same with the green beans. Toss the carrots, raw spinach leaves, green beans, and red pepper in a bowl and set aside. Heat a small amount of oil over high heat in a nonstick sauté pan. Make sure the scallops are completely dry. Place them in the pan, season with black pepper, and cook for 3 minutes on each side, until golden brown. Discard any that burn. Remove the scallops from the pan to a paper towel in order to drain off excess oil. For each serving, take a handful of the vegetables and put it on a plate, place three scallops on top of them, and drizzle with some of the lemon juice.

YIELD: Serves 4
SODIUM CONTENT: 151 mg. per serving

MUSHROOM, TOMATO, AND SHRIMP OMELET

You'll need little popcorn shrimp for this wonderful dish; look for them precooked at your fish counter, but be sure to verify they were steamed or boiled without salt. If they haven't been, buy fresh shrimp and steam them yourself.

2 tbsp. unsalted butter
2 c. sliced mushrooms
freshly ground black
** pepper to taste**
8 eggs
½ c. milk
2 medium tomatoes,
** diced**
½ lb. popcorn shrimp,
** cooked without salt**

Melt 1 tablespoon of butter in a skillet over medium heat. Add the mushrooms and season with pepper. Sauté until the mushrooms release their juices. Remove from the heat. Place 2 eggs in a bowl, season with pepper, add 2 tablespoons of milk and whisk until the milk, yolks, and whites are all well combined. Heat a separate nonstick pan over medium heat and add a small dab of butter. Add the egg mixture to the pan and cook until it starts to set. As it does, add one-fourth of the tomatoes, shrimp, and mushrooms, and distribute them evenly over the surface of the eggs. Finish cooking the omelet to the degree of firmness you like, then slide half of it onto a plate and flip the pan so that the other half folds on top of it. Repeat for the other three omelets. Serve immediately.

YIELD: Serves 4
SODIUM CONTENT: 232 mg. of sodium per serving

VIII. POULTRY

CHICKEN WITH MUSTARD SAUCE

Be sure to use garlic powder and onion powder, made only from dried garlic or onion, rather than garlic or onion salt.

FOR THE SAUCE:

⅓ c. salt-free
   mayonnaise
   (see page 15)
2 tbsp. salt-free Dijon
   mustard
dash of onion powder
dash of garlic powder
freshly ground black
   pepper to taste
2 tbsp. chopped parsley

FOR THE CHICKEN:

2 whole chicken breasts
   (4 half breasts)
½ c. flour
1 tbsp. corn oil
¼ c. low-sodium chicken
   broth

Put the ingredients for the sauce in a bowl; mix and set aside. Wash and pat the chicken breasts dry and dredge with flour. Heat the oil in a large skillet. When it is hot, slip the chicken into the skillet; brown quickly on both sides and remove. Deglaze the pan with the chicken broth (add the broth and stir to dissolve the residue on the bottom and sides of the pan), and cook until it is reduced by half. Then spoon in the sauce and stir. Add the chicken breasts and simmer for 15 to 20 minutes, or until the chicken is cooked through.

YIELD: Serves 4
SODIUM CONTENT: 125 mg. of sodium per serving

BALSAMIC GLAZED CHICKEN

½ c. balsamic vinegar
2 tbsp. olive oil
2 cloves garlic, crushed
1 tsp. ground sage
1 dash dried thyme
1 shallot, minced
freshly ground black
    pepper to taste
4-lb. roasting chicken

Combine all the ingredients except the chicken in a large bowl and stir to blend. Wash the chicken inside and out and pat dry with paper towels. Place the chicken in the bowl and spoon the marinade over it, making sure to coat the whole bird. Cover and marinate in the refrigerator for at least 3 hours, overnight if possible.

Preheat the oven to 375 degrees. Place the chicken on a rack in a roasting pan and pour the marinade over it. Roast for 1½ hours or until the juices run clear when a leg of the chicken is cut.

YIELD: Serves 6
SODIUM CONTENT: 119 mg. of sodium per serving

WHITE WINE BRAISED CHICKEN

olive oil
3 lbs. chicken pieces,
   washed and dried
½ c. white wine
2 tbsp. chopped fresh
   parsley
½ onion, chopped
4 fresh sage leaves
4 cloves garlic, chopped
freshly ground black
   pepper to taste

Preheat the oven to 350 degrees. On top of the stove, heat an ovenproof skillet or Dutch oven large enough to hold all the ingredients. When it has reached high heat, add enough oil to coat the bottom of the pan. Add the chicken pieces skin sides down to brown, then turn to brown the other sides. When the chicken has thoroughly browned, remove the pieces and deglaze the pan with the wine (add the wine and stir to dissolve the residue on the bottom and sides of the pan). Return the chicken pieces to the pan, add the rest of the ingredients, cover, and place in the oven to bake for 45 minutes. Serve the chicken with rice and generous spoonfuls of the pan juices.

YIELD: Serves 6
SODIUM CONTENT: 100 mg. of sodium per serving

BORDEAUX BRAISED CHICKEN

olive oil
1 c. chopped onion
1 c. chopped carrot
1 c. chopped green
    pepper
3 sprigs fresh tarragon
3 sprigs fresh sage
6 stalks fresh parsley
freshly ground black
    pepper to taste
2 c. Bordeaux wine
1 c. low-sodium chicken
    broth
8 small pieces of dark
    chicken meat
    (drumsticks and
    thighs)

Heat a pan large enough for all the ingredients to medium-high and coat the bottom with oil. Add the onion, carrot, and green pepper. Cook for about 10 minutes, stirring occasionally, then add the herbs and black pepper, and cook for another 5 minutes. Add the wine and the chicken broth; stir to blend. Cook the mixture until it is reduced by half. Add the chicken, cover, and allow to simmer very gently until the meat is falling off the bone, about 45 minutes. Remove the chicken to a serving plate. Strain the sauce and drizzle a little over the chicken, reserving the rest in a gravy boat to serve with the meat.

YIELD: Serves 4
SODIUM CONTENT: 153 mg. of sodium per serving

BAKED CHICKEN WITH APPLE CIDER AND APPLES

3 lbs. chicken pieces
2 c. apple cider
½ c. flour
1 tsp. ground ginger
1 tsp. ground cinnamon
freshly ground black
pepper to taste
2 tbsp. brown sugar
2 medium apples

Remove the skin and fat from the chicken pieces and wash them in cold water. Put the cider in a large bowl; add the brown sugar and stir to dissolve. Add the chicken pieces, cover, and allow to marinate for a few hours or overnight.

Preheat the oven to 350 degrees. Combine the flour, ginger, cinnamon, and pepper in another bowl and stir to blend. Remove the chicken from the cider marinade and reserve the liquid. Dip each chicken piece in the flour mixture and coat well, then place in a baking pan and bake for 30 minutes. Core the apples, cut into thin slices, and add them to the cider marinade. Remove chicken from the baking pan and pour in the cider-apple mixture. Return chicken to the pan and bake for another 25 minutes or until the chicken is cooked through.

Remove the chicken pieces to a serving dish. Deglaze the pan (use a wooden spoon to scrape bits of chicken and apple from the bottom and sides) and, if necessary, cook down the cider-apple mixture to make a sauce. If it has cooked down too much already, add a little cider. Serve the chicken pieces using the cider-apple mixture as a sauce.

YIELD: Serves 6
SODIUM CONTENT: 82 mg. of sodium per serving

CHICKEN BREASTS STUFFED WITH WILD MUSHROOMS

Assortments of wild mushrooms are an increasingly common sight in urban specialty food stores and some supermarkets. It's worth the effort to seek them out. Wild mushrooms have robust, meaty flavors that easily stand on their own without any need for salt. If you can't find chanterelles or shiitake, most others will do; the recipe also works with the cultivated mushrooms available in supermarkets nearly everywhere, though the flavor might not be as interesting.

3 large button mushrooms
4 chanterelle mushrooms
4 shiitake mushrooms
2 to 3 tbsp. olive oil
1 shallot, minced
1 clove garlic, minced
2 tbsp. balsamic vinegar
1 tbsp. dried parsley or 2 tbsp. chopped fresh parsley

2 whole boneless chicken breasts (4 half breasts) pounded between plastic wrap to ¼-inch thick
toothpicks

Chop the mushrooms, place them in a hot sauté pan with 1 tablespoon of olive oil (use more oil if needed), and reduce to moderate heat. Cook the mushrooms for 5 minutes, then add the minced shallot, parsley, and garlic. Cook for 5 more minutes; add the vinegar and deglaze the pan by stirring until all of the residue on the bottom of the pan has dissolved in it. This should take about a minute. Remove the mushroom mixture to a plate.

Preheat the oven to 350 degrees. When it is cool enough to handle, spread about 2 tablespoons of the mushroom mixture on each flattened piece of chicken and roll it up. Use toothpicks to secure the roll and keep it closed. Heat 1 to 2 tablespoons of olive oil in the pan you used to prepare the mushrooms and brown the chicken on all sides. Transfer the chicken rolls to a baking dish and cook in the oven until the chicken is cooked through, about 20 minutes.

YIELD: Serves 4
SODIUM CONTENT: 83 mg. of sodium per serving

CHICKEN TENDERS

This is a great dish for families where everyone works or goes to school— pick up the chicken breasts on the way home and get dinner on the table in 20 minutes. We like cumin and black pepper, but you can experiment with any spice you want to flavor the flour.

1 c. all-purpose flour
**1 tbsp. cumin or salt-
    free chili powder**
**freshly ground black
    pepper to taste**
**2 whole boneless
    chicken breasts
    (4 half breasts), cut
    into 1-inch cubes**
vegetable oil

Combine the flour, cumin or salt-free chili powder, and pepper in a paper bag. Put the chicken cubes in the bag and shake until all the pieces are evenly coated with the flour mixture. Pour enough oil into a large skillet to cover the bottom to a depth of ⅛ inch and heat to medium-high. Drop the chicken pieces into the oil and cook for about 5 minutes on one side, then turn and cook for another 5 minutes. Remove cooked pieces to a plate lined with a paper towel so that the oil drains off. Serve with a sprinkling of lemon juice, lemon wedges, salt-free hot sauce (see page 315) or dipping sauces (see pages 93–94).

YIELD: Serves 4
SODIUM CONTENT: 82 mg. of sodium per serving

GRILLED LEMON CHICKEN

3 whole boneless
  chicken breasts
  (6 half breasts)
juice of 1 lemon
freshly ground pepper
  to taste
1 tbsp. unsalted Dijon
  mustard
½ c. red wine vinegar
2 tbsp. chopped fresh
  parsley
4 basil leaves, chopped
1 tsp. dried oregano
¼ c. olive oil
pinch of ground sage

Make a marinade by combining all the ingredients except the chicken in a large bowl and mixing well. Wash the chicken and trim any excess fat. Put the chicken in the bowl with the marinade, turn the pieces to coat them, and put in the refrigerator to marinate for at least an hour. Prepare the charcoal or gas grill, and grill chicken pieces over medium heat until cooked through.

YIELD: Serves 6
SODIUM CONTENT: 88 mg. of sodium per serving

CHICKEN BREASTS
IN A PEANUT SAUCE

*This unsalted peanut
butter and tomato
concoction tastes a little
like Thai cuisine. If you
prefer, cut the chicken
into 1-inch cubes and
broil or grill it on skewers
to serve with rice.*

**2 whole boneless
   chicken breasts, cut
   into 4 half breasts**
¼ c. brown sugar
¼ c. white wine vinegar
**¼ c. salt-free peanut
   butter**
**¼ c. salt-free tomato
   paste**
**2 large cloves garlic,
   chopped**

Rinse the chicken breasts in cold
water, pat dry, and place them in a
shallow bowl. Whisk the rest of the
ingredients together in a small bowl;
pour the mixture over the chicken
pieces and turn them so they are
coated evenly. Marinate for at least an
hour. Cook the chicken pieces under
the broiler or on a charcoal grill,
basting with the remainder of the
marinade, until cooked through.

YIELD: Serves 4
SODIUM CONTENT: 91 mg. of sodium per serving

BROILED CHICKEN WITH MUSTARD AND HORSERADISH

Use salt-free Dijon mustard (see page 315) and salt-free mayonnaise (see page 15); if you don't have fresh horseradish, substitute a smaller amount of low-sodium prepared horseradish.

**3 whole boneless,
  skinless chicken
  breasts, cut in half
2 tbsp. unsalted Dijon
  mustard
2 tbsp. salt-free
  mayonnaise
½ tsp. ground cumin
1 tsp. cider vinegar
2 tbsp. grated fresh
  horseradish or 2 tsp.
  salt-free prepared
  horseradish
olive oil
freshly ground black
  pepper to taste**

Preheat the oven broiler. Rinse the pieces of chicken breast and dry completely with a paper towel. Combine the mustard, mayonnaise, cumin, vinegar, and 1 tablespoon of the grated horseradish (or all of the prepared horseradish) in a bowl, and stir until well blended. Use a pastry brush to coat the bottom of a shallow pan with olive oil. Place the chicken breasts in the pan, outer side down, then use a brush to add a light coating of oil to their exposed sides. Use the brush to spread the mustard-horseradish mixture on the exposed inner sides of the breasts, then turn them over and spread the mixture on the outer sides. Sprinkle with pepper and the rest of the grated horseradish. Place on the middle shelf of the oven under the broiler or on the lowest level of a separate broiler and cook until the breasts are golden brown on top and cooked through, about 15 minutes.

YIELD: Serves 6
SODIUM CONTENT: 115 mg. of sodium per serving

TANDOORI-STYLE CHICKEN

For the authentic dish, you need a tandoor, the conical clay oven common in Northern India and Pakistan; you can cook this salt-free version on a gas or charcoal grill.

3 whole boneless and skinless chicken breasts (or 6 half breasts)
1 pinch of saffron
1 tbsp. cumin
2 tsp. coriander
2 cloves garlic, crushed
1 c. plain yogurt

Rinse the chicken breasts, pat dry with a paper towel and cut into inch-thick strips. Mix all the spices, garlic, and yogurt together in a large bowl. Add the chicken to the bowl, cover, and allow to marinate for at least 2 hours.

Prepare the charcoal or gas grill; when it is at medium to medium-high heat, place the chicken pieces on it until they are cooked through, turning them from time to time so they cook evenly on all sides. This should take about 10 minutes. Serve with rice.

YIELD: Serves 6
SODIUM CONTENT: 97 mg. of sodium per serving

ROASTED PEPPERS STUFFED WITH CHICKEN

2 whole chicken breasts, cut into 4 half breasts, cleaned and trimmed of excess fat
½ c. balsamic vinegar
1 tbsp. olive oil
freshly ground black pepper to taste
2 tbsp. diced red onion
2 tbsp. chopped parsley
1 tbsp. chopped basil
1 tomato, diced
4 sweet red peppers

Marinate the chicken for about 20 minutes in the balsamic vinegar with the oil and black pepper. Grill the chicken over a charcoal grill or sauté it on top of the stove until cooked through. When it has cooled, chop it into very small pieces and place it in a bowl. Add the onion, parsley, basil, tomato, and black pepper; stir to combine. Roast the whole peppers until tender over the charcoal grill or a gas flame, or on a baking sheet in a 350-degree oven. Remove the stems, cut off the tops, remove the seeds, and fill each pepper with a generous amount of the chicken mixture. (If the peppers won't hold their shapes, spread pieces of them on plates and cover with the chicken mix.)

YIELD: Serves 4
SODIUM CONTENT: 83 mg. of sodium per serving

CHICKEN SCALOPPINE WITH MUSHROOMS

2 whole boneless
  chicken breasts cut
  into 4 half breasts
flour for dredging
2 to 3 tbsp. olive oil
1 c. sliced mushrooms
2 tsp. lemon juice
freshly ground black
  pepper to taste
½ c. grated low-sodium
  Gouda or Swiss cheese
parsley for garnish

Dredge a piece of chicken breast in flour, then sprinkle a little more flour on a piece of waxed paper and place the chicken on it. Pound the chicken flat, to a thickness of ¼ inch, using the bottom of a heavy skillet or pot. Repeat with the other pieces of chicken. Heat 2 tablespoons of oil in a large sauté pan; add the mushrooms and cook over medium heat to the point that they begin to wilt and give up their liquid. Sprinkle with 1 teaspoon of the lemon juice and a grinding of black pepper and stir to combine. Remove the mushrooms and put the chicken pieces in the pan, adding a bit more oil if necessary.

Turn up the heat and cook the chicken just until cooked on the bottom and the edges begin to turn white. Turn the chicken pieces over and place equal portions of mushrooms on top of each one, then sprinkle generously with grated cheese and with another teaspoon of lemon juice. Turn the heat down to low; cover and cook for a few more minutes until the cheese has melted and the chicken is cooked through. Serve garnished with parsley.

YIELD: Serves 4
SODIUM CONTENT: 78 mg. of sodium per serving

TWO CHICKEN STEW

2 tbsp. olive oil
2 medium onions,
  roughly chopped
1 bunch fresh sage
  (a dozen leaves
  or more)
1 bunch fresh thyme
1 bunch parsley
2 whole chickens (about
  3½ lbs. each)
4 quarts water
2 tbsp. whole black
  peppercorns
4 large carrots, peeled
  and cut into 1-inch
  lengths
10 new potatoes,
  quartered
2 medium tomatoes,
  diced

Heat the oil in a large pot or Dutch oven and sauté the onion and the herbs in it for about 10 minutes. Add the chickens, water, and peppercorns; bring to a boil. Turn down the heat and allow to simmer for 4 hours. Use a large spoon to skim off the fat as it collects on the surface.

After 4 hours, turn off the heat and allow to cool. Take the chickens out of the pot, and remove and discard the skin and fat. Separate the meat from the bones and break the meat into bite-sized pieces. Use a ladle to strain the liquid through a fine strainer or colander into a bowl, and return half of the liquid to the pot. Add the chicken, carrots, potatoes, and tomatoes; bring to a simmer and cook for 1½ hours.

YIELD: Serves 12
SODIUM CONTENT: 105 mg. of sodium per serving

CHICKEN CURRY
WITH COCONUT MILK

*The great depth of flavor
in this recipe depends on
the exotic combination of
coconut milk and
tamarind paste. Coconut
milk should be available
by the can in markets that
serve Hispanic or Asian
neighborhoods. We found
tamarind paste in a
Chinatown grocery,
though it may turn up in
East Indian markets as
well. If you can't find it,
there's an easy substitute:
¹/₃ cup of prune juice plus
2 tablespoons of lemon
juice. The 3 tablespoons
of curry powder made it
just hot enough for us; use
more or less as you prefer.*

3 boneless, skinless chicken breasts
   (6 half breasts)
½ c. all-purpose flour
freshly ground black pepper to taste
5 tbsp. unsalted butter
1 medium onion, chopped
2 cloves garlic, minced
2 green peppers, diced
3 tbsp. unsalted curry powder (see
   page 19)
2 c. diced tomatoes
2 tbsp. salt-free tomato paste
   dissolved in ¼ c. water
15-oz. can coconut milk
3 tbsp. tamarind paste dissolved in
   ½ c. water and strained
¼ c. dried currants
¼ c. golden raisins

(Continued)

Preheat the oven to 350 degrees. Rinse each piece of chicken breast and pat it dry, then cut it in half to create a total of 12 pieces of chicken. Combine the flour and black pepper and sprinkle over the chicken to coat each piece. Melt 3 tablespoons of the butter in a large skillet on top of the stove and brown the chicken pieces in it, then remove them and set them aside. Add the onion, garlic, and green pepper to the skillet along with the rest of the butter, and cook for several minutes over medium heat, stirring occasionally, until the onions begin to soften and turn brown. Add the curry powder; stir to blend, and cook for 2 minutes.

Add the tomatoes, dissolved tomato paste, and coconut milk, and stir to combine. Add the water with dissolved tamarind pulp, making sure you have strained out the skin and seeds (or add the mixture of prune juice and lemon juice if you don't have tamarind paste); stir to blend, then stir in the currants and raisins. Bring this mixture to a simmer, then remove it from the heat.

Put the chicken pieces in a large casserole or ovenproof Dutch oven and pour the curry–coconut milk mixture over them, then stir to combine. Cover and bake in the oven until the chicken is tender and the flavors are well developed, about 45 minutes. Allow the mixture to cool slightly before serving with rice and plain yogurt.

YIELD: Serves 6
SODIUM CONTENT: 34 mg. of sodium per serving

HUNTER'S CHICKEN

2 tbsp. olive oil
6 chicken drumsticks,
  washed and excess fat
  removed
6 chicken thighs,
  washed and excess fat
  removed
1 c. flour
3 carrots, chopped
3 celery stalks, chopped
1 small onion, sliced
freshly ground black
  pepper to taste
1 tbsp. ground thyme
1 tsp. ground sage
32-ounce can salt-free
  whole tomatoes or
  3 c. chopped fresh
  tomatoes
1 c. white wine
14 shiitake mushrooms,
  cleaned and sliced
2 cloves garlic
1 bay leaf

Heat the oil to medium-high heat in a large stew pot or Dutch oven. Roll the chicken in the flour. Add the chicken to the pan and brown well. When the chicken has browned, remove it and add carrots, celery, and onion. Season with black pepper, thyme, and sage. Cook for 10 minutes over medium heat until the vegetables have wilted. Add the chicken, tomatoes, and wine, and stir to combine. Then add mushrooms, garlic, and bay leaf. Bring the mixture to a simmer and cook for 1½ hours. Remove the bay leaf before serving. Serve with rice.

YIELD: Serves 6
SODIUM CONTENT: 147 mg. of sodium per serving

BULGUR STUFFING

Here's the salt-free family recipe tested on years of Thanksgiving turkeys. To make 4 cups of cooked bulgur, put 2 cups bulgur in a bowl, pour 2 cups of boiling water over it, and let it stand until the water is absorbed.

½ c. unsalted butter
   (one stick)
2 large onions, chopped
1½ tsp. ground
   coriander
½ tsp. ground cumin
1½ c. slivered, blanched
   almonds
1½ c. coarsely chopped
   dried apricots
1½ c. raisins
4 c. cooked bulgur
2 tsp. cinnamon
½ tsp. ground cloves
freshly ground pepper
   to taste

Melt the butter in large skillet. Add the onions, coriander, and cumin. Cover and cook, stirring occasionally, until the onion is translucent, about 10 minutes. Add the almonds, apricots, and raisins. Cook uncovered, stirring occasionally, until the almonds are golden. Transfer to a large bowl. Add the bulgur, cinnamon, cloves, and pepper, and mix well. Refrigerate before using to stuff a turkey before roasting.

YIELD: Serves 8
SODIUM CONTENT: 14 mg. of sodium per serving

CHESTNUT STUFFING

Use prepared unsalted bread crumbs (see page 315) or make your own by using a knife or food processor to chop up slices of toasted salt-free white or whole-wheat bread.

1 lb. chestnuts
1 tbsp. olive oil
1 medium onion, chopped
2 tbsp. finely minced fresh sage leaves
¾ lb. ground pork
freshly ground black pepper to taste
2 shallots, finely minced
½ c. chopped parsley
1 tbsp. fresh thyme or 1 tsp. dried thyme
2 cloves garlic, minced
2 c. salt-free bread crumbs
1 bay leaf

Prepare the chestnuts by cutting a cross in the flat side of each one, dropping them into a pot of boiling water, and allowing them to boil for about 5 minutes. Then turn off the heat and remove the chestnuts one by one, peeling off the inner and outer shells. Break the chestnut meats into small pieces with your fingers and put them in a large bowl.

Heat the olive oil in a skillet; add the onion and cook over medium heat, stirring occasionally, until the onion wilts and grows transparent. Add the sage and the bay leaf and cook for a few minutes more. Then add the ground pork and cook, breaking up the pork and stirring it with a heavy spoon so that it browns evenly. When the pork has browned, sprinkle generously with black pepper. Add the pork mixture to the chestnuts and stir to blend. Then add the rest of the ingredients, stir to combine, and sprinkle with a little more black pepper.

YIELD: Serves 8
SODIUM CONTENT: 35 mg. of sodium per serving

JALAPEÑO CORNBREAD STUFFING

One whole jalapeño pepper makes this ring four alarms for us; if you like it milder, use less.

1 c. milk
1 egg
1 tbsp. honey
1 jalapeño pepper, seeded and finely chopped
5 tbsp. unsalted butter
1 c. cornmeal
1 c. all-purpose flour
2 tbsp. low-sodium baking powder
2 c. sliced mushrooms
2 tsp. sage
freshly ground black pepper to taste

Preheat the oven to 350 degrees. Lightly grease an 8-inch square baking pan or loaf pan of similar size. Stir together the milk, egg, honey, and chopped pepper in a large bowl until well blended. Melt 3 tablespoons of the butter and add it to the milk mixture. Sift together the cornmeal, flour, and baking powder in a separate bowl and add them to the wet ingredients. Stir only until the dry ingredients are moistened. Pour the batter into the pan and bake for 20 to 25 minutes, until a toothpick dipped into the center of the cornbread comes out clean. Set aside to cool.

Melt the remaining butter in a small frying pan. Add the mushrooms and 1 teaspoon of the sage and cook over moderate heat, stirring constantly, for about 3 minutes, or until the mushrooms have begun to soften and absorb the butter. Crumble up the cornbread in a large bowl; add the mushrooms, the remaining sage, and the pepper. Stir until thoroughly blended.

YIELD: Serves 8
SODIUM CONTENT: 26 mg. of sodium per serving

TURKEY BREAST WITH CORNBREAD STUFFING

This recipe will make about twice the amount of cornbread you need for the stuffing; you can save the rest of the cornbread to eat with the meal, or you can halve the ingredients and bake in a smaller pan.

FOR THE CORNBREAD:

1 c. cornmeal
1 c. all-purpose flour
5 tsp. low-sodium baking powder
1 c. milk
1 egg
3 tbsp. unsalted butter, melted
1 tbsp. honey

FOR THE TURKEY AND STUFFING:

olive oil
1 medium onion, chopped
1 shallot, chopped
1 large clove garlic, minced
1 tbsp. chopped fresh sage leaves or 1 tsp. dried sage
1 c. sliced mushrooms
juice of ½ lemon
½ lb. ground pork
freshly ground black pepper to taste
4 tsp. salt-free chili powder
1 c. fresh or salt-free frozen corn
2 c. crumbled cornbread from this recipe
¼ c. parsley leaves
1 bay leaf
1 tsp. fresh thyme or ½ tsp. dried thyme
1 (4-lb.) boneless turkey breast
1 c. low-sodium chicken broth

To make the cornbread, preheat the oven to 350 degrees while you sift together the cornmeal, flour, and baking powder in a bowl. Put the milk in a separate bowl; add the egg and beat with a whisk to blend. Then slowly pour in the melted butter, stirring constantly, followed by the honey. Pour this mixture over the dry ingredients and stir only until the dry ingredients are well moistened. Pour the batter into a lightly greased 8" x 8" baking pan and bake for about 25 minutes until the top just begins to brown and a toothpick inserted into the center of the cornbread comes out clean. Allow to cool. Then crumble up enough of the cornbread to fill 2 cups.

To make the stuffing, heat 1 tablespoon of olive oil in a sauté pan. Add the onion, shallot, and garlic, and cook over medium heat,

(Continued)

stirring occasionally, until the onion begins to wilt. Add the sage leaves and cook for a few more minutes. Add the mushrooms and cook until they begin to soften. Sprinkle with lemon juice and stir to blend. Then add the ground pork and stir with a wooden spoon until it is evenly browned. Sprinkle with black pepper, add 3 teaspoons of the chili powder, and stir to blend. Transfer this mixture to a large bowl; add 2 cups of crumbled cornbread, corn, parsley, bay leaf, and thyme, and stir to combine.

Rinse the turkey breast and pat dry. Spread the meat out flat with the skin side down and "butterfly" the thick part of the breast: Start in the middle of the breast and cut about halfway through the thick section, cutting sideways toward the end, keeping the flat of the knife parallel with the work surface. Fold out the flap of meat created by this cut. Spread stuffing generously across the surface of the meat, using your fingers to press it down tightly. Then roll up the meat around the stuffing to form a cylinder, and use butcher's twine to tie it together. Start with one tie at the middle and add one or two more toward the ends.

Wipe the bottom of a roasting pan with olive oil and place the tied turkey breast in it, seam side down. Brush the top of the breast with olive oil and dust lightly with the remaining teaspoon of chili powder. Spread any leftover stuffing around the breast on the bottom of the pan, along with ½ cup of the chicken broth. Roast at 350 degrees until the breast meat is cooked through, basting occasionally with the rest of the chicken broth. Cooking time should be about 1½ hours. Transfer the breast and stuffing to a serving platter and garnish with parsley.

Allow the meat to cool a bit before slicing. To serve, cut slices from the end of the rolled breast so that the meat spirals around a portion of stuffing.

YIELD: Serves 10
SODIUM CONTENT: 103 mg. of sodium per serving

IX. MEAT

POT ROAST

*To cook pot roast so that
the meat flakes apart and
melts in your mouth, don't
allow it to boil for more
than a minute; instead
allow it to simmer under
the boiling point for
hours. If you don't have a
good salt-free beef broth
(see page 315) you can
take the dish in a slightly
different direction by
replacing the stock with a
6-ounce can of unsalted
tomato paste diluted with
1½ cups of water.*

2 tbsp. olive oil
3- to 4-lb. rump roast
1 onion, quartered
1 clove garlic, minced
1 green pepper, diced
1 large carrot, diced
¼ c. roughly chopped parsley
1 bay leaf
2 sprigs fresh thyme or
    1 tbsp. dried thyme
freshly ground black pepper to taste
½ c. red wine
1¾ c. salt-free beef broth

Heat the oil in a heavy pot or Dutch
oven. Add the meat to the pot and
brown well on all sides over medium
heat. Remove the meat and add the
onion, garlic, green pepper, carrot,
parsley, bay leaf, thyme, and black
pepper. Cook this mixture for about
10 minutes. When the onion is
translucent, add the wine and deglaze
the pot by using a wooden spoon to
scrape bits of meat off the bottom
and sides. Then return the meat to
the pot, add the broth, and bring the
liquid to a boil. Reduce the heat to a
simmer and cook for 3 to 4 hours,
covered, turning the meat every 30
minutes, until tender.

YIELD: Serves 8
SODIUM CONTENT: 139 mg. of sodium per serving

BEEF STROGANOFF
WITH NOODLES

For a lighter touch with this tasty dish, use sour half-and-half or reduced-fat sour cream.

2 tbsp. unsalted butter
1½ lbs. London broil sliced into thin 2- to 3-inch strips
freshly ground black pepper to taste
2 tbsp. balsamic vinegar
1 medium onion, chopped
½ c. dry vermouth or white wine
1½ c. sliced mushrooms
1 tsp. basil
1 tbsp. flour
2 tsp. unsalted Dijon mustard
½ c. sour cream

Melt the butter in a large frying pan and add the beef. Stir with a wooden spoon until the meat is browned on all sides. Sprinkle the meat with black pepper and balsamic vinegar; continue to cook over moderate heat, stirring, until the meat is cooked through. Remove the meat from the pan to a bowl and set aside. Add the onion to the frying pan and cook, stirring, until translucent, about 5 minutes. Add the vermouth, mushrooms, and basil, and cook, stirring, until the mushrooms have softened and the liquid is reduced by half. Turn the heat to low; add the flour and mustard, and stir, making sure all the flour is absorbed. Return the beef to the frying pan and stir to combine; then add the sour cream and stir to blend. Serve over noodles cooked without salt.

YIELD: Serves 6
SODIUM CONTENT: 79 mg. of sodium per serving

FLANK STEAK WITH PORTOBELLO MUSHROOMS AND WINE

1 flank steak
freshly ground black
   pepper to taste
dash of garlic powder
1 c. red wine
1 shallot, diced
2 portobello mushroom
   caps, cut into slices
   ¼-inch thick
1 c. drained salt-free
   canned tomatoes plus
   ½ c. of juice from the
   can
1 tbsp. dried parsley
pinch of dried oregano

Preheat the oven to 375 degrees and place a shallow roasting pan or ovenproof dish in the oven to heat up. Season the meat with pepper and garlic powder. Heat a heavy skillet to high heat on top of the stove. Sear the steak in the hot skillet on both sides so that it browns thoroughly and juices are sealed in. Transfer the steak to the pan in the oven to finish cooking (about 10 minutes for medium). Then remove it from the oven and set aside.

Meanwhile, use half of the wine to deglaze the skillet and allow it to cook until almost gone. Add the shallot and reduce the heat to low. Add the mushrooms; cook 2 minutes per side, then remove them from the skillet. Add the rest of the wine and allow it to cook until almost evaporated. Add the tomato, parsley, and oregano and cook at a simmer for 10 minutes. Return the mushrooms to the skillet on the stove and cook 1 minute to heat through. Slice the steak on the bias, arrange the slices on a plate with the mushrooms and sauce, and serve.

YIELD: Serves 4
SODIUM CONTENT: 161 mg. of sodium per serving

MARINATED PORK TENDERLOIN

**1 whole pork tenderloin
(about 2 to 3 lbs.)
¼ c. balsamic vinegar
juice of ½ lime
freshly ground black
pepper to taste
2 tbsp. chopped parsley
1 tsp. paprika
pinch of crushed red
pepper flakes
3 tbsp. olive oil
fresh parsley or
rosemary for garnish**

Remove the silvery membrane and any visible fat from the meat. Mix together all the other ingredients except the oil and parsley for garnish. Place the meat in a shallow dish and cover with the marinade mixture. Allow to sit for at least an hour (the longer it marinates, the better it will be); put it in the refrigerator if you are going to marinate it for several hours.

Preheat the oven to 375 degrees. Heat the oil in a heavy ovenproof skillet. When the oil begins to smoke, add the meat and sear it on all sides. Searing each side could take a few minutes. Then place the skillet in the oven and roast for 25 to 30 minutes until it is cooked through (no pink shows when you slice into the middle). To serve, slice the meat at an angle and arrange on a platter, garnished with fresh parsley or rosemary.

YIELD: Serves 6
SODIUM CONTENT: 112 mg. of sodium per serving

SPICY PORK TENDERLOIN

Our friend Sharon Zane served this excellent dish at a dinner party and we've never forgotten it. It's a great recipe to try cooking over wood coals.

1 whole pork tenderloin (2 to 3 lbs.)
1 tsp. salt-free chili powder, or more if desired
2 tsp. ground cumin
1 tsp. powdered ginger
¼ tsp. ground allspice
¼ tsp. paprika
freshly ground black pepper to taste
fresh lime wedges

Preheat broiler or prepare the charcoal gill. Wash and dry the pork tenderloin. Combine the spices in a bowl and spread them generously on the surface of the meat so that it is completely coated. Place the meat under the broiler, 4 inches from the heat source, or on the grill, and cook until the side nearest the heat has browned. Then turn it over and cook for another 15 minutes or so, depending on the thickness of the meat, until it is cooked through. The spices will form a crust. Serve with wedges of fresh lime.

YIELD: Serves 6
SODIUM CONTENT: 112 mg. of sodium per serving

PORK TENDERLOIN WITH MUSHROOM AND HERB SAUCE

1 whole pork tenderloin (2 to 3 lbs.)
freshly ground black pepper to taste
1 thin slice unsalted butter (about 1 tsp.)
10 white button or other mushrooms
2 tbsp. flour
1½ c. low-sodium chicken broth
½ c. heavy cream
1 tbsp. fresh lemon juice
1 tbsp. chopped fresh parsley
1 tbsp. chopped fresh basil
2 sage leaves, finely chopped
1 tbsp. olive oil

Preheat the oven to 400 degrees. Wash the pork tenderloin, pat dry, trim any excess fat, and sprinkle with black pepper. Heat oil to medium-high in an ovenproof pan. Sear the meat on all sides in the oil, then place in the oven to cook for at least 20 minutes.

In the meantime, prepare the sauce. Heat a saucepan to medium-high on top of the stove and add the butter and mushrooms. When they release their liquid, add the flour and cook for 5 minutes more, stirring to make sure the flour doesn't burn. Add the chicken broth and cream, whisk in the lemon juice, and bring to a boil. Lower the heat and simmer until the sauce is reduced by half, then add the herbs and continue to cook 5 minutes or more until the sauce thickens. Reduce the heat to just enough to keep the sauce warm.

When the meat has cooked through, remove from the pan and allow to stand for 5 minutes. To serve, slice the meat into thin rounds and arrange them on a plate, then smother them with the sauce.

YIELD: Serves 6
SODIUM CONTENT: 124 mg. of sodium per serving

PORK VINDALOO

This recipe bears an instructive tale. We made our first vindaloo in a cooking class devoted to various kinds of curries. Before the class, we asked the instructor, a chef and cookbook author of some renown, if the curries could be made without salt. He looked stunned, as if the idea had never occurred to him, then said, "Well, there are plenty of flavors going on here; I don't see why not. . . ." Then, for whatever reason, he made a point of pouring far more salt than his recipes required into the vindaloo and a couple of other dishes. When we tasted them, all we could taste was the salt. Perhaps we should have demanded our money back. Instead we went home determined to adapt the recipes for our salt-free diet. Here is one result; we think you'll agree that the chef doesn't know what he's missing.

Classic vindaloo is fiery hot; if you think you or your guests won't be able to handle it, reduce the cayenne pepper accordingly. You will also need a way to grind whole spices; a small electric spice grinder does the best job, but if you don't have one, use a mortar and pestle or a heavy mug and a spoon.

1½-lb. boneless pork loin, cut into
    1-inch cubes
vegetable oil
freshly ground black pepper to taste
2 c. finely chopped onion
1 tbsp. plus 2 tsp. minced garlic
1 tbsp. plus 2 tsp. peeled, minced
    fresh ginger
1½ tsp. cumin seeds
1½ tsp. mustard seeds
4 whole cloves
2½ tsp. cayenne pepper
1¼ tsp. paprika
1½ tsp. turmeric
1 tsp. ground cinnamon
1 c. low-sodium chicken broth
2 tbsp. prune juice
1 tbsp. lemon juice
1 tbsp. cider vinegar
1 tbsp. molasses
chopped cilantro leaves for garnish

(Continued)

If the pork is moist, pat it dry with paper towels. Heat a small amount of vegetable oil in a large pot or Dutch oven and brown the cubes of meat on all sides. Sprinkle the meat with black pepper and stir to distribute.

Remove the meat from the pot and set it aside. Add another tablespoon or two of oil to the pot; add the onion and cook over moderate heat, stirring frequently, for several minutes until it is well browned. Add the garlic and ginger; stir and continue to cook. Grind up the cumin, mustard seeds, and cloves, and mix them with the cayenne pepper, paprika, turmeric, and cinnamon. Add the spice mixture to the pot and continue to cook for a minute, stirring. Then return the browned meat to the pot and stir to combine.

Pour the chicken broth, prune juice, lemon juice, vinegar, and molasses over the mixture in the pot. Bring to a simmer; cover and continue to simmer over low heat for an hour, until the flavors are well blended and the meat is fork tender. If oil rises to the top, skim it off with a spoon. If the vindaloo seems too thin, turn up the heat and allow the sauce to cook down. Transfer to a serving dish and sprinkle fresh cilantro leaves across the top before serving.

YIELD: Serves 6
SODIUM CONTENT: 83 mg. of sodium per serving

TUSCAN-STYLE
BRAISED PORK LOIN

olive oil
1 large pork loin
(3 to 4 lbs.)
3 carrots, peeled and
chopped
2 stalks celery, chopped
1 onion, diced
1 bunch fresh thyme
2 sticks fresh rosemary
½ c. chopped parsley
28-oz. can unsalted
tomatoes or about
2 c. fresh tomatoes
1 c. white wine
2 (15-oz.) cans salt-free
navy beans (see page
315) or 4 c. dry
beans, cooked

Heat a small amount of oil to high in a large ovenproof pot or Dutch oven on top of the stove. Add the meat and sear on all sides. Remove the meat and add the carrots, celery, onion, black pepper, and herbs. Reduce the heat to medium and cook for 10 minutes, stirring occasionally to prevent burning.

Preheat the oven to 325 degrees. Add the tomatoes and wine to the pot, then stir and scrape the bottom and sides of the pan to deglaze. Drain the beans and add them to the pot, then return the pork to the pot, cover, and cook in the oven for about 2½ hours, until the pork is very tender.

YIELD: Serves 8
SODIUM CONTENT: 165 mg. of sodium per serving

GREEN CHILI STEW

Use long green chili peppers like Anaheims or poblanos for this tasty concoction. They are mildly hot and flavorful, not fiery like the smaller jalapeños or serranos.

olive oil
2½- to 3-lb. top round pork roast
freshly ground black pepper to taste
1 medium onion, diced
6 long green chilies, diced
12 c. water
1 c. red wine
1 tsp. dried thyme or 2 tsp. fresh thyme leaves
¼ c. finely chopped parsley
4 large potatoes, peeled and diced

In a large stew pot or Dutch oven, heat a little oil to medium-high heat on top of the stove. Season the meat with pepper, add it to the pot, and brown it on all sides. Remove the meat; add the onion and chiles, and cook for 10 minutes, stirring occasionally. Return the roast to the pot and add the water, wine, thyme, and parsley. Cover the stew and simmer for 2 hours.

Add the potatoes and cook for another ½ hour. Remove the roast from the pot and use a fork to pull it apart, shredding the meat. Return the meat to the pot and continue to cook until it is heated through. Serve with crusty salt-free bread.

YIELD: Serves 8
SODIUM CONTENT: 109 mg. of sodium per serving

BRAISED PORK CHOPS WITH PORTOBELLO MUSHROOMS

1 tbsp. olive oil
2 thick boneless pork
chops
2 portobello mushrooms,
sliced into strips
¼-inch thick
freshly ground black
pepper to taste
2 cloves garlic, diced
1 tbsp. unsalted tomato
paste
½ c. low-sodium chicken
broth

Heat the oil in a sauté pan and add the chops. Brown well on both sides, then remove to a plate. Add the mushrooms and black pepper and cook 5 minutes, then add the garlic and cook 2 minutes longer. Add the tomato paste and chicken broth, and stir together. Return the chops to the pan, and cook covered for 10 minutes, then remove the cover and cook for 5 minutes more, or until the chops are cooked through.

YIELD: Serves 2
SODIUM CONTENT: 104 mg. of sodium per serving

PORK CHOPS WITH TOMATOES AND PEPPERS

2 tbsp. olive oil
5 center-cut pork chops
1 c. white wine
2 cloves garlic, minced
1 medium onion,
    chopped
1 medium green
    pepper, roughly
    chopped
2 medium tomatoes,
    chopped, or 2 c. salt-
    free canned tomatoes
1 tbsp. fresh basil or
    2 tsp. dried basil
1 sprig of fresh thyme
    or 1 tsp. dried thyme
2 tbsp. balsamic vinegar

Heat the oil in a skillet large enough to hold all the pork chops. Brown the chops on both sides and remove to a plate. Pour ¼ cup of white wine into the pan and stir with a wooden spoon to deglaze (dissolve the residue of the meat in the wine to create a dark sauce). Add the garlic and onions and cook for several minutes, stirring, until the onions become translucent. Add the green pepper and cook for another minute or so, until it begins to soften. Add the tomatoes, basil, thyme, vinegar, and the rest of the wine. Allow the mixture to cook for about 2 minutes over medium heat so that the flavors begin to combine.

Return the pork chops to the pan, including any juice that has drained off them while they were out of the pan. Distribute the chops so that all are at least partially covered by the sauce. Bring the mixture to a boil, then reduce the heat to low; cover and simmer for about 40 minutes, until the pork chops are thoroughly cooked and tender. If the mixture seems too liquid after 30 minutes, remove the cover so that the sauce cooks down for the last several minutes. Serve with rice.

YIELD: Serves 5
SODIUM CONTENT: 80 mg. of sodium per serving

PORK CHOPS WITH APPLES

The sprinkle of calvados at the end of this recipe isn't necessary, but we love the special tinge it gives the apple flavor.

2 tbsp. vegetable oil
1 tbsp. unsalted butter
6 center-cut pork chops
¾ c. white wine
4 apples, peeled, cored, and cut into eight sections each
ground cumin
freshly ground black pepper to taste
2 tbsp. calvados (optional)

Preheat the oven to 350 degrees. Heat the oil in a large iron skillet, then melt the butter in it and stir to blend. Remove any excess fat from the pork chops. Brown them in the skillet on both sides, then remove. Add ¼ cup of the white wine and deglaze (stir to scrape bits of meat off the bottom and sides of the pan). Then add the pieces of apple, spreading them evenly in the pan. Rub a small amount of cumin on both sides of each pork chop, then return the chops to the pan, arranging them on top of the apples. Sprinkle them with black pepper and pour the rest of the wine over them, followed by the calvados. Put the pan on the middle rack of the oven and cook for about 40 minutes, until the pork chops are cooked through. Serve each chop smothered in apples.

YIELD: Serves 6
SODIUM CONTENT: 73 mg. of sodium per serving

STUFFED PORK CHOPS

1 tbsp. unsalted butter
1 shallot, minced
freshly ground black
    pepper to taste
10 mushrooms, sliced
    (use cremini or
    porcini, if you can
    find them—otherwise
    use supermarket
    button mushrooms)
¼ c. low-sodium
    chicken broth
2 tbsp. finely chopped
    parsley
1 tsp. chopped
    rosemary
4 thick pork chops
olive oil

Heat a skillet; add butter and shallot, and cook for 5 minutes over medium heat. Add the mushrooms and black pepper and allow the mushrooms to cook down for about 10 minutes, reducing the heat if necessary to prevent burning. Add the broth and deglaze the pan by stirring to dissolve cooked bits of vegetables clinging to the pan. Add parsley and rosemary; turn up the heat and reduce the liquid until the pan is almost dry. Remove this mushroom mixture to a plate and allow it to cool.

Preheat the oven to 350 degrees. Wash the pork chops and pat them dry. Use a sharp knife to cut sideways into each chop to create a pocket. Fill the pockets with the mushroom mixture. Heat a small amount of olive oil in the skillet and sear the chops on both sides. Transfer the chops to a baking dish, put them in the oven, and bake until cooked through, 20 to 30 minutes.

YIELD: Serves 4
SODIUM CONTENT: 80 mg. of sodium per serving

MELISSA FLOOD'S
PULLED PORK

For a family wedding we hired a caterer, Melissa Flood, and asked that everything she prepared be salt-free. She welcomed the challenge to modify one of her favorite creations, with highly successful results. This recipe is for twenty; you can scale it down for smaller parties.

FOR THE RUB:

2 tbsp. sugar
2 tbsp. brown sugar
2 tbsp. ground cumin
2 tbsp. salt-free chili powder
2 tbsp. freshly ground black pepper
1 tbsp. cayenne pepper
¼ c. Hungarian paprika

FOR THE PORK:

1 large boned pork loin (6 to 8 lbs.)
⅔ c. orange juice
⅔ c. molasses
⅓ c. cider vinegar or balsamic vinegar

Mix the spices for the rub together and spread them generously over the surface of the pork loin. Put the excess in a jar to save for future use. Allow the rubbed pork to sit for 2 hours.

Preheat the oven to 200 degrees. Put the pork in a roasting pan, cover it with aluminum foil, and roast it in the oven at this low heat until a meat thermometer inserted in the middle of the loin reaches 170 degrees. This could take a few hours.

Remove the loin from the oven, allow it to cool, and shred it into bite-sized pieces with your fingers. Return this "pulled" pork to the pan, and add ½ cup of water. Mix the orange juice, molasses, and vinegar, and pour the mixture over the pulled pork. Return the pork to the 200-degree oven and cook for another hour.

Taste the pork; if it seems too dry, add a bit of water and cook a bit more; if it seems too spicy, add a little molasses and orange juice. Serve it warm.

YIELD: Serves 20
SODIUM CONTENT: 103 mg. of sodium per serving

RIBS

Long, slow cooking makes all the difference here, and it is well worth the investment of time. We like baby back pork spareribs. If you prefer larger beef or pork ribs, simmer them for at least an hour, rather than 45 minutes.

2 racks baby back pork spareribs (1 lb. each), cut in half
1 onion
6 c. Andersons' Famous Barbecue Sauce (see page 81)

Bring a large pot of water to a boil on top of the stove, reduce the heat to a simmer, and add the ribs and onion. Simmer for 45 minutes, then remove the ribs and let them rest for 30 minutes (if you wish, you can simmer the ribs the day before and keep them in the refrigerator until ready to use).

Preheat the oven to 250 degrees. Add the ribs to a shallow roasting pan and cover with half the sauce. Put them in the oven and roast for 1½ hours, basting every 30 minutes with the rest of the sauce. The longer you cook them at low heat, the better they will be (we have cooked them for as long as 4 hours). If you are going to cook the ribs outdoors on a charcoal or gas grill, make sure that the heat is very low. Place the ribs on the grill and baste with sauce, turning frequently (every 10 minutes) for 40 minutes or longer.

YIELD: Serves 4
SODIUM CONTENT: 175 mg. of sodium per serving

VEAL CHOPS WITH MUSHROOMS AND PARSLEY

2 tbsp. olive oil
4 veal chops
1 shallot or ½ medium
 onion, chopped
½ c. white wine or dry
 vermouth
2 c. sliced mushrooms
 (cremini or porcini, if
 you can find them—
 otherwise use
 supermarket button
 mushrooms)
juice of ½ lemon
freshly ground black
 pepper to taste
½ c. chopped Italian
 parsley
2 sprigs fresh thyme or
 2 tsp. dried thyme

Heat the oil in a frying pan large enough to hold all the chops; brown the chops on both sides. Remove them from the pan and set them aside. Add the chopped shallot or onion to the pan and cook for several minutes until it turns translucent. Add 2 tablespoons of the wine to the pan and deglaze it by stirring with a wooden spoon so that the residue from browning the meat dissolves in the liquid. Add the mushrooms and allow them to cook, stirring occasionally, for about 5 minutes, until they begin to soften. Sprinkle the mushrooms with lemon juice and black pepper. Add parsley and thyme; stir them into the mushroom mixture and cook for another 3 to 5 minutes, until all the parsley wilts.

Return the chops and the juice that has drained off them to the pan and distribute them on top of the mushrooms. Add the rest of the wine, bring to a boil, then reduce the heat to low. Cover and simmer until the chops are cooked through, about 25 minutes. To serve, put a chop on a plate and cover it with a generous spoonful of mushrooms and sauce.

YIELD: Serves 4
SODIUM CONTENT: 160 mg. of sodium per serving

VEAL CHOPS
WITH RED PEPPER SAUCE

3 sweet red peppers
olive oil
4 veal chops or
medallions
freshly ground black
pepper to taste
1 shallot, minced
¼ c. white wine
2 tbsp. dry vermouth
1½ c. heavy cream
1 tbsp. finely chopped
parsley

Heat the oven to 350 degrees. Place the whole red peppers on a baking sheet, brush them with olive oil, and roast them on the middle rack of the oven until tender, about ½ hour.

In the meantime, rinse the meat and pat dry with a paper towel. Sprinkle both sides with black pepper and rub the pepper into the surface of the meat. Heat a small amount of oil over medium-high heat in a skillet, and sear the meat on both sides. Transfer the meat to a shallow pan and place it in the oven to finish cooking. This should take 15 to 20 minutes, depending on the thickness of the chops or medallions.

When the peppers are cooked, remove them from the oven, cut off the tops, and remove the seeds and pulp; use a blender or food processor to reduce them to a smooth purée. Then heat 2 tablespoons of oil in a saucepan; add the shallot and cook over medium heat for 3 or 4 minutes, until transparent. Be careful not to burn the shallot. Add the wine, vermouth, and heavy cream. Reduce the heat so the cream comes to a simmer without rising over the edges of the pot. When the cream has reduced by half, add the pepper purée and parsley, and stir to combine well. Sprinkle with black pepper. Keep the sauce warm on very low heat until the veal has cooked. To serve, ladle a generous portion of sauce over each veal chop or medallion.

YIELD: Serves 4
SODIUM CONTENT: 154 mg. of sodium per serving

VEAL CHOPS WITH SOUR CHERRY AND PORT WINE SAUCE

1 tbsp. unsalted butter
1 small shallot, minced
1 c. dried sour cherries
3 sage leaves, torn in
    half
1 c. port wine
¼ c. low-sodium chicken
    broth
1 tbsp. olive oil
freshly ground black
    pepper to taste
4 veal chops

To make the sauce, heat the butter in a saucepan, add the shallot, and sauté for 6 minutes. Add the cherries and sage and cook for another 5 minutes. Then add port wine and chicken broth, and cook at a simmer for 15 minutes. When it has cooked, strain the sauce and keep warm.

To cook the chops, preheat the oven to 400 degrees. Heat the oil in a sauté pan over medium-high heat, season the chops with black pepper, and add them to the pan, browning them well on both sides. Transfer the chops to a shallow roasting pan and put them in the oven until cooked through, about 12 to 15 minutes, depending on the thickness of the chops. Serve the sauce over the chops.

YIELD: Serves 4
SODIUM CONTENT: 176 mg. of sodium per serving

BRAISED DOUBLE THICK VEAL CHOPS

4 large tomatoes, or
    enough to make 3½
    to 4 c. of purée
½ c. heavy cream
1 shallot, peeled and
    quartered
3 cloves garlic
¼ c. roughly chopped
    parsley
freshly ground black
    pepper to taste
¼ tsp. ground thyme
1 tbsp. balsamic vinegar
olive oil
4 veal chops, about 1½-
    to 2-inch thick

Quarter and seed the tomatoes; put them in a blender or food processor and blend until liquefied. Add all the rest of the ingredients except the veal chops and olive oil, and blend until smooth. Place this mixture in a pan and cook over medium-low heat until reduced by one-third. Cover and set aside.

In a pan large enough to hold all the ingredients, bring a small amount of oil to high heat and sear the chops so that they are well browned on all sides. Add the sauce and turn the chops so that they are evenly coated with it. Cover the pot and simmer until the veal is very tender, about an hour or more. Serve hot.

YIELD: Serves 4
SODIUM CONTENT: 216 mg. of sodium per serving

ROASTED VEAL
WITH SHALLOTS

*This centerpiece for a
great dinner party begins
with your butcher: make
sure he or she does a
proper job of cutting,
rolling, and tying the veal
to form a good roast.*

2 tbsp. olive oil
**freshly ground black
    pepper to taste**
**4-lb. veal roast, rolled
    and tied**
**10 to 12 shallots, peeled
    and sliced**
1 c. white wine
**½ c. low-sodium chicken
    broth**
**3 cloves garlic, peeled
    and left whole**
2 fresh bay leaves
3 tbsp. chopped parsley

Heat the oil over medium-high heat in a large pot. Rub pepper into the surface of the roast; sear the roast on all sides, and remove it to a plate. Add the shallots; reduce the heat to medium-low and cook for 8 to 10 minutes. Add the wine and use a wooden spoon to deglaze the pot, scraping up the bits of meat that cling to the bottom. Add the broth, garlic, bay leaves, and parsley and return the meat to the pot. Cover and simmer at a gentle, low heat for 2½ to 3 hours, turning the roast from time to time so it cooks evenly.

YIELD: Serves 8
SODIUM CONTENT: 164 mg. of sodium per serving

BRAISED VEAL LOIN
WITH SAGE AND PEARS

*We prefer Seckel pears—
small, brown, and
wonderfully sweet—for
this remarkable dish; if
you can't find them, look
for Bosc pears or use the
more common Bartlett
pears that haven't ripened
to the point of softness.*

3 tbsp. olive oil
3½- to 4-lb. veal loin
**freshly ground black
    pepper to taste**
1 medium onion, diced
2 celery stalks, diced
3 carrots, diced
8 fresh sage leaves
**1 c. low-sodium chicken
    broth**
1 c. water
¼ c. chopped parsley
**5 Seckel pears,
    quartered and pitted,
    or 3 larger pears,
    quartered and pitted**

Preheat the oven to 325 degrees.
Heat 3 tablespoons of olive oil over
high heat on the top of the stove in a
large Dutch oven or other ovenproof
pot. Season the veal loin with pepper
and sear it on all sides in the oil.
Remove the veal from the pot, set
aside, and add the onion, celery, and
carrots. Reduce heat to medium. After
5 minutes, season with pepper. Add
sage leaves and cook for another
10 minutes, stirring occasionally to
prevent burning. Add broth and water,
and stir to deglaze the pot, scraping
up the bits of meat and vegetables
that cling to the bottom and sides.
Add the parsley and pears, and return
the veal loin to the pot. Cover and
place in the oven; cook for 2 to 2½
hours or until the meat is very tender.

YIELD: Serves 8
SODIUM CONTENT: 168 mg. of sodium per serving

OSSO BUCO

Osso buco, or "bone with a hole," relies on veal bone marrow for richness and flavor.

4 veal shanks with bones, 1½ inches thick (with marrow)
flour
2 tbsp. high-quality olive oil
1 c. finely chopped onion
⅔ c. finely chopped carrots
⅔ c. finely chopped green pepper
2 tsp. finely chopped garlic
1 c. dry white wine
1 c. low-sodium beef broth or water
1½ c. canned salt-free tomatoes or 2 medium fresh tomatoes
1 sprig fresh thyme
2 bay leaves
3 sprigs finely chopped parsley
freshly ground black pepper to taste

Preheat the oven to 350 degrees. Use butcher's twine to tie the meat around the bone so that it holds together while it cooks. Put some flour on a plate, and dredge the meat in the flour. Heat the oil on medium-high in a heavy bottomed pot large enough to hold all the pieces of meat without overlapping. When the oil begins to smoke, add the veal shanks and brown them quickly on all sides; remove the shanks from the pot. Add the onion, carrots, and green pepper to the pot and sauté for 6 to 8 minutes, until the onion becomes translucent and the vegetables release their flavor. Watch the heat to make sure the vegetables don't burn. Add the garlic and cook another 3 minutes. Then add the wine to deglaze the pot, scraping up bits of meat and vegetables from the bottom and sides, and cook down for 4 minutes.

Return the veal shanks to the pot; add the rest of the ingredients and bring to a simmer. Then place the pot, tightly covered, in the oven and cook for 4 hours. Baste and turn the meat at least every half hour. Remove thyme and bay leaves before serving.

YIELD: Serves 6
SODIUM CONTENT: 168 mg. of sodium per serving

VEAL SCALOPPINE

Be sure to add a bit of salt-free chili powder to the flour before you dredge the meat, and remember to sprinkle with pepper and lemon juice before serving. If you wish, you can deglaze the pan with white wine, scraping up bits of meat that cling to the bottom after sautéing the meat, then stir in a bit of unsalted butter and parsley to create a quick sauce.

½ c. flour
1 tsp. salt-free chili
  powder
freshly ground black
  pepper to taste
8 to 12 veal scaloppine
  slices (about 1 lb.),
  pounded to ¼-inch
  thick
2 tbsp. olive oil
2 tbsp. unsalted butter
juice of 1 lemon

Spread the flour on a plate; add the chili powder and a generous grinding of pepper, and stir to combine. Dredge the slices of meat in the flour mixture so they are lightly coated. Heat a sauté pan or skillet over medium-high heat, then add 1 tablespoon of the olive oil and 1 tablespoon of the unsalted butter. When the butter has melted, stir to combine it with the oil. Add the meat slices to the pan two or three at a time, and cook a minute or so on each side so that they just cook through. Add small amounts of oil and butter if the pan begins to dry out. As they cook, transfer the meat slices to a baking dish and sprinkle with lemon juice and a light grinding of pepper. Put the baking dish in a 250-degree oven to stay warm while you finish cooking the meat. Serve immediately.

YIELD: Serves 8
SODIUM CONTENT: 88 mg. of sodium per serving

IRISH LAMB STEW

2 lbs. lamb shoulder cut
  into 1-inch cubes
2 tbsp. flour
freshly ground black
  pepper to taste
1 tbsp. vegetable oil
1 c. boiling water
1 c. white wine
1 bay leaf
1 c. sliced carrots
  (½-inch slices)
1 c. cubed turnip
  (½-inch cubes)
1 c. peeled, cubed
  potato (½-inch cubes)
1 medium onion, sliced
2 tbsp. cider vinegar
2 tsp. fresh thyme or
  1 tsp. dried thyme
parsley or fresh thyme
  for garnish

Trim the fat off the cubes of meat and sprinkle them with flour and ground pepper. Heat oil in a heavy pot or Dutch oven; add the meat and turn the pieces until they are browned on all sides. Pour boiling water over the meat (watch out for splattering when the water hits the oil), then add wine and bay leaf. Simmer, covered, over low heat for an hour or until the meat becomes fork-tender. Stir occasionally to prevent the meat from sticking and burning on the bottom.

Add the vegetables, sprinkle with cider vinegar, thyme, and a grinding of fresh pepper, and stir to combine. Simmer another ½ hour, until the vegetables are cooked through. If the stew seems dry, add a little more water or white wine. Remove the bay leaf and serve garnished with parsley or a sprig of thyme.

YIELD: Serves 6
SODIUM CONTENT: 108 mg. of sodium per serving

SHISH KEBABS

Build a meal around this Middle Eastern tradition, starting off with hummus and baba ganouj (see pages 88–90).

FOR THE KEBABS:

1½ lbs. lamb, cut into
   1-inch cubes
several bay leaves
2 green peppers, diced
   in large pieces
1 large onion, diced in
   large pieces
2 pints cherry tomatoes
2 pints mushrooms,
   stalks removed

FOR THE MARINADE:

½ c. balsamic vinegar
½ c. olive oil
2 tbsp. salt-free Dijon
   mustard
2 cloves garlic, minced
freshly ground black
   pepper to taste

Place the cubes of meat in a shallow bowl. Whisk together the marinade ingredients, pour them over the meat, and stir to make sure all the cubes are covered in the liquid. Put in the refrigerator to marinate for 2 to 3 hours.

Prepare the charcoal grill: light the charcoal, and allow it to burn down until the coals turn gray and glow evenly. Put the meat on one set of skewers, interspersing pieces of bay leaf between cubes of meat. Put the vegetables on another set of skewers in order to cook them separately. Prepare the vegetable skewers by alternating tomatoes, mushroom caps, pieces of pepper, and onion. Place the meat skewers on the hottest part of the fire and the vegetable skewers on a cooler part. Cook, turning frequently to prevent burning, until meat and vegetables are cooked through. Serve immediately with rice.

YIELD: 6 kebabs
SODIUM CONTENT: 107 mg. of sodium per kebab

MEATBALLS

You can serve these meatballs on their own with pasta dishes, or you can add them to one of our tomato sauces for pasta (see pages 269–274), allowing them to simmer for 45 minutes in the sauce.

2 lbs. ground beef
¼ c. finely chopped parsley
6 cloves garlic, minced fine
freshly ground black pepper to taste
2 tbsp. finely chopped basil
1 egg
½ c. salt-free bread crumbs (see page 315)
olive oil

Place all the ingredients except the bread crumbs and oil in a bowl and use your fingers to mix them together, squeezing the other ingredients through the ground meat. Add bread crumbs sparingly in order to reduce the moisture in the mixture and tighten it up. Take small pieces of meat and form them into balls about 1½ inches in diameter by rolling them between your palms. Continue until all the meat is used up. Put the meatballs on a plate and set aside to rest for at least 15 minutes before cooking.

Heat a small amount of oil over medium-high heat in a nonstick frying pan. Cook a few meatballs at a time so as not to crowd the pan. Turn the meatballs as they cook to sear them on all sides. Leave them in the pan until cooked through; we like them best if still a little pink inside.

YIELD: 18 meatballs
SODIUM CONTENT: 115 mg. of sodium per 3-meatball serving

GREEN PEPPERS STUFFED WITH MEAT AND RICE

Unsalted horseradish (see page 16) adds a great dimension of flavor, but the dish works well enough without it if you aren't able to find fresh horseradish root.

4 medium green peppers
olive oil
1 medium onion,
  chopped
1 c. sliced mushrooms
1 tbsp. lemon juice
¾ lb. ground beef (at
  least 70 percent lean)
1 tbsp. balsamic vinegar
freshly ground black
  pepper to taste
1 tbsp. unsalted tomato
  paste
1 tbsp. fresh unsalted
  horseradish
1 tsp. fresh thyme or
  ½ tsp. dried thyme
1 c. cooked brown or
  white rice
¼ c. salt-free bread
  crumbs (optional, see
  page 315)

Preheat the oven to 350 degrees. Cut the tops off the peppers and remove the pulp and seeds to create shells. Place them cut side down on a baking sheet and brush the outsides lightly with olive oil. Put in the oven and bake for about 20 minutes, until the shells are tender but firm enough to hold their shape.

Meanwhile, heat 2 tablespoons olive oil in a large skillet, add the onion, and cook for several minutes, until translucent. Add the mushrooms and cook for about 5 minutes, until they begin to soften. Sprinkle with lemon juice. Add the meat and push it around with a wooden spoon until it is thoroughly browned. Sprinkle the meat with balsamic vinegar and ground pepper. Add the tomato paste, horseradish, and thyme, and stir to blend. Cook over moderate heat for about 5 minutes, stirring occasionally to prevent burning.

Add the rice to the meat mixture and stir to blend. Spoon the meat and rice into the pepper shells, filling them completely. If you wish, you can sprinkle the top of each one with salt-free bread crumbs. Place the stuffed peppers in a baking dish and return them to the oven for 15 minutes. Serve with a side dish of more rice.

YIELD: Serves 4
SODIUM CONTENT: 40 mg. of sodium per serving

MEATLOAF

Salt-free bread crumbs (see page 315) are important in this recipe. If you can't find them, toast a slice of salt-free bread and chop it up with a knife or pulverize it in a food processor.

2 lbs. lean ground beef
¼ c. finely chopped
   parsley
5 basil leaves, finely
   chopped
1 large onion, finely
   chopped
¼ c. salt-free bread
   crumbs
1 egg
¼ c. salt-free tomato
   purée
1 tbsp. Andersons' Steak
   Sauce (optional—see
   page 82)
1 tbsp. salt-free horse-
   radish (optional—see
   page 16)
a few drops salt-free hot
   sauce (see page 315)

Preheat the oven to 375 degrees. Put all the ingredients in a large bowl and squeeze together with your hands until thoroughly combined. If the mixture seems too moist, increase the bread crumbs. Press the meat mixture into a nonstick loaf pan and bake for 1 hour.

YIELD: Serves 8
SODIUM CONTENT: 103 mg. of sodium per serving

SOUTHWEST-STYLE RICE

1 tbsp. olive oil
1 medium onion,
  chopped
1 clove garlic, minced
1 medium yellow or red
  sweet pepper, cut into
  ½-inch pieces
1 lb. lean ground beef
freshly ground black
  pepper to taste
28-oz. can peeled
  unsalted tomatoes
1 bay leaf
1½ c. white or brown
  rice

Heat the oil in a large, deep skillet or saucepan over a medium flame; add the onion, garlic, and green pepper, and cook for several minutes until the onion becomes translucent. Add the ground beef and stir it around with a wooden spoon until it has browned evenly. Sprinkle black pepper over the meat and stir to blend. Add tomatoes, bay leaf, and rice. Bring to a boil, then reduce the heat and simmer, covered, until the rice has absorbed all the moisture and is well cooked—about ½ hour. Remove the bay leaf before serving. This is a great dish to serve with bread or black beans and a touch of Mr. Spice Tangy Bang hot sauce (see page 315) on the side.

YIELD: Serves 4
SODIUM CONTENT: 51 mg. of sodium per serving

SHEPHERD'S PIE

2 lbs. Yukon Gold
   potatoes
½ c. milk
1½ lbs. ground sirloin
2 tbsp. balsamic vinegar
freshly ground black
   pepper to taste
2 tbsp. olive oil
1 medium onion,
   chopped
2 c. sliced mushrooms
1 medium tomato,
   chopped
1 tsp. thyme, fresh or
   dried
juice of ½ lemon
1 c. roughly chopped
   parsley
unsalted butter

Peel and boil the potatoes until they
are tender. Mash them, adding the
milk, until smooth, and set aside.
Brown the meat in a heavy frying
pan, stirring with a wooden spoon so
that it cooks evenly. Add vinegar and
ground pepper and stir to blend. In a
separate pan, heat the olive oil and
add the onion. Cook for several
minutes until the onion turns
translucent. Add the mushrooms,
tomato, and thyme, and continue to
cook until the mushrooms begin to
soften. Sprinkle the mixture with
lemon juice and black pepper, and
stir to blend.

Preheat the oven to 350 degrees.
Transfer the mushroom mixture to the
meat; add the chopped parsley and
stir to distribute evenly. Cover and
cook over medium heat for 5
minutes. Transfer this mixture to an
ovenproof dish. Spread the mashed
potatoes on top to form a crust. Dot
the potatoes with butter. Bake for 20
minutes. Then turn the heat up to
broil for 5 minutes, or until the
potatoes are nicely browned.

YIELD: Serves 8
SODIUM CONTENT: 77 mg. of sodium per serving

MOUSSAKA

For this traditional Greek dish, it's important to limit the amount of oil used in preparing the filling and the eggplant slices; more than the barest minimum makes the final result too greasy. Touches of nutmeg in the sauce and cinnamon in the filling make a big difference.

FOR THE MEAT FILLING:

1 tbsp. olive oil
2 c. chopped onion
3 cloves garlic, finely minced
½ green pepper, finely chopped
1 lb. ground lamb
1 lb. ground sirloin
freshly ground black pepper to taste
2 c. chopped tomatoes
3 tbsp. unsalted tomato paste
¾ c. red wine
2 tbsp. balsamic vinegar
2 c. sliced mushrooms
½ c. fresh chopped parsley
1 tsp. thyme
1 tsp. cinnamon
2 tbsp. lemon juice

FOR THE EGGPLANT:

2 medium eggplants
1 tbsp. olive oil

FOR THE WHITE SAUCE:

½ c. flour
¼ tsp. nutmeg
½ c. unsalted butter, melted
4 c. milk
2 eggs
½ c. grated low-sodium Gouda or other low-sodium cheese

Heat the oil in a large skillet. Add the onions, garlic, and green pepper and cook for several minutes until the onions are translucent. Add the ground meat and cook, stirring with a wooden spoon, until browned. Sprinkle with black pepper; add the tomatoes and tomato paste, and stir to blend. Add the red wine and balsamic vinegar and stir; then add the mushrooms, parsley, thyme, cinnamon, and lemon juice, and stir to blend. Reduce the heat and simmer for 45 minutes.

Preheat the oven to 350 degrees. Cut the eggplant into slices ½-inch thick. Brush the olive oil on a baking sheet and spread the eggplant slices on it; brush a bit more olive oil on top of the eggplant. Be sure to use the olive oil sparingly. Cover the

(Continued)

baking sheet loosely with aluminum foil. Bake for 30 minutes, until the eggplant is tender.

To make the white sauce, stir the flour and nutmeg together in a bowl. Add the melted butter to the flour mixture; stir to combine. Place the mixture in the top of a double boiler over boiling water. Bring the milk almost to a boil in a separate pan, then add to the flour-butter mixture. Cook in the double boiler, stirring constantly, until the mixture begins to thicken. Remove from the heat and allow to cool for a few minutes. Beat the eggs in a bowl. Add half of the flour-butter mixture to the bowl, stirring constantly to prevent the eggs from scrambling. When the mixture is uniform, pour it back into the rest of the flour-butter mixture, stirring to blend. Return this mixture to the top of the double boiler over boiling water. Cook, stirring constantly, until the mixture thickens.

To assemble the moussaka, line the bottom of an ovenproof baking dish with rounds of eggplant; cover with a layer of the meat mixture; add another layer of eggplant rounds, followed by the rest of the meat mixture. Cover this with the white sauce; sprinkle it with the grated cheese. Place in a 350-degree oven and bake until the top has browned and the mixture has thoroughly cooked through, about 45 minutes.

YIELD: Serves 12
SODIUM CONTENT: 119 mg. of sodium per serving

VEALBURGERS

The horseradish (see page 16) makes a fine contribution here. If you wish, serve the vealburgers on thick slabs of salt-free bread brushed with olive oil and cooked until brown and crunchy over the same grill used for the burgers.

1½ lbs. ground veal
2 tbsp. fresh horseradish or low-sodium prepared horseradish
2 tbsp. finely chopped red onion
1 tbsp. finely chopped parsley
dash of ground sage
dash of salt-free garlic powder
freshly ground black pepper to taste

Combine all the ingredients in a bowl, working the horseradish, onion, and spices into the meat with your fingers. Form into patties, place on a plate, cover with plastic wrap, and allow to stand for about 20 minutes so that the flavors combine. Cook over the charcoal grill, or broil or pan-fry as you would hamburgers.

YIELD: 6 burgers
SODIUM CONTENT: 78 mg. of sodium per burger

CHILI CON CARNE

2 tbsp. olive oil
2 medium onions,
    chopped
1 medium green pepper,
    seeded and chopped
1 jalapeño or serrano
    pepper, seeded and
    minced
¾ lb. lean ground beef
¾ lb. ground pork
3 tbsp. salt-free chili
    powder
2 tbsp. ground cumin
1 tbsp. white wine
    vinegar
4 c. chopped fresh or
    salt-free canned
    tomatoes
1 bay leaf
freshly ground black
    pepper to taste
15-oz. can salt-free red
    kidney beans (see
    page 315) or
    2 c. cooked beans

Heat the olive oil in a large skillet or Dutch oven. Add the onion, green pepper, and hot pepper and cook for several minutes, until the onions and peppers begin to soften. Add the meat, breaking it apart and stirring until it is evenly browned and well combined with the other ingredients. Sprinkle the meat with chili powder, cumin, and balsamic vinegar, and stir to blend. Add the tomatoes, bay leaf, and black pepper, and stir to combine. Bring the mixture to a boil, reduce the heat, and simmer over low heat for 20 minutes. Add the kidney beans, including the water in which they are packed, and simmer for another half hour. Serve with rice or salt-free bread.

YIELD: Serves 8
SODIUM CONTENT: 61 mg. of sodium per serving

X. Vegetables

TARRAGON ROASTED
VEGETABLES

You can cook this dish in a skillet on top of the stove, but it tastes best if prepared on a charcoal grill. To do that, you will need a vegetable roasting pan designed for just that purpose—a rectangular pan with sloping sides and plenty of holes to let the charcoal smoke filter through. We've found them in housewares and some hardware stores.

2 bell peppers, seeded and cut into 1-inch squares
2 yellow squash cut into ½-inch rounds
2 zucchini cut into ½-inch rounds
1 medium eggplant cut into ½-inch rounds, then cut into semicircles
olive oil
freshly ground black pepper to taste
2 tbsp. chopped fresh tarragon
1 tbsp. butter

Heat the vegetable grill pan on the charcoal grill or the skillet on top of the stove to medium-high heat. Spread all the pieces of vegetables on a plate in one layer. Drizzle olive oil over them and season them with black pepper and tarragon. When the grill pan or skillet is hot, add the vegetables and cook, tossing them around so they don't burn. Cook until the vegetables are tender, but not mushy. Serve either hot or at room temperature.

YIELD: Serves 6
SODIUM CONTENT: 5 mg. of sodium per serving

RATATOUILLE

½ c. olive oil
2 medium green
  peppers, seeded and
  diced
1 c. chopped onion
2 cloves garlic, minced
2 medium zucchini,
  diced
1 medium eggplant,
  diced
4 medium tomatoes
1 tbsp. dried basil or 2
  tbsp. chopped fresh
  basil leaves
freshly ground black
  pepper to taste

Heat ¼ cup of the oil in a large skillet or heavy saucepan. Add the peppers, onion, and garlic, and sauté for about 5 minutes, until the onion is translucent and the peppers are tender. Remove and set aside. Heat 2 more tablespoons of oil, and add the zucchini. Cook for about 10 minutes, stirring frequently, until it becomes tender. Set aside the zucchini in a bowl and add the remaining 2 tablespoons oil to the pan. Add the eggplant and cook for about 5 minutes, until tender. Remove the cooked eggplant and combine with the cooked zucchini.

Cut the tomatoes into wedges, then cut each wedge in half. Return the cooked vegetables to the pan; add the tomatoes, basil, and ground pepper and stir to combine. Simmer over medium heat, stirring occasionally, until the vegetables cook down together, about 10 minutes. Serve hot or cold.

YIELD: Serves 6
SODIUM CONTENT: 10 mg. of sodium per serving

EGGPLANT AND PEPPERS

For canned salt-free chickpeas, see page 315. If you can't find them, substitute dried chickpeas soaked overnight and simmered for 1 to 2 hours until tender.

1 small eggplant
3 sweet red peppers
olive oil
freshly ground black
** pepper to taste**
8 fresh basil leaves,
** chopped**
2 cloves garlic, minced
1 c. salt-free chickpeas

Preheat the oven to 350 degrees. Place the whole eggplant and peppers on a baking sheet, drizzle them with oil, and sprinkle them with pepper. Roast them in the oven for 45 minutes to 1 hour, until the eggplant is completely tender.

Remove them from the oven and drain off any excess oil. Heat 1 tablespoon of oil to medium heat in a skillet or in a sauté pan on top of the stove, and add the garlic. Allow it to cook for a few minutes, being careful not to let it burn. Add the chickpeas, stir to combine, and cook for several minutes until they are warmed through. Cut the eggplant and the peppers into 1-inch pieces, put them in a bowl, add the chickpea mix and basil, and stir to combine. Serve warm.

YIELD: Serves 8
SODIUM CONTENT: 4 mg. of sodium per serving

FRESH MOZZARELLA
AND TOMATO NAPOLEON

12 tbsp. olive oil
12 tbsp. balsamic
   vinegar
4 small balls (about 2
   pounds) fresh
   unsalted mozzarella,
   sliced thin
1 bunch fresh basil
4 vine-ripe tomatoes,
   cut into ¼-inch slices
freshly ground black
   pepper to taste

Place six plates on the table. Drizzle 1 tablespoon of oil on each plate, followed by 1 tablespoon of vinegar. Place a slice of the cheese on each plate, then a basil leaf and then a slice of tomato. Repeat this process until all the slices of cheese and tomato are used up. Top each napoleon with another tablespoon of oil, another tablespoon of vinegar, and pepper to taste, and serve.

YIELD: Serves 6
SODIUM CONTENT: 8 mg. of sodium per serving

VEGETARIAN TERRINE

This hearty, flavorful dish depends on salt-free fresh mozzarella cheese, available from Italian butchers, delis, and cheese shops. If you can't find it, use salt-free Gouda for the internal layer of cheese—less authentic but every bit as satisfying.

olive oil
1 large eggplant, sliced
freshly ground black
   pepper to taste
several slices salt-free
   fresh mozzarella
   cheese, about ¾ lb.
2 medium yellow
   squash, sliced
2 medium zucchini,
   sliced
1 onion, diced
2 tomatoes, diced
2 tbsp. fresh chopped
   parsley
2 tbsp. fresh chopped
   basil
pinch of thyme
½ c. grated low-sodium
   Gouda cheese

Wipe the bottom and sides of a deep ovenproof baking dish with olive oil. Place all of the eggplant in the dish, and sprinkle with olive oil and black pepper. Add a few mozzarella cheese slices. Make a second layer using yellow squash, oil, pepper, and cheese, and a third layer with zucchini, oil, pepper, and cheese.

Preheat the oven to 350 degrees. Mix the onion and tomato with the parsley, basil, and thyme, and spread them evenly over the top. Sprinkle with grated Gouda cheese. Cover loosely with aluminum foil and bake for 30 minutes. Then remove the foil and bake for another 10 minutes, or until cooked through.

YIELD: Serves 8
SODIUM CONTENT: 48 mg. of sodium per serving if made with Gouda cheese, 73 mg. with salt-free mozzarella

REFRIED BLACK BEANS

olive oil
1 medium onion,
  chopped
1 clove garlic, minced
1 jalapeño pepper,
  minced
2 (15-oz.) cans salt-free
  black beans (see page
  315) or 4 c. cooked
  black beans
1 tbsp. ground cumin
1 tbsp. cider vinegar
several slices unsalted
  Gouda cheese
  (optional)
fresh cilantro leaves

Heat 2 tablespoons of oil in a large skillet with a cover. Add the onion, garlic, and jalapeño pepper, and cook uncovered over medium heat for several minutes, until the onion begins to turn golden brown. Drain the beans and reserve 1 cup of the liquid from the cans or cooking pot. Add the beans to the skillet, 1 cup at a time, mashing them with a fork and stirring them into the onion mixture. Continue to add and mash the beans until all are mashed and well mixed with the onions, garlic, and pepper.

Add the cumin and vinegar to the liquid from the beans and stir. Pour this mixture over the beans in the skillet, and stir to blend. Continue to cook over medium heat, stirring occasionally to prevent burning, until the liquid cooks down and the mixture begins to thicken. Turn off the heat and allow the refried beans to stand for 5 minutes; they will thicken more as they cool. Then spread the cheese on top of the beans, cover the skillet, and turn on the heat again to medium. Heat for just a few minutes, until the cheese melts. Sprinkle each serving with fresh cilantro leaves.

YIELD: Serves 4
SODIUM CONTENT: 65 mg. of sodium per serving

FRIED GREEN TOMATOES

½ c. flour
½ c. cornmeal
freshly ground black
 pepper to taste
4 green tomatoes, cut
 into slices ¼-inch thick
2 tbsp. vegetable oil
lemon juice or lemon
 wedges

Combine the flour, cornmeal, and a generous grinding of pepper on a plate. Dip each tomato slice into the mixture so that it is evenly coated. Heat the oil in a skillet over medium heat. Add the tomato slices so that each lies flat on the bottom of the pan, and allow to cook about 2 minutes on one side, then turn and cook for another minute, or until tender. Remove to a plate lined with a paper towel to drain before serving. Sprinkle with lemon juice or serve with lemon wedges.

YIELD: Serves 4
SODIUM CONTENT: 17 mg. of sodium per serving

SAUTÉED MUSHROOMS

These mushrooms make a fine sauce for hamburgers, pork chops, or green vegetables, turning such humble fare into a tasty, elegant dish for a quick supper. Use basic supermarket button mushrooms or, if you can find them, Italian varieties like porcini or cremini.

1 tbsp. olive oil
2 tbsp. finely chopped
   onion
2 c. sliced mushrooms
1 tbsp. lemon juice
2 tsp. finely chopped
   fresh thyme
freshly ground black
   pepper to taste

Heat the oil in a sauté pan and add the onion; cook for several minutes, until the onion turns translucent. Add the mushrooms and cook, stirring occasionally, until they wilt and give up their liquid. Sprinkle with the lemon juice, thyme, and pepper and cook for a few more minutes, stirring to make sure the lemon juice and pepper are well distributed. Serve immediately.

YIELD: 4 cups
SODIUM CONTENT: 2 mg. of sodium per ½-cup serving

ASPARAGUS
WITH LEMON BROTH

12 to 16 asparagus
   spears
vegetable oil
1 shallot, minced
1 clove garlic, minced
1 c. low-sodium chicken
   broth
juice of 1 lemon

Wash the asparagus spears and break off the tough, woody ends. Heat a small amount of oil over medium heat in a sauté pan large enough to hold all the ingredients. Add the shallot and garlic and cook for about 5 minutes. Then add the chicken broth, lemon juice, and sugar; stir to blend. Drop in the asparagus. Bring to a boil; reduce the heat to low, and simmer uncovered until the asparagus is just tender, about 8 to 10 minutes, depending on the thickness of the stalks. Remove the asparagus to a platter and pour the juice over it before serving.

YIELD: Serves 4
SODIUM CONTENT: 13 mg. of sodium per serving

SPAGHETTI SQUASH
WITH VEGETABLE MARINARA

Flesh of the spaghetti squash looks like pasta and has a wonderful sweet flavor. It's also a great discovery for people who love pasta but are trying to lose weight or avoid wheat. This recipe calls for cooking the squash by baking it in the oven, but you can also steam it or boil it. However you cook it, be sure to puncture the skin with a fork before cooking to release internal steam generated as the squash heats up; otherwise the squash will split open during cooking.

1 large spaghetti squash (about 4 pounds), pierced with a fork
1 tbsp. olive oil
1 medium onion, diced
2 cloves garlic, chopped
1 small zucchini, sliced
1 yellow squash, sliced
4 medium tomatoes, chopped
¼ tsp. dried basil
¼ tsp. dried thyme
½ lb. white button mushrooms, sliced

freshly ground black pepper to taste
½ c. white wine
fresh parsley or cilantro for garnish
grated low-sodium Gouda cheese

Preheat the oven to 350 degrees, and bake the whole spaghetti squash for 1 to 1½ hours. It is ready when it feels tender inside when poked with a fork.

To make the sauce, heat the oil in a large saucepan; add the onion and garlic and cook for several minutes until the onion turns translucent. Add zucchini and yellow squash and cook for 5 minutes longer. Then add tomato, herbs, mushrooms, black pepper, and wine. Stir and let simmer, partially covered, for an hour (you can do this while the squash cooks). If the sauce cooks down too much, add a little water.

When the squash has cooked, remove it from the oven and cut it in half lengthwise. Scoop out the seeds; remove the stringy flesh and arrange the flesh on a platter in a large circle or oval with a depression in the middle. Pour the sauce into the middle of the squash, garnish with fresh parsley or cilantro, and serve, sprinkling grated Gouda cheese on each serving.

YIELD: Serves 8
SODIUM CONTENT: 25 mg. of sodium per serving

VEGETARIAN VINDALOO

*This dish tastes best if
allowed to cool slightly
from piping hot; too much
heat tends to mask the
great mix of flavors.*

olive oil
2 c. chopped onions
2 tsp. whole cumin
  seeds
2 tsp. mustard seeds
6 whole cloves
1 tbsp. cayenne pepper
2 tsp. paprika
2 tsp. turmeric
1½ tsp. cinnamon
2 cloves garlic, finely
  minced
2 c. diced potatoes
  (½-inch cubes)
2 medium carrots, sliced
  (¼-inch slices)
2 tbsp. salt-free tomato
  paste dissolved in 2 c.
  water
2 c. cauliflower florets
2 c. broccoli florets
1 medium eggplant cut
  into 1-inch cubes
2 tbsp. lemon juice
2 c. finely chopped
  tomatoes
1 medium zucchini,
  sliced thin (¼-inch
  slices)

2 c. canned salt-free chickpeas (see
  page 315) or fresh chickpeas
  soaked overnight and cooked
  until tender
¼ c. raisins
2 tbsp. cider vinegar

Heat 2 tablespoons olive oil in a
heavy saucepan or Dutch oven, and
add the onion. Cook for about 10
minutes over low-medium heat,
stirring occasionally, until the onion
begins to caramelize (turn brown as
the natural sugar heats up).
Meanwhile, use an electric spice
grinder or a mortar and pestle to
grind up the cumin seeds, mustard
seeds, and cloves. Add them to the
cayenne pepper, paprika, turmeric,
and cinnamon and stir to blend.

When the onion has cooked, stir
in the garlic and cook for a minute;
then add the spice mixture and stir to
blend. Add a bit more oil if the
mixture seems too dry. Add the
potatoes and carrots and 1 cup of the
water-tomato paste mixture. Turn up
the heat to bring the liquid to a boil;
then turn it down so it simmers. Cook
at a low simmer for about 7 minutes,
then add the cauliflower and broccoli
and cook for another 7 minutes.

While these vegetables are
cooking, heat another tablespoon of

(Continued)

oil in a skillet over medium heat and cook the eggplant in it, stirring
to prevent burning, until it begins to soften. Sprinkle the eggplant
with lemon juice. Add the eggplant, tomato, zucchini, chickpeas, and
raisins to the main mixture and stir to blend. Pour the remaining
tomato paste and water mixture over the vegetables. Add the vinegar,
and simmer, covered, for another 10 minutes, until all the vegetables
are tender and the flavors are fully developed. Serve with rice and
plain yogurt.

YIELD: Serves 12
SODIUM CONTENT: 29 mg. of sodium per serving

STUFFED ACORN SQUASH

We used acorn squash for this tasty dish, but you can experiment with the other winter squashes. For bread crumbs, you can buy unsalted prepared bread crumbs (see page 315) or toast a slice of salt-free bread and reduce it to crumbs with a knife or food processor. The recipe yields two servings. Multiply the ingredients for the number of people you want to serve.

1 medium acorn squash
2 tbsp. unsalted butter
½ c. chopped onion
1 c. chopped
   mushrooms
3 tbsp. chopped parsley
freshly ground black
   pepper to taste
juice of ½ lemon
½ c. salt-free bread
   crumbs
1 c. grated low-sodium
   cheese (Gouda or
   Swiss)

Preheat the oven to 350 degrees. Cut the squash in half lengthwise and scoop out the seeds. Place the halves cut side down in a baking pan, add a ½-inch of water, and bake in the oven for about 30 minutes, or until the squash is soft when pierced with a fork. While the squash is cooking, melt the butter in a frying pan, add the onion, and cook for several minutes until it turns translucent. Add the mushrooms, parsley, and pepper, and continue cooking for a few minutes. Stir in the lemon juice. Transfer the onion-mushroom mixture to a bowl. When the squash has cooked, remove it from the oven and scoop out most of the flesh, reserving the shells. Stir the cooked squash into the mushroom mixture.

Combine the bread crumbs and grated cheese. Add about half of this mixture to the squash-onion-mushroom mixture, and stir to blend. Divide the resulting mixture in half and spoon into the shells of the squash. Spread the remaining cheese-bread crumb mixture on top of the stuffed shells. Put them on a baking sheet and return them to the oven to cook for about 15 minutes, until the cheese has melted and they are heated through.

YIELD: Serves 2
SODIUM CONTENT: 42 mg. of sodium per serving

ITALIAN ZUCCHINI

**3 medium zucchini,
thinly sliced**
**½ c. finely diced green
pepper**
**½ c. finely chopped
onion**
1 clove garlic, minced
**4 medium tomatoes,
diced**
1 tsp. oregano
**freshly ground black
pepper to taste**
**½ c. grated low-sodium
Gouda cheese**

Preheat the oven to 350 degrees. Put the zucchini slices in a casserole dish and stir in all the other ingredients except the cheese so that they are well distributed. Sprinkle the cheese over the top. Put the casserole in the oven and cook for about 45 minutes.

YIELD: Serves 6
SODIUM CONTENT: 23 mg. of sodium per serving

POTATO PANCAKES

A great potato pancake—golden and crunchy on the outside; creamy on the inside—requires a bit of technique as well as a good recipe. After you've made the batter, you may want to try a few experimental spoonfuls with different heat levels and amounts of oil. These pancakes are especially good if made with Yukon Gold potatoes.

**6 medium potatoes
(about 2 pounds)
2 eggs
2 tbsp. milk
1 medium onion, finely
chopped or grated
1 leek, finely chopped
2 tbsp. finely chopped
parsley
½ c. flour
1 tbsp. lemon juice
freshly ground black
pepper to taste
2 tbsp. vegetable oil**

Peel and wash the potatoes. Grate them on the coarse grid of a box grater. This will produce strands of potato about an inch long. Use a large knife to chop the potato into pieces about ⅛-inch long. Put the chopped potatoes in a large strainer or colander suspended over a bowl and press down on the potatoes to expel their juice. You may want to do this two or three times, allowing the potatoes to stand for a few minutes between each pressing.

Allow the juice to sit in the bottom of the bowl for a few more minutes so the potato starch collects at the bottom. Pour off the liquid so the starch remains at the bottom of the bowl.

Add the eggs and milk to the potato starch, and stir to combine. Then stir in the chopped onion, leek, parsley, and chopped potatoes. Add the flour and stir to combine; stir in the lemon juice and black pepper.

Heat the vegetable oil in a large skillet or on a griddle. Use a slotted spoon to lift about ¼ cup of the potato mixture out of the bowl and press out excess moisture. Drop the batter into the skillet, and press with a spatula to make a pancake. Cook

(Continued)

over moderate heat until golden brown on the bottom, then turn to brown the other side.

As the pancakes cook, remove them to a plate lined with a paper towel to drain off excess oil, and put the plate in a warmed oven while you finish cooking enough pancakes for the meal. Serve as soon as possible after cooking.

YIELD: 8 medium pancakes
SODIUM CONTENT: 28 mg. of sodium per pancake

HOT PEPPER PANCAKES

Savory flour-based pancakes are a welcome surprise as a side dish with chicken or meat dishes, or as the centerpiece for a vegetarian feast. Serve them with a dollop of quark, yogurt, or sour cream. Here is the first of three we've devised.

2 tbsp. olive oil
½ sweet red pepper, seeded and minced
½ jalapeño or serrano pepper, seeded and minced
½ c. white flour
½ c. cornmeal
2 tsp. low-sodium baking powder
1 egg
1 c. milk
1 tbsp. salt-free chili powder

Heat 1 tablespoon of the oil in a skillet and cook the red and hot pepper in it over moderate heat until the red pepper softens. Mix the flour, cornmeal, and baking powder together in a bowl. Beat the egg lightly with a whisk, and stir in the milk. Add the egg-milk mixture to the dry ingredients and stir until they are moistened. Then stir in the peppers and the chili powder. Heat the remaining tablespoon of oil on a griddle or large frying pan and drop spoonfuls of the batter on it; when bubbles form at the edges, turn and cook the other side until cooked through. Keep warm until ready to serve.

YIELD: 8 pancakes
SODIUM CONTENT: 24 mg. of sodium per pancake

SCALLION PANCAKES

The secret of a good scallion pancake and a good mushroom pancake is to use equal amounts of the vegetable mixture and the flour mixture. If you wind up with leftover flour mixture, you can save it in the refrigerator for a few days until you want to make another batch of pancakes.

2 tbsp. butter
1½ c. chopped scallions
¼ c. dry vermouth
freshly ground black
　　pepper to taste
½ c. whole-wheat flour
½ c. white flour
2 tsp. low-sodium
　　baking powder
1 egg
1 c. milk
1 tbsp. vegetable oil

Heat the butter in a sauté pan over medium heat. Add the scallions and cook until they begin to soften. Add the vermouth and pepper; stir to blend, and allow the mixture to cook down for a few minutes. Remove from the heat and set aside. Combine the flours and baking powder in a bowl. In another bowl, beat the egg lightly with a whisk; stir in the milk and add this mixture to the dry ingredients. Stir until the dry ingredients are fully moistened. Pour equal amounts of the scallion mixture and the flour mixture into another bowl and stir briefly to blend. Heat the vegetable oil on a griddle or frying pan. Drop spoonfuls of the pancake batter onto the griddle; when bubbles appear at the edges, turn and continue to cook until cooked through.

YIELD: 8 pancakes
SODIUM CONTENT: 18 mg. of sodium per pancake

MUSHROOM PANCAKES

1 tbsp. unsalted butter
2 c. finely minced
  cremini, porcini, or
  button mushrooms
¼ c. chopped fresh
  parsley
1 tbsp. dried thyme or
2 tbsp. fresh thyme
1 tbsp. lemon juice
freshly ground black
  pepper to taste
½ c. whole-wheat flour
½ c. white flour
2 tsp. low-sodium
  baking powder
1 egg
1 c. milk
1 tbsp. vegetable oil

Heat the butter in a sauté pan over medium heat. Add the mushrooms, parsley, and thyme. Cook until the mushrooms begin to soften; add the lemon juice and pepper, and stir to blend. Remove from the heat and set aside. Combine the flours and baking powder in a bowl. Beat the egg lightly with a whisk; stir in the milk, and add this mixture to the dry ingredients. Stir until the dry ingredients are fully moistened. Pour equal amounts of the mushroom mixture and flour mixture into another bowl and stir to blend. Heat vegetable oil on a griddle or frying pan; drop spoonfuls of the pancake batter onto the griddle; when bubbles appear at the edges, turn and continue to cook until cooked through.

YIELD: 8 pancakes
SODIUM CONTENT: 26 mg. of sodium per pancake

FRITTATA

2 medium potatoes
3 tbsp. olive oil
1 clove garlic, minced
1 small onion, chopped
½ c. diced green pepper
½ c. diced tomato
1 tsp. dried basil or 2
   tsp. fresh basil leaves
juice of ½ lemon
freshly ground black
   pepper to taste
6 eggs
1 c. fresh sweet corn or
   salt-free frozen corn
½ c. grated salt-free
   Gouda cheese

Peel the potatoes and put them in a pot to boil while you chop and dice the other vegetables. Boil the potatoes until they are not quite cooked through (a fork pushed into them resists at the center). Cut them into ½-inch cubes. Heat 2 tablespoons of the oil in a heavy metal frying pan on top of the stove.

Add the garlic, onion, and green pepper and cook for several minutes until the onion is translucent. Add the tomato, basil, lemon juice, and a grinding of pepper; cook for another 5 minutes, stirring to prevent the mixture from sticking. Transfer to a bowl and allow to cool. Put the potatoes in the pan (add a little more oil if necessary) and cook, stirring occasionally, until tender. Add them to the other vegetables and stir.

Preheat the broiler. Beat the eggs together in a bowl and stir in the cooked vegetables along with the corn. Reheat the remaining oil in the pan and pour the egg-vegetable mixture back into it. Cook for several minutes, until the egg has almost cooked through (cooking time will vary depending on the diameter of the pan and the depth of the egg mixture). Sprinkle the cheese on top of the frittata and place it under the broiler for a few minutes, until the rest of the egg has cooked and the cheese has melted. Serve immediately.

YIELD: Serves 8
SODIUM CONTENT: 71 mg. of sodium per serving

ASPARAGUS FRITTATA

6 asparagus spears
½ lemon
1 tbsp. unsalted butter
1 shallot, minced
6 eggs
¼ c. milk
freshly ground black
  pepper to taste
¼ tsp. tarragon
2 plum tomatoes, diced

Cut the tips off the asparagus spears, then cut the tender part of the stalks into ¼-inch pieces (discard the woody ends). Blanch the asparagus by immersing it for 5 minutes in 6 cups of simmering water with the half lemon. Strain, remove the asparagus to a bowl of ice water to stop the cooking, and drain. Melt the butter in an ovenproof sauté pan. Turn to medium heat; add the shallot and sauté for 6 minutes, then remove from the heat. Place the eggs in a bowl, add the milk and beat lightly, then stir in the black pepper and tarragon. Add the asparagus and diced tomato, and stir to blend.

Return the sauté pan with the shallots to the stovetop over low heat, and add the egg mixture. Cook on low until the eggs start to firm up. Then turn on the broiler and place the sauté pan under the broiler until the top of the frittata cooks through from the top. You can serve the frittata from the pan if you wish, or you can remove it by placing a plate on top of the pan and flipping it over, then placing another plate on the bottom of the frittata and flipping it back.

YIELD: Serves 8
SODIUM CONTENT: 61 mg. of sodium per serving

HORSERADISH MASHED POTATOES

For a full discussion of fresh horseradish root and its many virtues, see page 16.

6 large potatoes, peeled and sliced into quarters
4 tbsp. (½ stick) unsalted butter
1½ c. whole milk
freshly ground black pepper to taste
4 tbsp. finely grated fresh horseradish root

Add the potatoes to a large pot filled with water, bring to a boil, and cook until the potatoes are very tender, about 25 minutes. Drain the potatoes in a colander, then return them to the pot with the butter. Use a hand mixer or a potato masher to mash the potatoes, slowly adding the milk. When all the milk has been added, season with pepper, add the horseradish, and stir well to combine.

YIELD: Serves 6
SODIUM CONTENT: 40 mg. of sodium per serving

BASIL MASHED POTATOES

The classic flavor of basil gives a great lift to the basic potato. If you're trying to avoid fat, you can hold back on the butter without sacrificing that much flavor.

6 or 7 large potatoes
10 to 12 fresh basil
leaves
3 tbsp. unsalted butter
freshly ground black
pepper to taste
1 to 1½ c. milk

Peel and cut up the potatoes; cover them with water in a large pot. Bring the water to a boil; boil until the potatoes are very soft or fork tender, about 25 minutes. While the potatoes are boiling, add the basil leaves and the butter to a food processor and blend until there are no lumps of butter and the basil is finely chopped. Stir in a grinding of pepper. When the potatoes are cooked, drain and add to the basil and butter. Start to blend, and add the milk gradually. Blend until the lumps are gone and the mixture is smooth. Serve hot or transfer to a 200-degree oven until ready to serve.

If you don't have a food processor, chop the basil leaves as finely as you can with a knife, then put them and the butter in with the potatoes and add the milk as you mash them by hand.

YIELD: Serves 6
SODIUM CONTENT: 39 mg. of sodium per serving

WHIPPED POTATOES WITH ROSEMARY AND ROASTED GARLIC

1 whole head of garlic
2 tbsp. olive oil
6 large russet potatoes
½ c. (1 stick) unsalted
  butter
2 tbsp. finely chopped
  fresh rosemary
freshly ground black
  pepper to taste
1 c. milk

Preheat the oven to 375 degrees. Place the whole head of garlic in an ovenproof baking dish, drizzle the oil over it, and roast it for an hour. While it is roasting, peel and wash the potatoes, and cut them into equal sized pieces. In a large pot add enough water to cover the potatoes; bring the water to a boil and cook the potatoes until fork tender. When the garlic has cooked, remove it from the oven and use a sharp knife to slice off about ¼ inch of the pointed top. Then hold the garlic head over a small bowl and squeeze it so the cooked garlic oozes out like toothpaste.

When the potatoes are cooked, place the butter, garlic, rosemary, and a generous grinding of black pepper in a bowl large enough for all the ingredients. Drain the potatoes well and add them to the bowl. Use a hand mixer to whip the potatoes, incorporating the milk and blending the other ingredients. Serve warm.

YIELD: Serves 6
SODIUM CONTENT: 34 mg. of sodium per serving

POTATOES ROSTI

2 lbs. (6 medium)
   potatoes
4 tbsp. unsalted butter
2 tsp. onion powder
freshly ground black
   pepper to taste
grated low-sodium
   Gouda or Swiss
   cheese
sprigs of parsley

Peel the potatoes and boil or steam them until partially cooked, about 10 minutes. Use the coarse grid of a box grater to grate the potatoes until you have 4 cups. Melt 2 tablespoons of butter; pour the butter over the potatoes and stir to combine, then stir in the onion powder and black pepper. Melt the other 2 tablespoons of butter in a skillet over moderate heat. Put the potatoes in the skillet and use a spatula to press them flat. Reduce the heat to low and continue to cook for about 20 minutes, until a golden brown crust forms on the bottom of the potatoes. If you think it may be cooking too hard on the bottom (and you're not watching your cholesterol) work a bit more butter in around the sides of the pancake as it cooks.

When a nice crust has formed, slide a spatula underneath the pancake to loosen it. Then remove the skillet from the heat and place a large plate upside down over the skillet. Quickly flip the skillet over, holding the plate in place, so the pancake falls out onto the plate, crust side up. Sprinkle with the cheese and a few sprigs of parsley. To serve, cut in wedges.

YIELD: Serves 4
SODIUM CONTENT: 17 mg. of sodium per serving

SWEET POTATO SUPREME

**4 or 5 large sweet
  potatoes
2 tbsp. butter
1 shallot, finely chopped
3 tbsp. molasses
freshly ground black
  pepper to taste
1 c. milk**

Put the potatoes in the oven and roast at 350 degrees until tender. This could take as much as 1½ hours or more, depending on the size of the potatoes. (If you wish, you can roast the potatoes a day before.) Leave them unpeeled until ready for use. Heat a small slice of butter in a sauté pan over medium heat. Add the shallot and cook until wilted, taking care not to burn it. Allow the potatoes and shallot to cool while the milk and the rest of the butter warm to room temperature. When everything is ready, remove the potato skins and place the potato flesh in a bowl. Add the rest of the ingredients and mash them together with a hand potato masher. Just before serving, heat the mixture in a 350 degree oven.

YIELD: Serves 6
SODIUM CONTENT: 34 mg. of sodium per serving

SWEET POTATOES, CARROTS, AND SQUASH

Here's a dish based on the idea that foods of similar color taste good when mixed together. The dash of nutmeg is important.

1 tbsp. butter
4 large carrots, sliced into 1-inch pieces and steamed
3 sweet potatoes, baked and peeled
1 acorn squash, baked and peeled
½ tsp. nutmeg

Melt the butter in a sauté pan; add the steamed carrots, cooking for a few minutes so that they absorb the butter. Put the carrots, sweet potatoes, and squash in a food processor or blender and process until smoothly puréed. Transfer to a saucepan and stir in the nutmeg. Cook over moderate heat until heated through. Serve warm.

YIELD: Serves 6
SODIUM CONTENT: 24 mg. of sodium per serving

CHESTNUT CREAM

This recipe produces a thick sauce that makes a festive adornment for meat dishes or a fine addition to a vegetarian plate. This recipe goes heavy on the chestnuts; if you prefer a lighter sauce, reduce the nuts and increase the yogurt.

1 lb. chestnuts
1 medium bulb fennel
1 c. plain yogurt

Use a sharp knife to cut a cross in the flat side of each chestnut, then immerse in boiling water for 5 minutes. Turn off the heat, retrieve the chestnuts one by one, and peel off the outer and inner shells. Put the chestnut meats in a steamer basket in a saucepan with a little water. Bring the water to a boil and allow the chestnuts to steam for about 10 minutes, until tender. Clean and dice the fennel bulb and steam it, separately from the chestnuts, until tender, about 10 minutes. Then put the chestnuts, fennel, and yogurt in a blender or food processor and process to create a smooth cream. Serve warm.

YIELD: Serves 4
SODIUM CONTENT: 47 mg. of sodium per serving

ONION TART

FOR THE CRUST:

½ c. (1 stick) plus 2
tbsp. cold unsalted
butter or margarine
1¼ c. all-purpose flour
1 tsp. sugar
3 tbsp. ice water

FOR THE FILLING:

1 tbsp. butter
2 large onions, cut in
half and sliced thin
1 c. heavy cream
2 eggs
freshly ground pepper
to taste

To make the crust, slice the butter into small pieces and put them in a food processor fitted with a metal blade. Combine the flour and sugar, add them to the food processor, and process until the butter and flour begin to mix. Dribble in the ice water while the processor continues to run. When the dough comes together in a ball, remove to a bowl, wrap in waxed paper, and refrigerate. (To make the dough by hand, combine the flour and sugar and cut them into the butter with a pastry blender, two knives, or your fingertips. Add the water and continue to mix until the dough clings together.)

To make the filling, heat the butter in a pan; add the onion, and cook over medium heat for 15 minutes, making sure not to burn the onion. The onions should caramelize, turning brown and sweet. While the onions are cooking, put the cream and eggs in a bowl; beat them together, and add a generous grinding of pepper. When the onions are cooked, allow them to cool down.

Preheat the oven to 375 degrees. Roll out the dough to form a circle less than ¼-inch thick. Press it gently into a 9-inch pie tin and trim off any dough that hangs over the edges. When the onions have cooled off, add them to the cream and egg mixture, and stir to combine. Pour this filling into the pie shell, put it on the middle rack of the oven, and bake for 35 to 45 minutes, until a toothpick stuck in the mixture comes out clean.

YIELD: Serves 8
SODIUM CONTENT: 32 mg. of sodium per serving

MUSHROOM AND ONION QUICHE

FOR THE CRUST:

½ c. (1 stick) plus 2 tbsp. cold unsalted butter or margarine
1¼ c. all-purpose flour
1 tsp. sugar
3 tbsp. ice water

FOR THE QUICHE:

1 tbsp. butter
1 onion, diced
2 c. sliced white button mushrooms
4 eggs
1 c. milk
1 c. heavy cream
pinch of nutmeg
freshly ground black pepper to taste

To make the crust, slice the butter into small pieces and put them in a food processor fitted with a metal blade. Combine the flour and sugar, add them to the food processor, and process until the butter and flour begin to mix. Dribble in the ice water while the processor continues to run. When the dough comes together in a ball, remove to a bowl, wrap in waxed paper, and refrigerate. (To make the dough by hand, combine the flour and sugar and cut them into the butter with a pastry blender, two knives, or your fingertips. Add the water and continue to mix until the dough clings together.)

To make the quiche, melt the butter in a frying pan over medium-high heat; add the onion and cook for 5 minutes. Add the mushrooms and cook for another 7 to 10 minutes until they release their liquid. While the mushrooms and onions are cooking, beat the eggs in a bowl and add the milk and heavy cream. Stir in the nutmeg and pepper.

Preheat the oven to 350 degrees. Roll out the dough to line a 9-inch pie tin. Bake the crust for 15 minutes. While the crust bakes, remove the mushroom mixture from the frying pan and let cool. Spread the cooled mushroom mixture in the baked crust. Then pour the egg mixture over the mushrooms and bake for about 40 minutes, until the top is golden brown. Test for doneness by sticking a knife in the middle of the custard mixture. When it comes out clean, the quiche is done.

YIELD: Serves 8
SODIUM CONTENT: 63 mg. of sodium per serving

BRUSCHETTA

We like to make this classic Italian appetizer with thick slices of our olive oil and basil bread (see page 61), but you can use any French- or Italian-style loaf of salt-free bread.

**4 slices salt-free bread
good quality olive oil
2 medium tomatoes, seeded and cut into ½-inch cubes
1 tbsp. balsamic vinegar
1 tsp. lemon juice
freshly ground black pepper to taste
1 whole clove garlic, peeled
4 slices low-sodium Gouda or fresh salt-free mozzarella cheese (about 6 oz. altogether)
4 fresh basil leaves**

Put the slices of bread on a baking sheet and place them under the broiler until lightly toasted. Turn them over and brush the untoasted side with olive oil, then return them to the broiler until that side is lightly toasted. Meanwhile, combine the tomatoes, balsamic vinegar, and black pepper in a bowl and stir to blend.

Rub the clove of garlic over the oiled, toasted slices of bread, then spoon equal portions of the tomato mixture onto each one. Top each one with a slice of cheese and return to the broiler just long enough to melt the cheese. Place a fresh basil leaf on top of each bruschetta before serving.

YIELD: Serves 4
SODIUM CONTENT: 24 mg. of sodium per serving if Gouda cheese is used, 69 mg. with fresh mozzarella

XI. PASTA, RICE, AND PIZZA

EGG NOODLES WITH PEAS AND GARLIC DRESSING

½ c. low-sodium chicken broth
1½ c. fresh or salt-free frozen peas
1 tbsp. unsalted butter
1 small shallot, finely chopped
4 cloves garlic, finely minced
1 pound egg noodles, cooked without salt and drained
freshly ground black pepper to taste
2 tbsp. chopped parsley

Heat the chicken broth and peas in a saucepan; bring to a boil and cook until the liquid is almost gone. Add the butter, shallot, and garlic and cook for 5 minutes. Add the egg noodles. Stir to combine, and cook until heated through. Sprinkle with the pepper and chopped parsley; stir and serve.

YIELD: Serves 4
SODIUM CONTENT: 19 mg. of sodium per serving

ASPARAGUS AND SPINACH WITH PASTA

2 tbsp. olive oil
2 cloves garlic, minced
1 medium sweet red
   pepper, seeded and
   diced
5 c. raw spinach leaves,
   stems removed,
   packed
12 stalks asparagus
2 tbsp. balsamic vinegar
freshly ground black
   pepper to taste
grated low-sodium
   Swiss or Gouda
   cheese
1 lb. linguini, ziti, or
   small shells cooked
   without salt and
   drained

Heat the oil in a large skillet, and add the garlic and sweet pepper. Cook over medium heat, stirring occasionally, until the pepper softens. Add the spinach leaves and stir to combine. Cover and reduce the heat to very low as the spinach cooks down. Meanwhile, cut off the tips of the asparagus, then cut the rest of each stalk into 1-inch lengths, discarding the tough, woody ends. Put the pieces of asparagus in a steamer basket in a saucepan over an inch of water; bring to a boil, cover, and steam for about 5 minutes, until the asparagus turns bright green. It should be tender but still a bit crunchy. Combine the steamed asparagus with the spinach mixture; sprinkle with the balsamic vinegar and pepper, and toss to blend. Serve over linguini, ziti, or small shells sprinkled with grated cheese.

YIELD: Serves 4
SODIUM CONTENT: 67 mg. of sodium per serving

SHRIMP WITH PASTA AND PESTO

2 tsp. olive oil
1 lb. shrimp, shelled
and deveined
2 cloves garlic, finely
chopped
½ c. white wine
¼ c. plus 1 tbsp.
salt-free pesto
(see page 88)
½ c. low-sodium chicken
broth
1 lb. pasta cooked
without salt and
drained

Heat the oil in a pot large enough to hold all the ingredients. Add the shrimp and garlic and cook for 2 minutes, then remove the shrimp from the pot. Add the wine and deglaze, using a wooden spoon to scrape bits of shrimp and garlic from the bottom of the pot. Then add the pesto and the chicken broth, and cook until it starts to simmer. Add the pasta and toss together. To serve, spoon pasta onto a plate, then arrange several shrimp on top of it.

YIELD: Serves 4
SODIUM CONTENT: 179 mg. of sodium per serving

CHICKEN AND PASTA SALAD WITH VEGETABLES

We've used asparagus, peppers, zucchini, and carrots, but you might also use broccoli, sautéed mushrooms, eggplant, or whatever else looks good at the market.

1 lb. elbow macaroni, ziti, or other small pasta
1 c. olive oil
1 boneless chicken breast (2 half breasts)
2 tbsp. fresh thyme or 1 tbsp. dried thyme
freshly ground black pepper to taste
3 medium carrots, peeled and cut into 2-inch strips
1 yellow sweet pepper, seeded and cubed
1 red sweet pepper, seeded and cubed
1 medium zucchini, cut into julienne strips
12 stalks asparagus, washed and cut into 2-inch pieces
1 jalapeño or serrano pepper, minced
¼ c. balsamic vinegar
3 cloves garlic, minced
juice of ½ lemon

Cook the pasta according to the directions on the package, omitting salt. Drain and toss with a little of the olive oil, and transfer to a large bowl to cool. Preheat the oven to 350 degrees. Brush the chicken with olive oil and sprinkle with 1 tablespoon of the fresh thyme (1 teaspoon dried) and black pepper. Place in an ovenproof pan or dish and roast in the oven until cooked through, about ½ hour. Remove and allow to cool.

Meanwhile, steam the carrots, peppers, zucchini, and asparagus one at a time until tender. Cut the chicken into thin 2-inch strips; add to the pasta and stir to combine. Then stir in the steamed vegetables, one at a time. Sprinkle the minced hot pepper over the mixture and stir once more.

Prepare the dressing by whisking together the remaining olive oil, vinegar, garlic, and the rest of the thyme. Pour this mixture over the pasta-chicken mixture and stir. Sprinkle with black pepper and lemon juice and stir once more. If you wish, add a bit more vinegar, lemon juice, or black pepper to taste before serving.

YIELD: Serves 6
SODIUM CONTENT: 44 mg. of sodium per serving

STUFFED SHELLS
WITH SPINACH AND PARSLEY

The addition of spinach and parsley lightens up this tasty dish. We get mascarpone cheese at upscale supermarkets and specialty food shops. We've yet to find it with salt, but check the label to be sure.

FOR THE SAUCE:

1 tbsp. olive oil
½ medium onion, chopped
1 clove garlic, minced
2 c. salt-free canned tomatoes or coarsely chopped fresh tomatoes
2 tbsp. red wine
1 tsp. balsamic vinegar
1 tsp. lemon juice
1 tsp. dried basil or 2 tsp. chopped fresh basil leaves
½ tsp. sugar
freshly ground black pepper to taste

FOR THE SHELLS:

olive oil
½ medium onion, chopped
1 clove garlic, minced
2 c. raw spinach
1 c. parsley leaves, tightly packed
juice of ½ lemon
1 c. mascarpone cheese
1 c. plain yogurt
24 large pasta shells
3 to 4 tbsp. grated low-sodium Gouda cheese

To make the sauce, heat the olive oil in a heavy saucepan. Add the onion and garlic, and cook over medium heat until the onion begins to wilt. Add the rest of the sauce ingredients, bring to a simmer, and cook for at least an hour. If you prefer a smooth sauce, transfer the cooked mixture to a blender or food processor and process until smooth.

To make the filling, heat 1 tablespoon of olive oil in a sauté pan. Add the onion and garlic, and cook over medium heat until the onion begins to wilt. Then add the spinach and cook, stirring, until the spinach cooks down to about half its volume. Add the parsley and lemon juice, and cook for a few more minutes until the parsley softens. Transfer this mixture to a food processor or blender, and

(Continued)

process briefly so that all the ingredients are chopped fine and well distributed. Combine the mascarpone and yogurt in a bowl, add the spinach-parsley mixture and stir until well blended.

Preheat the oven to 350 degrees. Cook the shells according to package directions (omitting salt) until they just begin to turn tender. Don't overcook, since they will cook more when filled. Lightly oil the bottom of a baking dish with olive oil. Drain the shells and fill each one with a spoonful of the spinach-parsley mixture. Place them seam side up in the baking dish. Pour the tomato sauce over and around the shells, then sprinkle the whole dish with grated cheese. Cover loosely with aluminum foil and bake until the cheese has melted and the shells are heated through, about 20 minutes.

YIELD: Serves 6
SODIUM CONTENT: 67 mg. of sodium per serving

CHICKEN AND SUN-DRIED TOMATOES WITH PASTA

Exploring the possibilities for salt-free sun-dried tomatoes (see page 315), we adapted this recipe from a cookbook provided by Timber Crest Farms of Healdsburg, California. To reconstitute dried tomatoes, put them in a bowl, cover with boiling water, allow to stand for 20 minutes, and drain.

8 ounces elbow macaroni, ziti, or other small pasta
2 boneless chicken breasts (4 half breasts)
2 tbsp. olive oil
4 cloves garlic, minced
½ tsp. salt-free chili powder
juice of ½ lemon
freshly ground black pepper to taste
3 c. low-sodium chicken broth
½ c. chopped parsley
½ c. reconstituted dried tomatoes (20 tomato halves), cut into small pieces
8 green onions, chopped

Cook the pasta according to package directions, omitting salt. Rinse the chicken breasts, trim off any fat and skin, and cut the flesh into strips about ½ inch wide and 2 inches long. Heat the olive oil to medium in a large sauté pan or skillet, add the garlic, and cook for a few minutes until it softens. Add the chicken and cook for a few more minutes, until cooked through. Sprinkle with chili powder, lemon juice, and black pepper, and stir to blend. Remove the chicken from the pan and set aside.

Add the chicken broth, parsley, tomatoes, and green onions to the pan; bring to a boil and allow to cook down for several minutes, until the liquid is reduced by a third or more. Then return the chicken to the pan; stir. Cook for a few more minutes so that the flavors are well blended. Put the pasta in a large bowl, pour the sauce over it, and stir to combine before serving.

YIELD: Serves 6
SODIUM CONTENT: 81 mg. of sodium per serving

RISOTTO

It's possible to make risotto with either water or chicken broth, but we strongly recommend salt-free chicken broth—make your own or look for one of the commercial products. As with any other starch, you are likely to notice the lack of salt in rice prepared without it. That makes the other flavoring ingredients important, and chicken broth here makes a big difference.

1 tbsp. unsalted butter
3 whole cloves garlic
1 shallot, finely chopped
6 medium mushrooms, sliced
1½ c. arborio rice
5 to 6 c. salt-free chicken broth or water
¼ c. grated salt-free Gouda cheese
freshly ground black pepper to taste

Put the butter, garlic, shallot, and mushrooms into a deep pot and sauté over medium heat for 5 minutes or so. Add the rice and 2 cups of the broth or water and stir to combine. As the mixture cooks down add a cup at a time of the remaining broth or water until the rice is done. This will take about 30 minutes. After 20 minutes, add the cheese and stir until smooth. Add freshly ground pepper to taste and serve immediately.

YIELD: Serves 6
SODIUM CONTENT: 34 mg. of sodium per serving

BASIL RISOTTO

2 tbsp. unsalted butter
½ shallot, finely diced
1 c. arborio rice
3 to 4 c. low-sodium
 chicken broth or
 water
freshly ground black
 pepper to taste
10 basil leaves, finely
 chopped

Heat a pot to medium heat; add 1 tablespoon of the butter and the shallot. Cook for 5 minutes, then add the rice, stirring to coat the rice with the butter. Continue to cook for 6 minutes or so, making sure not to let the rice burn. Then add 1 cup of the chicken broth or water. Stir in the liquid, bring to a simmer, and cook until reduced by at least half. Add ½ cup of the liquid, bring to a simmer again, and allow to cook down; repeat this process until the rice is soft and the liquid is almost gone. The rice should have a creamy appearance and texture. This may occur before all of the liquid is used up—if the rice has a good texture after adding 2½ or 3 cups of liquid, don't continue to add more. Finally, add the pepper, basil, and the rest of the butter, stir until the butter is incorporated. Serve immediately.

YIELD: Serves 4
SODIUM CONTENT: 33 mg. of sodium per serving

ROASTED TOMATO RISOTTO

2 tomatoes, halved and
   seeded
1 clove garlic, sliced
2 tbsp. olive oil
freshly ground black
   pepper to taste
2 tbsp. unsalted butter
1 shallot, minced
1½ c. arborio rice
5 to 6 c. low-sodium
   chicken broth
6 basil leaves, chopped

Preheat oven to 400 degrees. Place the tomato halves cut side up on a baking sheet, and put two slices of garlic in each half. Drizzle oil over the tomatoes and sprinkle them with pepper. Roast them in the oven for 25 minutes. While the tomatoes are roasting, heat up a pot large enough for the risotto on top of the stove. Add 1 tablespoon of unsalted butter to the pot; add the shallot and cook for about 8 minutes, until thoroughly wilted. Add the rice and the other tablespoon of butter; stir to blend, and cook until the butter has melted. Add enough of the chicken broth just to cover the rice, and reduce the heat to low. When the broth has cooked down, add more, allow it to cook down, and repeat until the rice is soft.

When the tomatoes are roasted, remove them from the oven and allow them to cool to the point where you can easily handle them. Cut them up, add them to the rice with the basil, and stir to blend. Serve hot.

YIELD: Serves 6
SODIUM CONTENT: 36 mg. of sodium per serving

CARAMELIZED ONION RISOTTO

2 tbsp. unsalted butter
1 leek, white part only,
    rinsed and finely
    chopped
1 small onion, finely
    chopped
freshly ground black
    pepper to taste
1½ c. arborio rice
5 to 6 c. low-sodium
    chicken broth

In a pot large enough for all the
ingredients, melt 1 tablespoon of the
butter over medium heat; add the
leek and onion. Season with pepper,
and cook over medium to low heat
for about 15 minutes, stirring to
prevent burning. The onion should
turn golden brown. Add the rice and
the second tablespoon of butter. Stir
the rice to coat evenly with melted
butter. Add 1 cup of broth and allow
it to cook down slowly over low heat.
When it is almost completely
absorbed, add another cup, repeating
this process until rice is tender. If the
rice seems to need more liquid, add a
cup of water.

YIELD: Serves 6
SODIUM CONTENT: 35 mg. of sodium per serving

RISOTTO WITH ACORN SQUASH, SAGE, AND CHICKEN

1½ tbsp. unsalted butter
2 pinches allspice
1 acorn squash, cut in half, seeds removed
1 boneless chicken breast (2 half breasts)
½ shallot, finely minced
1⅓ c. arborio rice
5 to 6 c. water or low-sodium chicken broth
8 fresh sage leaves, finely chopped
freshly ground black pepper to taste

Preheat the oven to 375 degrees. Place 2 small slices of the butter on a baking sheet and sprinkle a pinch of allspice on each. Cover each piece of butter with a half of the squash, cut side down, and roast in the oven for 45 minutes to 1 hour, until very soft. While the squash is roasting, prepare the chicken. Trim the skin and fat off the breasts and cook them either by sautéing in a little oil over medium heat on top of the stove or by putting them on a baking sheet and baking them in the oven. Be sure they are cooked through.

In a large pot heat the rest of the butter; add the shallot and cook for several minutes, until it begins to soften. Add the rice and cook for another 4 minutes or so, stirring so the rice doesn't burn. Add just enough water or chicken broth to the pot to cover the rice. Allow to simmer uncovered, stirring every couple of minutes. When the liquid is absorbed, add another cup, repeating this process until the rice is tender.

When the rice is cooked, remove it from the heat and add sage, chicken, and black pepper. Scoop the flesh from the squash—it should be soft and creamy—and add it to the mixture; stir to incorporate. Serve in bowls, garnished with fresh sage.

YIELD: Serves 6
SODIUM CONTENT: 55 mg. of sodium per serving

LENTILS, RICE, AND ONIONS

1 c. white rice
1 c. lentils
4 c. salt-free chicken
  broth
2 tbsp. olive oil
2 c. chopped onion
¼ tsp. salt-free chili
  powder
1 tsp. lemon juice
½ tsp. ground cumin
freshly ground black
  pepper to taste

Put the rice and lentils in separate saucepans, and cover each with 2 cups of chicken broth. Bring both pans to a boil, reduce to a simmer, and cook until the rice and the lentils are just tender (about 15 minutes). Meanwhile, heat the oil in a large skillet or sauté pan, add the onions and cook, stirring occasionally, until they turn a deep brown and develop a full, sweet flavor.

Preheat the oven to 350 degrees. When the lentils are cooked, sprinkle them with the chili powder, lemon juice, and cumin, and stir to blend. When the rice is cooked, sprinkle it with a generous grinding of black pepper, and stir to blend. To assemble the final dish, stir the rice and lentils together in an ovenproof casserole. Press the rice and lentils down to create a flat surface, then spread a thick layer of onions on top of it. Place the dish on the middle rack of the oven and bake until the flavors develop, about 15 minutes. Serve warm.

YIELD: Serves 6
SODIUM CONTENT: 31 mg. of sodium per serving

ORZO WITH SUMMER VEGETABLES

1 tbsp. unsalted butter
1 tbsp. corn oil
2 medium zucchini, diced
2 medium yellow squash, diced
1 red bell pepper, diced
1 small red onion, diced
freshly ground black pepper to taste
1 lb. orzo cooked according to package directions, without salt, and drained
¼ c. chopped parsley

Heat the butter and oil in a large skillet over medium heat. Add zucchini, squash, red pepper, and onion. Season with black pepper. Cook, stirring occasionally, for about 12 minutes. Remove the vegetable mixture from the heat and combine with the cooked orzo in a large bowl. Add the parsley and toss. Serve warm or cool.

YIELD: Serves 6
SODIUM CONTENT: 25 mg. of sodium per serving

BASIC TOMATO SAUCE

2 tbsp. olive oil
1 medium onion,
 chopped
2 carrots, finely diced
½ tsp. dried thyme or
 3 to 4 sprigs of fresh
 thyme
4 cloves garlic, chopped
1 c. red wine
10 fresh basil leaves,
 chopped
1 bunch parsley, roughly
 chopped
2 (15-oz.) cans salt-free
 whole tomatoes or
 4 c. chopped fresh
 tomatoes
freshly ground black
 pepper to taste

In a pot large enough for all the ingredients, heat the oil over medium-high heat. Add the onion and cook for several minutes, until it turns translucent. Add the carrots, thyme, and garlic, and cook for another 6 minutes. Add the wine, basil, parsley, and tomatoes, crushing the tomatoes with a wooden spoon or a potato masher. Stir well to combine. Season with pepper and simmer for 1 hour.

YIELD: Serves 4
SODIUM CONTENT: 24 mg. of sodium per serving

MEAT SAUCE FOR PASTA

2 tbsp. olive oil
1 medium onion,
   chopped
4 cloves garlic, chopped
1½ lbs. lean ground
   beef
2 tbsp. balsamic vinegar
freshly ground black
   pepper to taste
2 (15-oz.) cans salt-free
   tomatoes or 4 c.
   chopped fresh
   tomatoes
1 bunch parsley, roughly
   chopped
8 fresh basil leaves,
   chopped, or 1 tbsp.
   dried basil
1 tbsp. fresh oregano
   leaves, or 1 tsp. dried
   oregano
1 c. red wine

Heat the oil in a large skillet or Dutch oven; add the onion and garlic and cook over medium heat for several minutes until the onion turns translucent. Add the meat and use a wooden spoon or potato masher to push it down so it cooks evenly. When the meat has browned, sprinkle it with the balsamic vinegar and black pepper, then stir to blend. Add the rest of the ingredients, stirring to blend. Allow the mixture to come just to a boil, then turn down to a low simmer and cook for an hour or more.

YIELD: Serves 8
SODIUM CONTENT: 67 mg. of sodium per serving

FRESH TOMATO SAUCE

A good fresh tomato sauce has dozens of uses: for starters, serve it over a thick slice of salt-free Tuscan bread brushed with olive oil and run under the broiler, or spoon it over chicken or fish as they come off the charcoal grill or sauté pan. Preparation is simple enough—get good ripe tomatoes and cut them up with everything else. The secret is to let it all stand for a half hour or so before serving.

5 fresh, ripe tomatoes, seeded and diced
½ c. chopped fresh basil leaves
2 cloves garlic, minced
3 tbsp. olive oil
2 tsp. balsamic vinegar
juice of ½ lemon
½ tsp. salt-free chili powder
freshly ground black pepper to taste

Combine the diced tomatoes, basil, and garlic in a bowl and stir to distribute evenly; add the olive oil, vinegar, and lemon juice and stir to blend. Sprinkle with the chili powder and a generous grinding of black pepper. Stir again to blend, and allow to stand for at least ½ hour before serving.

YIELD: Serves 6
SODIUM CONTENT: 14 mg. of sodium per serving

GRILLED PEPPER
AND TOMATO SAUCE

4 sweet red peppers
2 large ripe tomatoes,
cut in half
olive oil
½ red onion, finely
chopped
¼ c. chopped fresh
parsley
2 tbsp. chopped fresh
tarragon
8 basil leaves, chopped
freshly ground black
pepper to taste

Rub the peppers and tomatoes with olive oil and place over the charcoal grill or a medium open flame on top of the gas range. Let the skin of the peppers get black, then remove the peppers from the fire. Allow the tomatoes to grill only until they get a little mushy. When the peppers are cool enough to handle, remove the skin under cool water. Cut them into large chunks, and remove the membranes and seeds from the inside. Place the tomatoes and the peppers in a blender and blend to a smooth purée. Heat a tablespoon of oil in a saucepan over low to medium heat and sauté the onion in it for 10 minutes. Add the purée, along with the rest of the ingredients, and cook for about 45 minutes over low heat.

YIELD: Serves 4
SODIUM CONTENT: 15 mg. of sodium per serving

PASTA SAUCE
WITH SUN-DRIED TOMATOES

**16 salt-free sun-dried
tomato halves
3 tbsp. olive oil
2 cloves garlic, minced
2 (15-oz.) cans salt-free
tomatoes or
4 c. chopped fresh
tomatoes
8 basil leaves, chopped
juice of ½ lemon
freshly ground black
pepper to taste**

Put the sun-dried tomatoes in a bowl, cover with boiling water, and set aside to soften for about 15 minutes. Heat the olive oil in a large sauté pan or pot. Add the garlic, and cook for 5 minutes over medium heat. Add the fresh tomatoes, basil, lemon juice, and pepper, and stir to blend. Bring the mixture to a simmer. When the sun-dried tomatoes have softened, remove them from the water, drain, and use a scissors or sharp knife to cut them into small pieces. Add the sun-dried tomatoes to the tomato mixture and allow to cook for another 20 minutes or so, until the liquids reduce and the flavors develop.

YIELD: Serves 6
SODIUM CONTENT: 21 mg. of sodium per serving

FESTIVE TOMATO SAUCE

1 tbsp. olive oil
2 cloves garlic, minced
1 medium onion,
   chopped
2 (15-oz.) cans salt-free
   tomatoes or 4 c.
   chopped fresh
   tomatoes
¼ c. red wine
2 tsp. balsamic vinegar
2 tsp. lemon juice
1 tsp. dried basil or
   2 tsp. chopped fresh
   basil leaves
1 tsp. dried oregano or
   2 tsp. fresh oregano
   leaves
2 tbsp. dried parsley or
   ¼ c. chopped fresh
   parsley
1 large sprig fresh
   tarragon
1 tsp. sugar
freshly ground black
   pepper to taste
¾ c. fresh zucchini cut
   in 1-inch julienne
   strips
¾ c. sliced fresh
   mushrooms

Heat the olive oil in a heavy saucepan. Add the garlic and onion, and cook for several minutes, until the onion becomes translucent. Add the rest of the ingredients except for zucchini and mushrooms; stir to blend thoroughly and simmer, partially covered, for at least an hour. Then add zucchini and mushrooms and cook for no more than 15 minutes, so that zucchini strips remain al dente and retain their color.

YIELD: Serves 6
SODIUM CONTENT: 14 mg. of sodium per serving

PIZZA DOUGH

It's not that hard to make good pizza at home, especially if you are willing to invest in a couple of essential tools: a clay tile or "brick" to put in the oven, a baker's peel (the paddle-shaped implement for shoving pies into the oven and hauling them out), and perhaps a pizza wheel, a little gadget fitted with a sharp-edged disk for slicing up the pie. All are available at reasonable prices in kitchenware stores or from mail-order catalogs. You can also make tolerable pizza without the brick and the peel, if you can't find them; assemble the pie on a baking sheet lined with baker's parchment or spread with a thin layer of cornmeal.

Here is a recipe for basic pizza dough. You may want to improvise with the flour, substituting a cup of rye or whole wheat for some of the all-purpose for a crust with a bit more flavor.

2 packages or 4½ tsp. dry yeast
2 c. lukewarm water
2 tbsp. olive oil
1 tbsp. honey
4-plus c. all-purpose flour

Dissolve the yeast in ½ cup of the water and allow to stand for a few minutes until it begins to foam. Add the oil, honey, and the rest of the water and stir to blend.

Add 1 cup of flour, and stir. Add the rest of the flour, ½ cup at a time, stirring until the dough becomes too stiff to stir with a spoon. Remove it to a floured board and knead for about 5 minutes, until it feels soft and elastic and the texture is uniform.

(If you have a mixer with a dough hook, you can use it to knead the dough. After stirring in the first cup of flour by hand, put the mixture in the mixer's bowl, add 2 more cups of flour and run the mixer on slow speed. Add more flour ¼ cup at a time until the dough holds together in a ball and no longer sticks to the sides of the bowl. After removing the dough from the bowl, knead by hand a few times to make sure the texture is uniform.)

(Continued)

Wipe the inside of a clean bowl with olive oil; place the dough in it to rise and cover loosely with plastic wrap. For a faster rise, put the bowl in a sink partly filled with hot water. The dough is ready to use for pizza crusts when it has doubled in bulk. There should be enough for four medium-sized pies.

YIELD: 24 slices
SODIUM CONTENT: less than 1 mg. of sodium per slice

BASIC PIZZA

For the sauce, use basic tomato sauce (page 269), pasta sauce with sun-dried tomatoes (see page 273), or a good off-the-shelf salt-free tomato sauce. You can elaborate on this basic pie by adding slices of green or red pepper, broccoli florets, mushrooms, or salt-free meatballs (see page 209).

salt-free pizza dough for one pie, risen once (¼ of pizza dough recipe on page 275)
cornmeal
1 c. salt-free tomato sauce
½ lb. salt-free fresh mozzarella cheese, sliced thin
1 tbsp. dried basil or 2 tbsp. chopped fresh basil leaves
1 tbsp. dried oregano or 2 tbsp. fresh oregano leaves
1 tbsp. high-quality olive oil
¼ c. grated low-sodium Gouda cheese

Place a baking tile (if you have one) on the bottom rack of the oven and preheat it to 500 degrees.

Using first the heel of your palm, then your fingertips, flatten the ball of risen dough on a floured board so that it forms a large circle no more than ¼-inch thick. Forget the twirling and tossing of pizza parlor bakers; the best crusts are shaped by using the fingertips to push the edges of the dough out from the center of the circle.

Spread enough cornmeal across the surface of a baker's peel so the dough will slide off it easily. Transfer the flattened dough to the peel. (If you don't have a peel, transfer the dough to a large baking sheet lined with baker's parchment or spread with a thin layer of cornmeal.) Spread the tomato sauce evenly on the crust, followed by slices of the mozzarella cheese. Sprinkle with basil, oregano, and olive oil, then with the grated Gouda cheese. Be careful not to load the crust up with too much sauce and cheese, or it won't slide off the peel easily.

Open the oven door and carefully shift the pie to the baking tile, shoving the peel forward in short strokes so that the pie slides forward onto the tile. (If using a baking sheet, rest it on

(Continued)

the tile. If you aren't using a tile, put the baking sheet on the bottom rack of the oven.) Close the door and cook the pie until the cheese bubbles on the surface and the edges of the crust turn dark brown, about 15 to 20 minutes. Slide the peel under the cooked pie and remove it from the oven. Cut into pieces with a sharp knife or a pizza wheel.

YIELD: 6 slices
SODIUM CONTENT: 62 mg. of sodium per slice

SPRING AND SUMMER PIZZA

4 stalks fresh asparagus
1 large ripe tomato
1 medium summer
   squash
1 medium zucchini
1 medium onion
1 medium green pepper
salt-free pizza dough for
   one pie, risen once
   (¼ of pizza dough
   recipe on page 275)
cornmeal
1 tbsp. olive oil
1 tbsp. dry basil or
   2 tbsp. fresh leaves
1 tbsp. dry oregano or
   2 tbsp. fresh leaves
freshly ground black
   pepper to taste
¼ lb. Swiss Lorraine
   cheese (see page 11),
   sliced thin

Place a baking tile (if you have one) on the bottom rack of the oven and preheat it to 500 degrees. Cut the tough ends off the asparagus stalks and slice them lengthwise. Use a sharp knife to prepare paper-thin (if possible) slices of tomato, squash, zucchini, onion, and green pepper.

Using first the heel of your palm, then your fingertips, flatten the ball of risen dough on a floured board so that it forms a large circle ¼-inch thick. Spread enough cornmeal across the surface of a baker's peel so that the dough will slide off it easily. Transfer the flattened dough to the peel. (If you don't have a peel, transfer the dough to a large baking sheet lined with baker's parchment or spread with a thin layer of cornmeal.)

Brush a thin layer of olive oil on the crust and arrange vegetable slices, in equal portions, on top of it. Do not use so many vegetable slices that they make the crust too heavy to slide easily off the peel. Sprinkle with basil, oregano, and ground pepper. Place slices of the cheese on the vegetables.

Open the oven door and carefully shift the pie to the tile, shoving the peel forward in short strokes so the pie slides forward onto the tile. (If using a baking sheet, rest it on the tile. If you aren't using a tile, put the

(Continued)

baking sheet on the bottom rack of the oven.) Close the door and cook the pie until the cheese melts and the edges of the crust turn brown, about 15 to 20 minutes. Slide the peel under the cooked pie and remove it from the oven. Cut into pieces with a sharp knife or a pizza wheel.

YIELD: 6 slices
SODIUM CONTENT: 28 mg. of sodium per slice

FRESH PIZZA

2 medium ripe
  tomatoes, chopped
10 fresh basil leaves,
  chopped, or 2 tbsp.
  dried basil
1 tbsp. balsamic vinegar
1 clove garlic, finely
  minced
freshly ground black
  pepper to taste
olive oil
salt-free pizza dough for
  one pie, risen once
  (¼ of pizza dough
  recipe on page 275)
cornmeal

Place a baking tile (if you have one) on the bottom rack of the oven and preheat it to 500 degrees. In a bowl, combine the tomatoes, basil, vinegar, garlic, a sprinkling of pepper, and

1 tablespoon of olive oil; stir to combine and set aside. Place the dough on a floured board and use your fingertips and the heels of your palms to flatten it into a large circle no more than ¼-inch thick.

Transfer the flattened dough to a baking sheet lined with baker's parchment or spread with a thin layer of cornmeal. Brush a little olive oil on the crust, and place the baking sheet on the tile in the oven (or on the bottom rack if you don't have a tile). Bake for about 15 minutes, until the crust turns golden brown and crisp.

To serve, cut the crust into sections with a sharp knife or pizza wheel and spoon a generous helping of topping onto each one. If the topping mixture seems too liquid, use a slotted spoon.

YIELD: 6 slices
SODIUM CONTENT: 5 mg. of sodium per slice

XII. DESSERT

BERRY PIE

3½ c. fresh blueberries
or raspberries
¼ c. minute tapioca
½ c. sugar
½ c. water
2 tsp. lemon juice (if
using blueberries)
9-inch precooked
salt-free crumb or
pastry crust (see
pages 22-24)

Put 2 cups of fresh berries along with all the remaining ingredients for the filling in a saucepan, stir to blend, and bring to a boil on top of the stove over medium heat. When the mixture reaches a full boil, remove it from the heat. Add the remaining 1½ cups of fresh berries, and stir gently to distribute. The fresh berries will cook a bit and the mixture will thicken up as it cools. Allow to cool before pouring into the crust. If you want a top crust for a pie with a pastry bottom crust, bake strips or circles of pastry and float them on the filling. Sprinkle loose crumbs on a pie with a crumb crust.

YIELD: Serves 6
SODIUM CONTENT: 3 mg. of sodium per serving

AMARETTO CREAM PIE

A crust based on amaretto cookies (see page 24) is pretty sweet, since the already sweet cookies come covered with big grains of sugar. If you prefer the crust less sweet, try brushing the sugar off the cookies before crushing them.

FOR THE CRUST:

1½ c. amaretto cookie crumbs (about 17 cookies)
6 tbsp. unsalted butter or margarine, melted

FOR THE FILLING:

½ c. sugar
½ c. flour
2 c. milk
3 egg yolks, lightly beaten
1 tbsp. butter
1 tsp. vanilla

FOR THE MERINGUE:

2 egg whites
¼ tsp. cream of tartar
2 tbsp. sugar
½ tsp. vanilla

Preheat oven to 350 degrees. To make crumbs for the crust, grind up cookies in a blender or food processor or crush them with a rolling pin between two sheets of waxed paper. Put the crumbs in a bowl and stir in the melted butter until thoroughly blended. Press the crumbs into a 9-inch pie tin, pushing them against the bottom and sides of the tin with your fingertips to form a crust of uniform thickness. Put the tin in the oven and bake for 10 minutes. Allow to cool before filling.

To make the filling, put the sugar, flour, and milk in the top of a double boiler. Boil water in the bottom half and cook the sugar mixture over it until it begins to thicken. Remove it from the heat and pour half of it into a bowl containing the beaten egg yolks, stirring to blend. Then pour the egg mixture back into the rest of the sugar mixture and return it to cook over the boiling water, stirring until it thickens. Remove from the heat and add the butter and vanilla, continuing to stir until they are well blended. Allow the mixture to cool for a few minutes before pouring it into the amaretto crust.

When separating egg whites for the meringue, be extremely careful not to let any egg yolk contaminate the whites. If it does, the whites won't

(Continued)

beat up into a thick meringue. To make meringue, beat the egg whites until they begin to foam; then add the cream of tartar and beat until they form stiff peaks that droop a bit as you pull the beater out of the bowl. Then stir in the sugar until thoroughly blended, followed by the vanilla.

Spread the meringue evenly on top of the cream filling, and put the pie in the oven to bake for about 10 minutes, until the peaks of the meringue are lightly browned.

YIELD: Serves 8
SODIUM CONTENT: 53 mg. of sodium per serving

LEMON CUPS

In this classic "sponge custard," flour and egg whites rise to the surface to form a light sponge cake, while egg yolks, milk, sugar, and lemon juice form a delicious custard below. We found the recipe one day in our mother's file. Her last written comment on it ("excellent") is dated March 6, 1938. She used to divide the recipe and cook it in individual ovenproof custard cups, by far the most elegant way to serve the dish. If you don't have them, you can cook the whole thing in a single casserole dish, though you may need to bake it for a bit longer than 45 minutes.

1 c. sugar
¼ c. all-purpose flour
2 tbsp. unsalted butter, melted
¼ c. plus 1 tbsp. lemon juice
rind of 1 lemon, finely grated
1½ c. milk
3 egg yolks, beaten well
3 egg whites, beaten stiff

Preheat the oven to 350 degrees. Blend the sugar and flour and stir them together with the melted butter. Add the lemon juice and lemon rind and stir to blend. In a separate bowl, stir the milk into the beaten egg yolks. Then add the sugar-lemon-flour mixture to the eggs and milk and stir well. Fold in the beaten egg whites gently and evenly. Pour the mixture into 6 lightly greased ovenproof cups and place them in a shallow pan of hot water. Bake them for 45 minutes until the tops are golden brown.

YIELD: Serves 6
SODIUM CONTENT: 60 mg. of sodium per serving

BOURBON BREAD PUDDING

**4 c. salt-free white or
whole-wheat bread
cubes, crusts
removed**
2¾ c. warm milk
3 egg yolks
½ c. sugar
splash of vanilla
¼ c. bourbon

Preheat the oven to 350 degrees.
Place the bread in a bowl and cover
with warm milk. (Be sure the milk is
warm and not hot, so you don't
scramble the egg yolks you will be
adding.) While the bread is soaking,
mix the egg yolks with the sugar, and
stir with a whisk until well combined.
Add the vanilla and the bourbon, and
whisk again. Add the yolk mixture to
the bread, and stir to combine. Place
the pudding in an ovenproof dish;
place it in a larger pan, and add hot
water to half the depth of the
pudding dish. Put the whole thing in
the oven and cook for 45 minutes.

YIELD: Serves 6
SODIUM CONTENT: 58 mg. of sodium per serving

RICE PUDDING

If you like, you can add a small handful of raisins or dried currants when cooking the rice with the milk.

½ c. long-grain rice
3 c. milk
½ c. sugar
1 tbsp. honey
1 tsp. cinnamon
2 large egg yolks
¼ tsp. vanilla

Put the rice and milk in a saucepan and bring to a boil. Reduce the heat and simmer for 1 hour.

Combine the rest of the ingredients in a bowl and stir to blend. When the rice has cooked, add this mixture to it in small amounts, stirring constantly to avoid scrambling the egg yolks, and cook 5 minutes more until the pudding thickens. Pour the pudding into serving bowls, cover with plastic wrap, and refrigerate for 2 hours before serving.

YIELD: Serves 6
SODIUM CONTENT: about 64 mg. of sodium per serving

AMARETTO APPLE CRISP

If you can't find amaretto cookies, use 1 cup of dry rolled oats and increase the brown sugar to 1¹/₂ cups.

1¹/₂ c. amaretto cookie crumbs (about 20 cookies)
6 c. peeled, cored, and thinly sliced apples
1 tsp. cinnamon
8 tbsp. (1 stick) butter
¹/₂ c. brown sugar
¹/₂ c. all-purpose flour
¹/₂ tsp. almond extract

Preheat the oven to 350 degrees. To prepare amaretto crumbs, grind up cookies in a blender or food processor or crush them with a rolling pin between two sheets of waxed paper. Put the apples in a bowl; add cinnamon, and stir until it is evenly distributed. Transfer the apples to a baking dish.

Cut the butter into small pieces and put them in a food processor. Add the sugar, flour, crushed cookies, and almond extract. Process for a few minutes until the mixture is thoroughly blended. (Or cut the butter into the rest of the ingredients in a bowl, using a pastry cutter, two knives, or your fingertips.) Spread the mixture over the apples and press it down into them to create a uniform crust. Bake on the middle rack of the oven until the crust has browned and the apples are cooked through, about 45 minutes. Allow to cool a bit before serving.

YIELD: Serves 8
SODIUM CONTENT: 12 mg. of sodium per serving

BLUEBERRY COBBLER

We like a cobbler—a crumbly pastry crust over fruit filling—with blueberries, even if we have to get them frozen out of season. But this recipe will also work with other berries or fruits, like strawberries, raspberries, or peaches.

FOR THE CRUST:

1¾ c. all-purpose flour
1 tbsp. sugar
1 tbsp. low-sodium
   baking powder
5 tbsp. chilled butter,
   cut into 1-inch pieces
¾ c. heavy cream

FOR THE FILLING:

3 c. fresh or frozen
   blueberries
⅔ c. sugar
1 tbsp. flour

Preheat the oven to 425 degrees. To make the crust, sift the flour, sugar, and baking powder together in a bowl, and add the chilled butter. Combine the butter with the dry ingredients by squeezing the mixture gently through your fingers. When it consists of marble-sized balls, add the heavy cream, and continue to mix with your fingers only until the cream is absorbed. The dough should be crumbly, not smooth. Wrap in plastic wrap and refrigerate while you make the filling.

Heat the blueberries with the sugar and flour in a saucepan. Stir as the sugar melts; bring the mixture to a boil, then turn it off. Lightly grease a 9" × 9" ovenproof baking dish with butter. Add the berries and spread them out so that they cover the bottom of the dish. On a floured surface, roll out the dough just until it is large enough to cover the filling; the dough should be thick. Place the dough on top of the filling. Put the cobbler in the oven and bake for about 30 minutes, until the dough begins to brown. Allow to cool slightly before serving with vanilla ice cream.

YIELD: Serves 12
SODIUM CONTENT: 9 mg. of sodium per serving

APPLE WALNUT CAKE

The calvados makes a nice addition; if you don't have it, try rum or brandy.

2 c. all-purpose flour
4 tsp. low-sodium baking powder
¾ tsp. cinnamon
¾ tsp. ground cloves
¾ tsp. ground ginger
¼ tsp. nutmeg
1 c. brown sugar, packed
1 c. plain yogurt
¾ c. vegetable oil
1 egg
1 tsp. vanilla
2 tbsp. calvados
1½ c. peeled, seeded, and chopped apples
¾ c. chopped walnuts

Preheat the oven to 350 degrees. Lightly grease an 8" × 8" baking pan. In a large mixing bowl, combine the flour, baking powder, spices, and brown sugar, and stir to blend, making sure to break up any lumps in the sugar. In a separate bowl, stir together the yogurt and oil; add the egg, vanilla, and calvados. When this mixture is thoroughly blended, add the apples and walnuts, and stir to combine. Add the liquid mixture to the flour mixture and stir only until all the dry ingredients are moistened. Pour the batter into the baking pan, spreading it evenly with a rubber scraper. Bake on the middle rack of the oven for about an hour, or until a toothpick inserted into the center of the cake comes out clean.

YIELD: Serves 12
SODIUM CONTENT: 22 mg. of sodium per serving

ANGEL FOOD CAKE

An angel food cake recipe deserves a place in every salt-free kitchen since it depends entirely on the egg whites for leavening— there's no need to worry about finding low-sodium baking powder. You'll need a good tube pan to make it work, as well as well-sifted cake flour made from soft winter wheat. (Be careful NOT to get a "self-rising" cake flour loaded up with salt and baking soda.)

12 egg whites
1 tbsp. water
1 tsp. cream of tartar
½ tsp. vanilla
½ tsp. almond extract
1½ c. sugar
1 c. cake flour

Preheat the oven to 350 degrees. Combine the egg whites, water, cream of tartar, vanilla, and almond extract in a large bowl; beat with an eggbeater or hand-held electric mixer until more than quadrupled in volume.

Do not beat beyond the point where the whites form a soft foam. Then continue to beat while adding ¾ cup sugar in small amounts until the whites form soft peaks.

Sift together the cake flour and the remaining ¾ cup sugar. Then sprinkle small amounts of this mixture over the egg whites, using a rubber scraper to fold the flour in each time. Fold gently and carefully; take care not to overmix.

Pour this mixture into an ungreased 10-inch tube pan, and spread gently so that it fills the pan evenly. Bake on the middle rack of the oven until a thin knife or bamboo skewer inserted into the middle of the cake comes out clean (about 35 minutes). Arrange three water glasses or jars in a triangle so they will support the rim of the pan when inverted. Set the pan upside down on the glasses and allow the cake to cool completely.

To remove the cake, run a thin knife around the circumference of the pan and of the tube without cutting into the cake. Then tap the pan on a hard surface and the cake should come out. If you have the kind of pan with a removable bottom, remove it with the cake and run the knife underneath the cake to separate it from the bottom of the pan.

YIELD: 12 slices
SODIUM CONTENT: 51 mg. of sodium per slice

PINEAPPLE UPSIDE-DOWN CAKE

The pineapple upside-down cake was supposedly invented as a way to promote sales of canned pineapple, and most of the recipes we've seen for it depend on the canned product. Feeling a little perverse, we decided to try it with a fresh pineapple, and the results were memorable. Some recipes insist that it be baked in an iron skillet, but we had no problem with an ovenproof baking dish.

FOR THE GLAZE:

8 tbsp. (1 stick) unsalted butter or margarine
½ c. packed dark brown sugar
6 large slices (½-inch thick) of ripe fresh peeled pineapple with the fibrous core removed (or 8 to 10 canned pineapple rings)
24 pecan halves
2 tbsp. maple syrup

FOR THE CAKE BATTER:

1 c. sugar
¾ c. unsalted butter or margarine
3 eggs
1 tsp. vanilla
1 more slice of fresh pineapple (or 2 canned rings)
3 c. all-purpose flour
1 tbsp. low-sodium baking powder
1 tsp. ground ginger

Preheat the oven to 350 degrees.

To prepare the glaze: Melt the butter or margarine and pour it into a 9" × 13" ovenproof baking dish. Add the brown sugar; stir to blend, and spread the mixture evenly across the bottom of the dish. Distribute the pineapple rings in two lines, pressing them into the sugar mixture. Press two pecan halves, curved side down, into the center of each ring, and distribute the others in the spaces between rings. Drizzle with the maple syrup.

To prepare the batter: Cream the sugar together with butter or margarine, and stir in the eggs and vanilla. Use a blender or food processor to grind up the single slice of fresh pineapple (or two slices of canned); add this purée to the butter-sugar-egg mixture and stir. Sift

(Continued)

together the flour, baking powder, and ginger and add them to the liquid mixture, stirring to blend.

To assemble the cake: Pour the batter over the glaze in the baking dish, and use a rubber scraper to spread it to an even depth. Cook on the middle rack of the oven for 30 to 40 minutes until the cake has turned golden brown and a toothpick inserted into it comes out clean of batter (don't stick it all the way down to the glaze). Remove the cake from the oven and allow to cool for several minutes right side up. Run a knife around the edge to separate the cake from the sides of the dish. Place a tray or baking sheet large enough to cover the baking dish on top of it, then, using heavy potholders to protect your hands, quickly invert the baking dish and tap the bottom of it so that the cake drops onto the tray. If any glaze clings to the bottom of the baking dish, use a rubber scraper to remove it, and add it to the top of the upside-down cake. Serve warm.

YIELD: Serves 10
SODIUM CONTENT: 25 mg. of sodium per serving

GINGERBREAD

Try serving this gingerbread with light lemon sauce (see page 301). This recipe produces a dark gingerbread; if you prefer it lighter in color and somewhat milder in flavor, use light brown sugar and light molasses. The crystallized ginger is expensive, but it adds a lot of flavor.

¼ c. unsalted butter, softened
¼ c. vegetable shortening
¼ c. dark brown sugar
¼ c. white sugar
1 egg
¼ c. molasses
2 c. flour
1 tbsp. low-sodium baking powder
2 tsp. ground ginger
2 tsp. cinnamon
½ tsp. ground cloves
3 tbsp. chopped crystallized ginger
½ c. boiling water

Preheat the oven to 350 degrees. Beat together the butter and shortening until thoroughly blended, then mix in the sugars, egg, and molasses. Sift together the flour, baking powder, ground ginger, cinnamon, and ground cloves. Add the dry ingredients to the liquid ingredients, stirring until just blended, then stir in the crystallized ginger. Add the boiling water and stir to blend. Lightly grease a 9-inch square baking pan, and fill it with the batter. Bake on the middle rack of the oven for 35 to 40 minutes, until a toothpick or knife blade inserted in the center comes out clean.

YIELD: Serves 12
SODIUM CONTENT: 15 mg. of sodium per serving

FRUIT SALAD WITH PORT

Use a good port wine to enhance the flavor of fresh summer fruit. It makes a fine simple dessert on a warm night, or serve it with salt-free cottage cheese for a light supper.

2 peaches, peeled and sliced
1 small bunch seedless grapes, stems
removed
2 bananas, sliced
1 pint fresh strawberries, halved
2 tbsp. port wine
1 tbsp. brandy (optional)

Place all the ingredients in a bowl and toss them together gently. Chill before serving.

YIELD: Serves 4
SODIUM CONTENT: 3 mg. of sodium per serving

PEARS IN WINE

4 Bosc pears
1 c. Chianti wine
1 c. sugar
2 tbsp. honey

Preheat the oven to 350 degrees. Place the pears upright in a baking dish and pour in the wine and sugar. Bake for 1 hour.

Remove the pears to a plate and cover lightly with aluminum foil. Allow the sauce to stand and cool; as it does, it will thicken up. Place a pear on a serving dish and spoon sauce over it, followed by about ½ tablespoon of honey.

YIELD: Serves 4
SODIUM CONTENT: 5 mg. of sodium per serving

POACHED PEACHES

4 peaches
6 c. water
2 c. sugar
¼ c. lemon juice

Place all the ingredients in a saucepan, and bring to a boil. Reduce the heat to a simmer and cook, covered, for 1 hour.

Remove the peaches from the pot; turn up the heat to medium and cook the liquid until it reduces to a syrup. Allow it to cool slightly. Peel each peach and slice it into wedges. To serve, arrange the wedges on 4 plates, and pour syrup over them.

YIELD: Serves 4
SODIUM CONTENT: 1 mg. of sodium per serving

DRUNKEN BANANAS

2 bananas
juice of 1 lemon
½ c. brown sugar
½ c. dark rum
¼ tsp. cinnamon

Cut the bananas in half, then divide each half lengthwise. Place the lemon juice, sugar, rum, and cinnamon in a sauté pan and cook over medium heat until reduced to a syrup. Drop the pieces of banana in the pan and cook them for a few minutes in the syrup, turning them so they are completely coated. To serve, place two pieces of banana on a plate and spoon some of the syrup over them.

YIELD: Serves 4
SODIUM CONTENT: 9 mg. of sodium per serving

MAPLE WALNUT BAKED APPLES

½ c. raisins and hot
  water to cover
4 large apples
½ c. chopped walnuts
½ c. maple syrup
1 tbsp. lemon juice
2 tbsp. unsalted butter
1 c. apple juice or water

Put the raisins in a bowl; cover with hot water and allow to stand for an hour, or until soft.

Preheat the oven to 375 degrees. Core each apple, leaving about ½ inch of flesh at the base of the hole you create. Take care not to poke through the bottom of the apple. Beginning at the edge of the hole in the top of the apple, peel away the skin about a third of the way down.

Drain the raisins, then put them in a small bowl with the walnuts, and stir to combine. Set the apples in a shallow baking pan and pack each core loosely with the walnut mixture, then pour in maple syrup to fill. Sprinkle a little lemon juice over each apple, then drizzle a bit more maple syrup on the exposed flesh. Place a thin slice of butter on the packed core of each apple. Pour the apple juice or water into the pan so it covers the bottom to a shallow depth. Bake on the middle rack of the oven until the apples are cooked through (test with a toothpick); this should take 35 to 40 minutes.

YIELD: Serves 4
SODIUM CONTENT: 11 mg. of sodium per serving

LIGHT LEMON SAUCE

*The basic recipe for this
simple sauce calls for no
eggs or butter; if you
prefer something a little
richer and less pure,
however, you can stir a
tablespoon or two of
unsalted butter into the
warm sauce just before
serving. Serve with
gingerbread or apple cake.*

½ **c. sugar**
1 tbsp. cornstarch
1 c. water
¼ **c. lemon juice**
2 tsp. grated lemon rind

Stir the sugar and cornstarch together
in a saucepan until well blended. Add
the water, lemon juice, and lemon
rind, and stir to combine. Bring the
mixture to a boil, continuing to stir
until it thickens. Serve warm.

YIELD: Serves 4
SODIUM CONTENT: less than 1 mg. of sodium per serving

UNFORGETTABLE FUDGE SAUCE

This family recipe unites the flavors of three tropical beans—cocoa, coffee, and vanilla—with condensed milk, cinnamon, and sugar for a fudge sauce people won't forget. It's so robust that you can use evaporated skim milk, rather than condensed whole milk, to hold down the fat with no sacrifice of flavor.

3 to 4 oz. high-quality bittersweet chocolate
12-oz. can evaporated skimmed milk
½ c. sugar
1 tsp. vanilla
2 tsp. cinnamon
2 tbsp. brewed coffee

In a medium saucepan, melt the chocolate in the evaporated milk over moderate heat, stirring constantly. When all of the chocolate has melted, stir in the sugar, vanilla, and cinnamon. Continue to cook just under the boil, stirring frequently, until the sauce begins to thicken. Add the brewed coffee, and return the sauce to the heat, continuing to stir. When bubbles rise and burst slowly, as if in a lava flow, the sauce is thick enough to serve.

YIELD: Serves 6
SODIUM CONTENT: 70 mg. of sodium per serving

GOOD MACAROONS

Use only pure shredded coconut from a health-food store or high-end supermarket. The packaged product you find in the baking section of most supermarkets is usually loaded with sugar, salt, and other sodium compounds.

2 egg whites
½ c. sugar
3 tbsp. honey
1 tsp. vanilla extract
1 tsp. almond extract
⅓ c. flour
3 c. unsweetened dried coconut

Preheat the oven to 375 degrees. Beat the egg whites until they are soft, then stir in the sugar, honey, and vanilla and almond extract. Use a mixer to beat the mixture until it is very stiff. (This will take at least 10 minutes.) Fold in the flour and coconut and stir to distribute them evenly. Drop spoonfuls of the mixture onto a greased baking sheet. Bake on the top shelf of the oven for about 10 minutes or until the macaroons turn golden brown. Allow them to cool before removing them to a rack.

These are excellent when coated with semisweet chocolate. Melt the chocolate in a pan, and dip each macaroon into it so it is half covered with the chocolate. Place on waxed paper until the chocolate has cooled and hardened. Serve with fresh strawberries.

YIELD: 12 macaroons
SODIUM CONTENT: 13 mg. of sodium per macaroon

CURRANT COCONUT
CASHEW COOKIES

Substitute raisins if you can't find dried currants, though in our view, the loss of alliteration means a loss of special mystique as well. Again, be sure to use pure grated coconut rather than the packaged product processed with sugar, salt, and other sodium compounds.

½ c. **unsweetened dried coconut**
½ c. **(1 stick) unsalted butter**
½ c. **sugar**
1 **egg, lightly beaten**
2 **tbsp. honey**
1 **tsp. vanilla**
1¼ c. **all-purpose flour**
1 **tbsp. low-sodium baking powder**
⅔ c. **chopped cashews**
½ c. **dried currants**

Preheat the oven to 350 degrees. Spread the coconut on a baking sheet and put it in the oven to toast for a few minutes until it begins to turn golden brown. Cream the butter and sugar together, then add the egg, honey, and vanilla, and stir to combine. Sift together the flour and baking powder in a large bowl. Add the toasted coconut, cashews, and currants, and stir to combine. Add the liquid ingredients, and stir to blend. Drop walnut-sized balls of batter onto a lightly greased baking sheet, and bake on the middle rack of the oven until the cookies begin to brown, about 15 minutes.

YIELD: 32 cookies
SODIUM CONTENT: 4 mg. of sodium per cookie

LEMON COCONUT COOKIES

*Here, too, stick with pure
grated coconut to avoid
the sugar, salt, and sodium
compounds in the
packaged brands.*

**½ c. shredded
  unsweetened coconut**
**½ c. (1 stick) unsalted
  butter**
½ c. sugar
¼ c. maple syrup
1 egg
zest of 1 lemon
3 tbsp. lemon juice
1 c. flour
**1 tbsp. low-sodium
  baking powder**

Preheat the oven to 350 degrees.
Spread the coconut in a baking pan
and toast in the oven until golden
brown. Cream together the butter,
sugar, and maple syrup. Add the egg,
and stir to combine. Add the lemon
zest and lemon juice. Stir in the
toasted coconut. Sift together the
flour and baking powder in a small
bowl or on a sheet of waxed paper.
Add to the liquid ingredients and stir
to combine. Drop teaspoonfuls of the
batter onto a lightly greased baking
sheet. Cook on the middle rack of the
oven until the edges of the cookies
begin to turn brown and they resist
on the top when touched with a
fingertip.

YIELD: 24 cookies
SODIUM CONTENT: 4 mg. of sodium per cookie

MOLASSES COOKIES

*This recipe is adapted
from one we learned from
Mary Elliott, who spends
summers in Maine near
the Appalachian Trail.
Mary likes to leave freshly
baked tins of cookies in a
lean-to on the trail as an
anonymous gift (she signs
herself "the cookie lady")
for hikers stopping off at
the end of the day.*

1 c. sugar
¾ c. unsalted butter or
   margarine
¼ c. molasses
1 egg
2 c. flour
1 tbsp. low-sodium
   baking powder
1 tsp. cinnamon
¾ tsp. ground ginger
¾ tsp. ground cloves

Preheat the oven to 375 degrees.
Cream the sugar with the butter or
margarine, then stir in the molasses
and egg. Sift together the flour,
baking powder, and spices. Mix the
dry ingredients with the wet, stirring
to combine them well. Drop balls of
dough the size of walnuts onto a
lightly greased baking sheet. Bake on
the middle rack of the oven for 10 to
12 minutes, until the tops are no
longer puffed up and soft.

YIELD: 16 cookies
SODIUM CONTENT: 10 mg. of sodium per cookie

OUR FAVORITE
OATMEAL COOKIE

This version of a classic treat, our all-time favorite, is adapted from one found in an old Fannie Farmer cookbook, which calls it a "Cape Cod" oatmeal cookie without explaining why.

1½ c. all-purpose flour
1 tbsp. low-sodium baking powder
1 tsp. cinnamon
1 c. (2 sticks) melted unsalted butter or vegetable shortening
1 tbsp. molasses
1 c. sugar
1 egg
¼ c. milk
1¾ c. uncooked rolled oats
½ c. raisins

Preheat the oven to 350 degrees. Sift the flour, baking powder, and cinnamon together in a mixing bowl. Combine the melted butter or shortening with the molasses and sugar in a small bowl, then stir into the flour mixture. Whisk the egg together with the milk, and stir into the batter. Fold in the rolled oats and raisins. Drop teaspoonsful of the batter onto a lightly greased cookie sheet, and bake for 10 to 15 minutes. When the edges turn brown, remove from the oven and place on a rack to cool.

YIELD: 18 cookies
SODIUM CONTENT: 9 mg. of sodium per cookie

PEANUT BUTTER COOKIES

Here the absence of salt in both the peanut butter (see page 20) and the dough itself allows for a purer marriage of delicate peanut flavor with brown sugar and vanilla.

½ c. brown sugar
½ c. white sugar
½ c. (1 stick) unsalted butter, softened
1 egg
1 tsp. vanilla
1 c. salt-free peanut butter
2 tsp. low-sodium baking powder
1¼ c. all-purpose flour

Preheat the oven to 350 degrees. Cream together the sugars and butter until thoroughly blended. Stir in the egg and vanilla, followed by the peanut butter. Sift together the baking powder and flour; add to the wet ingredients, and stir to blend. To make the classic cookie, roll the dough into balls, drop them on a greased baking sheet, and press them flat with a fork to create a crosshatch pattern. If you wish, you may also roll out this dough to a thickness of ¼ inch and use a glass to cut circles or cookie cutters to cut shapes.

YIELD: 12 cookies
SODIUM CONTENT: 12 mg. of sodium per cookie

AUNT LEN'S CHRISTMAS COOKIES

Our great aunt, Lena Schwenk, put salt in these lebkuchen, but we find it's totally unnecessary. Dates, raisins, anise, and a splash of bourbon create a deeply flavorful cookie that could easily become a tradition in your family, as it did in ours. If you don't have bourbon handy, you can substitute white wine.

½ c. (1 stick) unsalted
  butter
½ c. brown sugar
1 egg
½ c. light molasses
1 tbsp. crushed anise
  seeds
1 tsp. cinnamon
1 tsp. nutmeg
1 tsp. ground cloves
¼ c. bourbon whiskey
1 c. finely chopped
  dates

1 c. golden raisins
1 c. roughly chopped walnuts
2½ to 3 c. all-purpose flour
2 tsp. low-sodium baking powder

Cream together the butter and brown sugar. Stir in the egg and molasses. Add the anise seeds, cinnamon, nutmeg, and cloves, and stir to blend. Stir in the bourbon, followed by the dates, raisins, and walnuts. Sift the flour with the baking powder, and stir into the moist ingredients. Put the dough in the refrigerator to chill for 15 minutes.

Preheat the oven to 350 degrees. Use a rolling pin to roll out the dough on a floured board to a thickness of ¼ inch in the shape of a large rectangle. (You may want to divide the dough into pieces and roll out each piece.) Cut individual cookies into rectangular shapes measuring about 2 inches by 3 inches. Place the cookies on a lightly greased baking sheet, and bake for 10 to 15 minutes, until they are cooked through and the edges turn slightly brown.

YIELD: 18 cookies
SODIUM CONTENT: 11 mg. of sodium per cookie

PECAN PUFFS

½ c. (1 stick) **unsalted**
butter
2 tbsp. sugar
1 tsp. vanilla
1 c. finely ground
pecans
1 c. plus 2 tbsp.
all-purpose flour
confectioners' sugar

Preheat the oven to 300 degrees.
Cream the butter with the sugar. Add
the vanilla and ground pecans, and
stir to blend. Add the flour, and stir
until evenly incorporated. Shape
small pieces of the dough into balls
about 1 inch in diameter. Place them
on a lightly greased cookie sheet.
Bake until slightly brown, about 30 to
40 minutes. While still warm, roll
each puff in confectioners' sugar so
that it is completely coated. Allow to
cool completely, then dust each puff
with confectioners' sugar a second
time, covering areas where the first
coating of sugar melted.

YIELD: 12 puffs
SODIUM CONTENT: 1 mg. of sodium per puff

THE BEST BROWNIES

*Not surprisingly, the secret
of a great brownie is in
the chocolate. It's worth
paying extra for a superior
sweet ground chocolate,
and for a bar of powerful
bittersweet, like Valrhona,
to chop up and stir into
the batter.*

2 eggs
¾ c. sugar
1 tsp. vanilla
**½ c. (1 stick) unsalted
    butter, melted**
⅔ c. sifted flour
**¾ c. ground sweet
    chocolate**
**1 tsp. low-sodium
    baking powder**
**½ c. semisweet
    chocolate chips or
    coarsely chopped
    bittersweet chocolate**
**½ c. coarsely chopped
    walnuts (optional)**

Preheat oven to 350 degrees. Stir
together the eggs, sugar, and vanilla
in a large bowl. Add the melted
butter. Sift the flour, ground
chocolate, and baking powder
together onto a piece of waxed
paper. Stir these dry ingredients into
the egg mixture; add chocolate chips
or pieces and walnuts, and stir to
distribute. Spread the mixture in a
greased 9" × 9" baking pan and bake
for 20 to 30 minutes, until you can
stick a toothpick or knife blade into
the center of the batter and it comes
out clean. Allow to cool before
cutting into brownies.

YIELD: 12 brownies
SODIUM CONTENT: 16 mg. of sodium per brownie

SNICKERDOODLES

1 c. sugar
½ c. (1 stick) butter or
    shortening
1 egg
½ tsp. vanilla
1 tbsp. low-sodium
    baking powder
½ c. milk
12-oz. package
    semisweet chocolate
    bits
2 c. sifted all-purpose
    flour
2 tbsp. cinnamon
2 tbsp. sugar

Preheat the oven to 350 degrees. Cream the sugar with the shortening or butter, stir in the egg and vanilla. Stir the baking powder into the milk and add it to the shortening-sugar mixture, stirring to blend thoroughly. Add the chocolate bits and stir to distribute, then add the flour, stirring until well blended. Spread the mixture in a lightly greased 9" × 12" baking tin, and sprinkle cinnamon and sugar over the top. Bake for about 30 minutes, until a toothpick or knife blade inserted into the center of the batter comes out clean. Allow to cool and then cut into bars.

YIELD: 12 bars
SODIUM CONTENT: 17 mg. of sodium per bar

RESOURCES

A Guide to Products

Here is a partial list of low-sodium products we find useful and refer to in recipes. Look for them in health-food stores, high-end supermarkets, and specialty food shops. Many are also available by phone or online from Healthy Heart Market (1-888-685-5988; *www.healthyheartmarket.com*).

Baking powder: Featherweight baking powder—Hain Food Group, Uniondale, NY.

Beans: Eden organic no-salt-added beans (black, kidney, pinto, chickpeas [garbanzos], and more)—Eden Foods, Inc., Clinton, MI.

Bread: Salt-free whole wheat bread available by mail order by telephone—The Baker, Milford, NJ (1-800-995-3989); Ezekiel 4:9 low-sodium bread—Food for Life Baking Company, Corona, CA; 4C salt-free bread crumbs—4C Foods Corp., Brooklyn, NY; Toufayan salt-free pita bread and pitettes—Toufayan Bakeries, Inc., North Bergen, NJ and Orlando, FL.

Broth: Perfect Addition stocks (chicken, beef, vegetable, fish)—Perfect Addition, Inc., Newport Beach, CA; Health Valley no-salt-added broth (chicken or beef)—Health Valley Company, Irwindale, CA.

Catsup: Hunt's no-salt-added catsup—Hunt-Wesson, Inc., Fullerton, CA; Westbrae no-salt-added fruit-sweetened catsup—Hain Food Group, Uniondale, NY; Enrico's no-salt-added ketchup—Ventre Packing Company, Syracuse, NY.

Condiments: Mr. Spice sauces (Tangy Bang hot sauce, Indian Curry, Thai Peanut, Hot Chicken Wings)—Lang Naturals, Newport, RI.

Mayonnaise: Hain eggless mayonnaise—Hain Food Group, Uniondale, NY.

Mustard: Maitre Jacques low-sodium Dijon mustard—American Marketing Team, Bloomfield, NJ; Westbrae natural no-salt-added stoneground mustard—Hain Food Group, Uniondale, NY.

Pickles: B&G no-salt-added pickles (various varieties, including relish)—Bloch and Guggenheimer, Inc., Hurlock, MD; Pickle Eaters salt-free pickles—New Morning, Acton, MA.

Seasonings: Bell's all-natural seasoning—William G. Bell Co., East Weymouth, MA; Mrs. Dash salt-free original blend—Alberto Culver USA, Inc., Melrose Park, IL; Salt-free Spike all-purpose natural seasoning—Modern Products, Milwaukee, WI.

Sun-Dried Tomatoes: Timber Crest Farms (many salt-free variations)—Healdsburg, CA (1-707-433-8251; *www.timbercrest.com*)

Sodium Content of Common Foods

COMPILED FROM THE UNITED STATES DEPARTMENT OF
AGRICULTURE NUTRIENT DATABASE

FOOD	AMOUNT	SODIUM CONTENT
Allspice, ground	1 tsp.	2 mg.
Anise seed	1 tsp.	0.3 mg.
Apples, raw, with skin	1 medium	0 mg.
Apple juice, canned or bottled, unsweetened	1 c.	7 mg.
Applesauce, canned, sweetened, without salt	1 c.	8 mg.
Applesauce, canned, unsweetened	1 c.	5 mg.
Apricots, raw	1 c. halves	2 mg.
Apricots, dried, sulfured, uncooked	1 c. halves	13 mg.
Apricots, canned, water packed, with skin, solids and liquids	1 c. halves	7 mg.
Artichokes, (globe or French), raw	1 medium	120 mg.
Asparagus, raw	1 medium spear (5¼"–7" long)	0.3 mg.
Asparagus, cooked, boiled, drained	4 spears	7 mg.
Avocados, raw	1 avocado	20 mg.
Bacon, cured, raw	1 thick slice, packed ½ lb.	277 mg.
Bacon, cured, cooked, broiled, pan-fried, or roasted	3 medium slices, after cooking	303 mg.
Baking powder, double-acting, sodium aluminum sulfate	1 tsp.	488 mg.
Baking powder, low-sodium	1 tsp.	4.5 mg.
Baking soda	1 tsp.	1259 mg.
Bananas, raw	1 medium (7"–7⅞" long)	1 mg.
Basil, raw	2 tbsp.	0 mg.
Basil, ground	1 tsp.	.5 mg.
Bass, sea, mixed species, raw	3 oz.	58 mg.
Bass, sea, mixed species, cooked, dry heat	3 oz.	74 mg.
Bay leaf, crumbled	1 tsp.	0.1 mg.
Beans, snap, green, raw	1 c.	7 mg.
Beans, snap, green, boiled without salt	1 c.	4 mg.
Beans, kidney, mature seeds, sprouted, raw	1 c.	11 mg.
Beans, kidney, all types, mature seeds, cooked, boiled, without salt	1 c.	4 mg.
Beans, lima, raw	1 c.	32 mg.
Beans, lima, immature seeds, frozen, baby, boiled, drained, without salt	½ c.	26 mg.
Beans, lima, immature seeds, frozen, fordhook, boiled, drained, without salt	½ c.	46 mg.
Beans, navy, mature seeds, cooked, boiled, without salt	1 c.	2 mg.

FOOD	AMOUNT	SODIUM CONTENT
Beef, bottom round, trimmed to ¼" fat, raw	1 lb.	249 mg.
Beef, bottom round, trimmed to ¼" fat, roasted	3 oz.	54 mg.
Beef, brisket, whole, trimmed to ¼" fat, raw	1 lb.	290 mg.
Beef, brisket, whole, trimmed to ¼" fat, braised	3 oz.	52 mg.
Beef, chuck, arm pot roast, trimmed to ¼" fat, raw	1 lb.	268 mg.
Beef, chuck, arm pot roast, trimmed to ¼" fat, braised	3 oz.	50 mg.
Beef, cured, corned beef, brisket, raw	1 lb.	553 mg.
Beef, cured, corned beef, brisket, cooked	3 oz.	964 mg.
Beef, flank, trimmed to 0" fat, raw	4 oz.	80 mg.
Beef, flank, trimmed to 0" fat, broiled	3 oz.	69 mg.
Beef, ground, lean (21 percent fat), raw	4 oz.	78 mg.
Beef, ground, lean (21 percent fat), broiled or pan fried medium	3 oz.	65 mg.
Beef liver, raw	4 oz.	82 mg.
Beef liver, braised	3 oz.	60 mg.
Beef ribs, whole, (6–12), trimmed to ¼" fat, roasted	3 oz.	54 mg.
Beef, top sirloin, trimmed to ¼" fat, raw	1 lb.	240 mg.
Beef, top sirloin, trimmed to ¼" fat, broiled	3 oz.	4 mg.
Beer, regular	12 fl. oz.	18 mg.
Beer, light	12 fl. oz.	11 mg.
Beet greens, boiled without salt	½ c. 1" pieces	174 mg.
Beets, raw	1 c.	106 mg.
Beets, boiled without salt	½ c. slices	65 mg.
Blueberries, raw	1 c.	9 mg.
Bluefish, raw	3 oz.	51 mg.
Bluefish, cooked dry heat	3 oz.	65 mg.
Bread, white, commercially prepared	1 slice	135 mg.
Bead, whole-wheat, commercially prepared	1 slice	148 mg.
Bread, rye, commercially prepared	1 slice	211 mg.
Bread, pumpernickel, commercially prepared	1 slice	174 mg.
Broccoli, raw	1 c. chopped	24 mg.
Broccoli, boiled without salt	½ c.	20 mg.
Brussels sprouts, raw	1 c.	22 mg.
Brussels sprouts, boiled without salt	½ c.	16 mg.
Butter, with salt	1 tbsp.	118 mg.
Butter, without salt	1 tbsp.	2 mg.
Buttermilk, cultured, low fat	1 c.	257 mg.
Cabbage, raw	1 c. shredded	13 mg.
Cabbage, boiled without salt	½ c. shredded	6 mg.
Cabbage, red, raw	1 c. shredded	8 mg.
Cabbage, red, boiled without salt	½ c. shredded	6 mg.
Cabbage, Chinese (bok choy), raw	1 c. shredded	46 mg.
Cantaloupe, raw	1 medium	50 mg.

FOOD	AMOUNT	SODIUM CONTENT
Caraway seeds	1 tsp.	.4 mg.
Cardamom, ground	1 tsp.	.4 mg.
Carrots, raw	1 large carrot (7¼"–8½" long)	25 mg.
Carrots, boiled without salt	½ c. slices	51 mg.
Cashew nuts, dry-roasted, without salt	1 c. halves and whole	22 mg.
Cauliflower, raw	1 c.	30 mg.
Cauliflower, boiled without salt	½ c.	9 mg.
Celery, raw	1 medium stalk	35 mg.
Celery, boiled without salt	1 c. diced	137 mg.
Celery seed	1 tsp.	3 mg.
Chard, Swiss, raw	1 c.	77 mg.
Chard, Swiss, boiled without salt	1 c. chopped	313 mg.
Cheese, blue	1 oz.	396 mg.
Cheese, Camembert	1 oz.	239 mg.
Cheese, Cheddar	1 oz.	176 mg.
Cheese, cream	1 oz.	84 mg.
Cheese, Gouda	1 oz.	232 mg.
Cheese, Gouda, low-sodium	1 oz.	10 mg.
Cheese, Gruyere	1 oz.	95 mg.
Cheese, Limburger	1 oz.	227 mg.
Cheese, mozzarella, whole milk	1 oz.	106 mg.
Cheese, Muenster	1 oz.	178 mg.
Cheese, Parmesan, grated	1 oz.	528 mg.
Cheese, provolone	1 oz.	248 mg.
Cheese, ricotta, whole milk	½ c.	104 mg.
Cheese, Romano	1 oz.	340 mg.
Cheese, Roquefort	1 oz.	513 mg.
Cheese, Swiss	1 oz.	74 mg.
Cherries, sour, red, raw	1 c.	5 mg.
Chestnuts, European, roasted	1 c.	3 mg.
Chervil, dried	1 tsp.	.5 mg.
Chicken, broilers and fryers, light meat and skin, raw	½ chicken	126 mg.
Chicken, broilers and fryers, light meat and skin, roasted	½ chicken	99 mg.
Chicken, broilers and fryers, dark meat and skin, raw	½ chicken	194 mg.
Chicken, broilers and fryers, dark meat and skin, roasted	½ chicken	145 mg.
Chicken liver, raw	1 liver	25 mg.
Chicken liver, simmered	1 c. chopped or diced	71 mg.
Chives, raw	1 tsp. chopped	.03 mg.
Chocolate, baking, unsweetened, squares	1 square (1 oz.)	4 mg.
Cinnamon, ground	1 tsp.	.6 mg.
Clams, mixed species, raw	9 large or 20 small	101 mg.

FOOD	AMOUNT	SODIUM CONTENT
Clams, mixed species, cooked, moist heat	3 oz.	95 mg.
Cloves, ground	1 tsp.	5 mg.
Coconut meat, raw	1 c. shredded	16 mg.
Coconut milk, raw		
(liquid expressed from grated meat and water)	1 c.	36 mg.
Cod, Atlantic, raw	3 oz.	46 mg.
Cod, Atlantic, cooked, dry heat	3 oz.	66 mg.
Cod, Pacific, raw	3 oz.	60 mg.
Cod, Pacific, cooked, dry heat	3 oz.	77 mg.
Coriander leaf, dried	1 tsp.	1 mg.
Coriander seeds	1 tsp.	.6 mg.
Corn grits, white, regular, quick, unenriched,		
cooked with water, without salt	1 c.	0 mg.
Corn, sweet, white, raw	1 large ear	
	(7³/₄"–9" long)	21 mg.
Corn, sweet, white, boiled without salt	½ c.	14 mg.
Corn, sweet, yellow, raw	1 medium ear	
	(6³/₄"–7½" long)	14 mg.
Corn, sweet, yellow, boiled without salt	½ c.	14 mg.
Cornmeal, whole-grain, white	1 c.	43 mg.
Corn oil, salad or cooking	1 tbsp.	0 mg.
Cornstarch	1 c.	12 mg.
Corn syrup, dark	1 c.	508 mg.
Corn syrup, light	1 c.	397 mg.
Crab, Alaska king, raw	3 oz.	711 mg.
Crab, Alaska king, cooked, moist heat	3 oz.	911 mg.
Crab, blue, raw	3 oz.	249 mg.
Crab, blue, cooked, moist heat	3 oz.	237 mg.
Crab, Dungeness, raw	3 oz.	251 mg.
Crab, Dungeness, cooked, moist heat	3 oz.	321 mg.
Crab, queen, raw	3 oz.	458 mg.
Crab, queen, cooked, moist heat	3 oz.	587 mg.
Cranberries, raw	1 c. whole or chopped	1 mg.
Cranberry sauce, canned, sweetened	1 c.	80 mg.
Cranberry juice cocktail, bottled	1 c. (8 fl. oz.)	5 mg.
Cream, fluid, light (coffee cream or table cream)	1 c.	95 mg.
Cream, fluid, heavy whipping	1 c. fluid	
	(yields 2 c. whipped)	89 mg.
Cream, fluid, half and half	1 c.	98 mg.
Cucumber, raw	1 cucumber (8¼")	6 mg.
Cumin seeds	1 tsp.	4 mg.
Curry powder	1 tsp.	1 mg.
Dandelion greens, raw	1 c. chopped	42 mg.
Dandelion greens, boiled without salt	1 c. chopped	46 mg.
Dates, domestic, natural and dry	1 c. pitted, chopped	5 mg.
Dill weed, dried	1 tsp.	2 mg.

FOOD	AMOUNT	SODIUM CONTENT
Dill weed, fresh	5 sprigs	.6 mg.
Dill seeds	1 tsp.	.4 mg.
Egg, whole, raw, fresh	1 large	63 mg.
Egg, whole, hard boiled	1 large	62 mg.
Eggplant, raw	1 eggplant	16 mg.
Eggplant, boiled without salt	1 c. cubed	3 mg.
Endive, raw	½ c. chopped	6 mg.
Fennel seeds	1 tsp.	2 mg.
Fenugreek seeds	1 tsp.	2 mg.
Figs, dried, uncooked	1 fig	2 mg.
Flounder (and other sole species), raw	3 oz.	69 mg.
Flounder (and other sole species), cooked, dry heat	3 oz.	89 mg.
Flour, white wheat, all-purpose, enriched, bleached	1 c.	3 mg.
Flour, whole-grain wheat	1 c.	6 mg.
Fruit cocktail (peach, pineapple, pear, grape, cherry), canned, light syrup	1 c.	15 mg.
Fruit salad (peach, pear, apricot, pineapple, cherry), canned, light syrup	1 c.	15 mg.
Garlic, raw	1 tsp.	.5 mg.
Garlic powder	1 tsp.	.7 mg.
Gelatin dessert, dry mix	1 package	216 mg.
Ginger root, raw, sliced	¼ c.	3 mg.
Ginger, ground	1 tsp.	.6 mg.
Grapefruit, raw	½ medium	0 mg.
Grapes, red or green, raw	1 c. seedless	3 mg.
Grape juice, canned or bottled, unsweetened, without added vitamin C	1 c.	8 mg.
Grape juice drink, canned	1 c. (8 fl oz.)	3 mg.
Haddock, raw	3 oz.	58 mg.
Haddock, cooked, dry heat	3 oz.	74 mg.
Halibut, Atlantic and Pacific, raw	3 oz.	46 mg.
Halibut, Atlantic and Pacific, cooked, dry heat	3 oz.	59 mg.
Ham, fresh, separable lean and fat, raw	1 lb.	213 mg.
Ham, fresh, separable lean and fat, roasted	3 oz.	51 mg.
Honey, strained or extracted	1 tbsp.	.8 mg.
Honeydew melon, raw	1 wedge (⅛ of 5¼"-diameter melon)	13 mg.
Ice cream, vanilla	½ c. (4 fl. oz.)	53 mg.
Jams and preserves	1 tbsp.	6 mg.
Kale, raw	1 c. chopped	29 mg.
Kale, boiled without salt	1 c. chopped	30 mg.
Kidneys, beef, raw	4 oz.	202 mg.
Kidneys, beef, simmered	3 oz.	114 mg.
Kohlrabi, raw	1 c.	27 mg.

FOOD	AMOUNT	SODIUM CONTENT
Kohlrabi, boiled without salt	1 c.	35 mg.
Lamb, leg, whole, separable lean and fat, trimmed to ¼" fat, raw	1 lb.	254 mg.
Lamb, leg, whole, separable lean and fat, trimmed to ¼" fat, roasted	3 oz.	56 mg.
Lamb, shoulder, whole, separable lean and fat, trimmed to ¼" fat, raw	1 lb.	277 mg.
Lamb, shoulder, whole, separable lean and fat, trimmed to ¼" fat, braised	3 oz.	56 mg.
Lemons, raw, with peel	1 fruit without seeds	3 mg.
Lemon juice, canned or bottled	1 tbsp.	3 mg.
Lemonade, frozen concentrate, white, prepared with water	1 c. (8 fl oz.)	7 mg.
Lentils, mature seeds, raw	1 c.	19 mg.
Lentils, mature seeds, cooked, boiled, without salt	1 c.	4 mg.
Lettuce, butter head (includes Boston and Bibb types), raw	1 head (5" diameter)	8 mg.
Lettuce, iceberg (includes crisp head types), raw	1 head (6" diameter)	49 mg.
Lettuce, cos or romaine, raw	½ c. shredded	2 mg.
Lime, raw	1 fruit (2" diameter)	1 mg.
Lobster, northern, raw	3 oz.	252 mg.
Lobster, northern, cooked, moist heat	3 oz.	323 mg.
Mace, ground	1 tsp.	1 mg.
Mango, raw	1 c. sliced	3 mg.
Mango, raw	1 fruit without refuse	4 mg.
Maple syrup	1 tbsp.	2 mg.
Margarine, hard, corn and soybean (hydrogenated) and cottonseed (hydrogenated), with salt	1 stick	1070 mg.
Margarine, hard, corn and soybean (hydrogenated) and cottonseed (hydrogenated), without salt	1 stick	2 mg.
Marjoram, dried	1 tsp.	.5 mg.
Matzo crackers, plain	1 matzo	.6 mg.
Milk, fluid, 3.25 percent milk fat	1 c.	120 mg.
Milk, low fat, fluid, 1 percent milk fat, with added vitamin A	1 c.	123 mg.
Milk, nonfat, fluid, protein fortified, with added vitamin A (fat free and skim)	1 c.	144 mg.
Milk, canned, evaporated, without added vitamin A	1 c.	267 mg.
Milk, canned, condensed, sweetened	1 c.	389 mg.
Milk, dry, nonfat, regular, with added vitamin A	1 c.	642 mg.
Mushrooms, raw	1 c. pieces	3 mg.
Mushrooms, boiled without salt	1 c. pieces	3 mg.
Mustard greens, cooked, boiled, drained, without salt	1 c. chopped	22 mg.
Mustard seeds, yellow	1 tsp.	.15 mg.

FOOD	AMOUNT	SODIUM CONTENT
Nectarines, raw	1 fruit (2½" diameter)	0 mg.
Noodles, egg, cooked, enriched	1 c.	11 mg.
Nutmeg, ground	1 tsp.	.4 mg.
Oil, olive, salad or cooking	1 tbsp.	.005 mg.
Oil, corn, vegetable, salad or cooking	1 tbsp.	0 mg.
Oil, peanut, salad or cooking	1 tbsp.	.015 mg.
Oil, sesame, salad or cooking	1 tbsp.	0 mg.
Okra, raw	1 c.	8 mg.
Okra, cooked, boiled, drained, without salt	½ c. slices	4 mg.
Olives, ripe, canned (small–extra large)	1 small	28 mg.
Onions, raw	1 c. chopped	5 mg.
Onions, boiled without salt	1 c.	6 mg.
Onion powder	1 tsp.	1 mg.
Oranges, raw	1 large	0 mg.
Orange juice, fresh	1 c.	2 mg.
Orange juice, frozen concentrate, unsweetened, diluted with 3 volume water	1 c.	2mg.
Oregano, ground	1 tsp.	.2 mg.
Oysters, eastern, farmed, raw	6 medium	150 mg.
Oysters, eastern, farmed, cooked, dry heat	6 medium	96 mg.
Oysters, eastern, wild, raw	6 medium	177 mg.
Oysters, eastern, wild, cooked, dry heat	6 medium	177 mg.
Papaya, raw	1 small	5 mg.
Paprika	1 tsp.	.7 mg.
Parsley, raw	1 tbsp.	2 mg.
Parsley, dried	1 tbsp.	6 mg.
Parsnips, raw	1 c., slices	13 mg.
Parsnips, boiled without salt	½ c. slices	8 mg.
Peaches, raw	1 medium (2½" diameter— about ¼ lb.)	0 mg.
Peaches, canned, water packed, solids and liquids	1 c. halves or slices	7 mg.
Peaches, canned, light syrup packed, solids and liquids	1 c. halves or slices	13 mg.
Pear, raw	medium (about 6 oz.)	0 mg.
Pears, canned, water packed, solids and liquids	1 c., halves	5 mg.
Peas, green, raw	1 c.	7 mg.
Peas, green, boiled without salt	1 c.	5 mg.
Pepper, black	1 tsp.	1 mg.
Pepper, red or cayenne	1 tsp.	.5 mg.
Pepper, white	1 tsp.	.1 mg.
Peppers, sweet, green, raw	1 medium (approx. 2¾" long, 2½" diameter)	2 mg.
Peppers, sweet, green, boiled without salt	½ c. chopped	1 mg.
Perch, mixed species, raw	3 oz.	53 mg.
Perch, mixed species, cooked, dry heat	3 oz.	67 mg.
Persimmons, native, raw	1 fruit without refuse	.3 mg.

FOOD	AMOUNT	SODIUM CONTENT
Persimmons, Japanese, raw	1 fruit (2½" diameter)	2 mg.
Pheasant, raw, meat and skin	½ pheasant	160 mg.
Pineapple, raw	1 c. diced	2 mg.
Pineapple, canned, juice packed, solids and liquids	1 c. crushed, sliced, or chunks	2 mg.
Plums, raw	1 c. sliced	0 mg.
Plums, canned, purple, light syrup packed, solids and liquids	1 c. pitted	50 mg.
Popcorn, air-popped	1 oz.	1 mg.
Poppy seeds	1 tbsp.	2 mg.
Pork, fresh, loin, center rib (chops or roasts), separable lean and fat, raw	1 chop	41 mg.
Pork, fresh, loin, center rib (chops or roasts), separable lean and fat, broiled	1 chop	46 mg.
Pork, fresh, loin, whole, separable lean and fat, broiled	3 oz.	53 mg.
Pork, fresh, loin, whole, separable lean and fat, roasted	3 oz.	50 mg.
Pork, fresh, spareribs, separable lean and fat, braised	3 oz.	79 mg.
Pork sausage, fresh, cooked	1 link (raw: 4" long x ⅞" diameter)	168 mg.
Potatoes, boiled, cooked in skin, flesh, without salt	1 potato	5 mg.
Potatoes, French fried, unsalted frozen, heated in oven without salt	9 oz.	59 mg.
Prunes, dried, uncooked	1 prune	.3 mg.
Prunes, dried, stewed	1 c. pitted	5 mg.
Prune juice, canned	1 c.	10 mg.
Pumpkin, raw	1 c.	1 mg.
Pumpkin, boiled without salt	1 c. mashed	2 mg.
Pumpkin, canned, without salt	1 c.	12 mg.
Pumpkin pie spice	1 tbsp.	3 mg.
Radishes, raw	1 small	.5 mg.
Raisins, seedless	1 miniature box (.5 oz.)	2 mg.
Raspberries, raw	1 c.	0 mg.
Raspberries, frozen, red, sweetened	1 c. unthawed	3 mg.
Relish, pickle, sweet	1 tbsp.	122 mg.
Rhubarb, raw	1 c. diced	5 mg.
Rhubarb, frozen, cooked, with sugar	1 c.	2 mg.
Rice, brown, medium-grain, raw	1 c.	8 mg.
Rice, brown, medium-grain, cooked	1 c.	2 mg.
Rice, white, medium-grain, raw, enriched	1 c.	2 mg.
Rice, white, medium-grain, cooked	1 c.	0 mg.
Rosemary, dried	1 tbsp.	2 mg.
Rutabaga, raw	1 c. cubed	28 mg.
Rutabaga, boiled, drained, without salt	1 c. cubed	34 mg.

FOOD	AMOUNT	SODIUM CONTENT
Saffron	1 tsp.	1 mg.
Sage, ground	1 tsp.	.07 mg.
Salami, cooked, beef	1 slice (4" diameter x ⅛" thick)	270 mg.
Salmon, Atlantic, farmed, raw	3 oz.	50 mg.
Salmon, Atlantic, farmed, cooked, dry heat	3 oz.	52 mg.
Salmon, pink, canned, solids with bone and liquid	3 oz.	471 mg.
Salmon, pink, canned, without salt, solids with bone and liquid	3 oz.	64 mg.
Salt, table	1 tsp.	2325 mg.
Sauerkraut, canned, solids and liquids	1 c.	939 mg.
Savory, ground	1 tsp.	.3 mg.
Scallops, mixed species, raw	3 oz.	137 mg.
Soy sauce made from soy and wheat (*shoyu*)	1 tbsp.	871 mg.
Soy sauce made from soy and wheat (*shoyu*), low sodium	1 tbsp.	600 mg.
Soy sauce made from soy (*tamari*)	1 tbsp.	1005 mg.
Soy sauce made from hydrolyzed vegetable protein	1 tbsp.	1024 mg.
Spinach, raw	1 c.	24 mg.
Spinach, boiled, drained, without salt	1 c.	126 mg.
Spinach, frozen, chopped or leaf, boiled, drained, without salt	½ c.	82 mg.
Squash, summer, all varieties, raw	1 c. sliced	2 mg.
Squash, summer, all varieties, boiled, drained, without salt	1 c. sliced	2 mg.
Squash, summer, zucchini, includes skin, raw	1 c. sliced	3 mg.
Squash, summer, zucchini, includes skin, boiled, drained, without salt	1 c. sliced	5 mg.
Squash, winter, acorn, cooked, baked, without salt	1 c. cubed	8 mg.
Strawberries, raw	1 pint	4 mg.
Strawberries, frozen, sweetened, whole	1 package (10 oz.)	3 mg.
Sugar, brown, packed	1 c.	86 mg.
Sugar, brown, unpacked	1 c.	57 mg.
Sugar, granulated	1 c.	2 mg.
Sugar, powdered	1 c. unsifted	1 mg.
Sunflower seed kernels, dried	1 c.	4 mg.
Sweet potato, raw	1 sweet potato (5")	17 mg.
Sweet potato, baked in skin, without salt	1 medium	11 mg.
Tangerines (mandarin oranges), raw	1 large (2½" diameter)	1 mg.
Tarragon, ground	1 tsp.	1 mg.
Thyme, fresh	1 tsp.	.07 mg.
Thyme, ground	1 tsp.	.08 mg.
Tomatoes, red, ripe, raw, year round average	1 c. chopped or sliced	16 mg.
Tomatoes, red, ripe, boiled without salt	1 c.	26 mg.
Tomatoes, red, ripe, canned, whole, no salt added	1 c.	24 mg.

FOOD	AMOUNT	SODIUM CONTENT
Tomato paste, canned, without salt added	1 tbsp.	14 mg.
Tongue (beef), raw	4 oz.	78 mg.
Tongue (beef), simmered	3 oz.	51 mg.
Turmeric, ground	1 tbsp.	3 mg.
Turkey, all classes, meat only, roasted	1 c. chopped or diced	98 mg.
Turnips, boiled, drained, without salt	1 c. cubed	78 mg.
Turnips, boiled, drained, without salt	1 c. mashed	115 mg.
Turnip greens, raw	1 c. chopped	22 mg.
Turnip greens, boiled, drained, without salt	1 c. chopped	42 mg.
Veal, loin, separable lean and fat, roasted	3 oz.	79 mg.
Vinegar, cider	1 tbsp.	.15 mg.
Water chestnuts, Chinese, canned, solids and liquids	½ c. sliced	6 mg.
Watercress, raw	1 c. chopped	14 mg.
Watermelon, raw	1 wedge (about ¹/₁₆ of melon)	6 mg.
Wheat germ oil	1 tbsp.	0 mg.
Wine, red	1 wine glass (3.5 fl. oz.)	5 mg.
Wine, white	1 wine glass (3.5 fl. oz.)	5 mg.
Wine, dessert, dry	1 wine glass (3.5 fl. oz.)	9 mg.
Wine, dessert, sweet	1 wine glass (3.5 fl. oz.)	9 mg.
Whitefish, mixed species, raw	3 oz.	43 mg.
Whitefish, mixed species, cooked, dry heat	3 oz.	55 mg.
Whitefish, mixed species, smoked	3 oz. cooked, flaked	866 mg.
Yams, raw	1 c. cubed	14 mg.
Yams, boiled, drained, or baked, without salt	1 c. cubed	11 mg.
Yeast, baker's, compressed	1 cake	5 mg.
Yeast, baker's, active dry	1 package	4 mg.
Yogurt, plain, whole milk, 8 grams protein per 8 oz.	1 c.	114 mg.
Yogurt, plain, low fat, 12 grams protein per 8 oz.	1 c.	172 mg.
Yogurt, plain, skim milk, 13 grams protein per 8 oz.	1 c.	187 mg.

•